Growing Up, Following Jesus

Also by Adrian Plass

Silver Birches: A Novel

The Sacred Diary of Adrian Plass, Aged 37¾

The Sacred Diary of Adrian Plass, Christian Speaker, Aged 45¾

And Jesus Will Be Born: A Collection of Christmas Poems, Stories and Reflections

The Best in Plass

The Sacred Diaries: Encounters with Leonard Thynn and Andromeda Veal

You, Me and Mark

Keeping Up with the Robinsons

Growing Up, Following Jesus

Growing Up, Following Jesus

Internationally
BESTSELLING AUTHOR
ADRIAN PLASS

ZONDERVAN®

ZONDERVAN.com/
AUTHORTRACKER
follow your favorite authors

ZONDERVAN

Growing Up, Following Jesus
Copyright © 2010 by Adrian Plass

The Growing Up Pains of Adrian Plass
Copyright © 1989 by Adrian Plass

Why I Follow Jesus
Copyright © 2010 by Adrian Plass

Requests for information should be addressed to:
Zondervan, Grand Rapids, Michigan 49530

ISBN 978-0-310-25227-6

Cover design, illustration, and hand-lettering: Kristi Smith / Juicebox Designs
Interior design: Michelle Espinoza

Printed in the United States of America

10 11 12 13 14 15 /DCI/ 23 22 21 20 19 18 17 16 15 14 13 12 11 10 9 8 7 6 5 4 3 2 1

Contents

Book 1:

The Growing Up Pains of Adrian Plass

9

Book 2:

Why I Follow Jesus

199

Book 1:

The Growing Up Pains of Adrian Plass

Introduction

God really brought me down to earth once. He's rather good at that sort of thing.

We'd gone to Cornwall for a winter holiday, something that we'd always yearned to do as a family. It was early December, bitingly cold, but brilliantly lit by one of those water-colour winter suns that seem to drip liquid light through the atmosphere. Our little white rented cottage overlooked an indescribably beautiful part of the northern coast. That coast must have been planned, built and illuminated by a creator with time on his hands, and a fine, excited eye for detail.

One morning, after a long, lingering, excessive breakfast, we all dressed in layer upon layer of the warmest clothes we could find, and set off, a procession of human barrels, to go for a walk in the ice-cream air. We went a new way. Through a white farm gate, and across an expanse of wind-flattened, metallic green grass, towards what looked like a cliff edge a few hundred yards away. Beyond that the sea stretched away for ever, merging with the sky in the strange pale distance.

I walked with Matthew, aged eight, whose every utterance at that time began with an interrogative. My wife, Bridget, strolled beside four-year-old Joseph, deep and thoughtful beyond his years. The smallest barrel, David, aged two, ran ahead of us chuckling delightedly, applauding the seagulls who keeled around us for a few minutes, performing impossible aerobatics with casual vanity.

As we neared the edge of the cliff, I reflected on the fact that we were happy – all of us. We are a close family, but it didn't often happen that we all achieved contentment, all at the same time, when we were all together. You have to work hard to keep a family of five reasonably happy. It's like the circus act where all those plates are kept spinning on the top of tall, thin sticks by someone rushing from one to the other at great speed. The difference with a family is that you never get a chance to stop and take a bow. You just carry on, and get tired. Holidays had always been an opportunity for Bridget and myself to enjoy an awareness of our whole selves, and to give some thought to what we needed to keep our plates spinning.

We had reached the edge. Far beneath us, enclosed by a horseshoe of unscaleable cliffs, lay one of the most magically secluded bays I had ever seen. Perfect shape, perfect sea, perfect sand, perfect rock pools. There was no way down. We could never use it. We could only look at it. It was as though one of God's successful creation prototypes had been overlooked when the workbench was cleared.

I forgot everything else as I gazed out over this hidden corner of the world. I felt a sudden surge of pride about belonging to the same world as the vast shining sea, the blue-white wash of the sky, and the massive, granulated bulk of the cliffs. These, surely, were symbols of God. Huge, beautiful, sublime, desirable, yet impossible to contain or define narrowly. I was lost in wonder ...

'Daddy, want to go loo, daddy!'

My youngest son's voice arrived in my consciousness with urgent haste. David's little face was strained with the knowledge that disaster was imminent. As I struggled to reduce his Michelin-like proportions to an appropriate state of undress, I spoke to God in my mind with some truculence.

'Goodness knows,' I complained, 'I get little enough time as it is to actually relax and enjoy beautiful things. Why should I have to come down from where I was to cope with little problems like this?'

'I did,' said God.

Chapter 1

Early photographs show that I was little more than a huge pair of ears mounted on two long skinny legs. In most of those early pictures I look slightly troubled and very earnest.

Each week I attended the local church at the other end of the village, an activity that seemed to me to have very little to do with God. The Roman Catholic chapel in Rusthall was a converted private house, and therefore lacked the atmosphere of sublime mystery and divine confidence that I rather enjoyed on our occasional visits to St Augustine's, the huge and ornate mother church in Tunbridge Wells. There were few points of interest for a small child in an hour spent in one of three physical postures, listening to someone speaking a language that he didn't understand, to a God who seemed as distant and irrelevant as the dark side of the moon. Some of those services seemed to be several days long. Afterwards, my father, my two brothers and I would proceed sedately back along the path into the village, all my little springs of boredom and tension popping and pinging into relaxation as I looked forward to Sunday lunch and the traditional midday comedy half-hour on the radio.

Nowadays I have a great respect and fondness for the Roman Catholic Church and many friends who are members of it, but if you had asked me at the age of eight or nine to tell you what I enjoyed most about the mass, I could have named only one thing. I did rather look forward to that point in the proceedings when the priest placed a wafer in the open mouths of the communicants, as they knelt in a semicircle around him. There was a satisfyingly repellent fleshiness about all those extended tongues, and a fascinating vulnerability about the grown-ups, waiting like baby birds to be fed with something that, once inside them, (I was told) would turn into the body of Jesus Christ and nourish them in a way that I couldn't begin to understand.

That the church seemed to me to have very little to do with God may have had something to do with the fact that, while my father was a convert to the Catholic Church, my mother, whose religious background was the Congregational Church, remained a Protestant and didn't come to church with us on Sundays.

We frequently experienced our own domestic version of 'The Troubles' and I can recall how, as a small child, I felt painfully bewildered about the religious separation between my parents.

Why didn't mummy come to church with us? Did she know a different God? No? Well, in that case why didn't she come to church with us? I would understand when I was older, I was told.

The shadow of conflict darkened those Sunday morning services throughout my early childhood and had a strongly negative effect on my feelings about God, who clearly wouldn't or couldn't sort out our family.

If my poor father had been a more secure man the boredom of the services and even the parental conflict over religion might not have mattered too much. As it was, his inability to trust the love of his family resulted in twenty-five very difficult years for my mother, and, in my case, a very confused and troubled perception of what love, adulthood and Christianity meant. Two incidents spring to mind as being typical of the kind of emotional half-nelson that he was expert in applying and which must have contributed heavily to the emotional constipation which led to a breakdown in my own life years later in 1984, and from which I am only just emerging as I write.

The first concerned my father's black prayer book. It was a small, plump, much thumbed little volume, whose wafer-thin pages were edged with gold. As a child it seemed to me a miniature treasure chest, filled with immense wealth that had somehow been compressed into a tiny space for easy portage.

Dad's prayer book was part of him, like the little round boxes of Beecham's pills, the tin full of old and foreign coins, the trilby hat, and the tortoise-shell reading spectacles that made my sight worse when I was allowed to try them on, before they were put away again in the case that snapped shut with a pleasing hollow 'plock' sound.

One day we had all been naughty – all three of us. One of my brothers was two years older than me, the other was two years younger. I must have been about eight years old at the time. We seemed to spend our lives pursuing one of three activities. The first involved the consumption of vast slices of white crusty bread, spread thickly with butter and marmalade. We often accounted for three long loaves in a single day.

The second activity was simply playing together, and the third, which usually grew naturally out of the second, was simply fighting each other. Today, the eating and playing stages had passed all too quickly. We three boys had argued and squabbled and cried and fought for most of a long rainy Saturday. My parents' patience had been tried and tested in a way that, with three boys of my own, I now fully understand. They had tried everything: the gentle rebuke, the not-so-gentle rebuke, the appeal to reason, the bribe, the threat, the repeated threat, the repeated-yet-again threat, the last chance option and finally the shriek of fury. Nothing had worked. My father had long since abandoned any attempt to play an adult role in the proceedings. He was an angry child, hurt by our refusal to make it easy for him to be grown-up. His idea of an appropriate solution to this problem was bizarre, to say the least. He picked up his prayer book from its place next to the biscuit barrel on the sideboard, and holding it dramatically over his head, announced that if we didn't behave ourselves, we would drive him to the point where he would be forced to throw it at us, and if he had to do *that*, it really would be 'the end'.

Children believe things.

The end of what? Pictures flashed through my mind of the

little book, stuffed with condensed divinity, crashing to the floor, bursting like some ripe, heavy fruit, and losing all its goodness for ever. Was that what he meant? Would I be to blame for that? Had I said or done something in the course of that long day of bickering, that was more serious – more wicked than I had realised? When he did finally, with a sort of orgasmic zeal, fling the book in the general direction of my younger brother and me, I was surprised to find that the world seemed unaffected by the gesture. No thunderbolts – no voice from heaven. The book lay, almost unharmed, on the floor, one or two pages detached by the impact and protruding slightly from the others, but otherwise, just the same.

I wasn't just the same though. I had made my father throw his prayer book at me, and he had said that it would be 'the end'. That book contained God. I had made him throw God away.

The devils grinned as they snapped home the padlock on another chain of guilt.

The other incident was so painful, that, even now, I find it difficult to record.

My father was a very jealous man. He found it almost impossible to believe that he was loved and wanted by those closest to him. Happiness and peace were just clever devices designed to lull him into a state where he could more easily be cheated and victimised, especially by his wife – my mother – who was, and still is, one of the most loving and innocent people I have ever met. People outside the family were 'all right'. They could never give him things that he feared losing in the same way. It was us, the family, and my mother particularly, who were obliged to trip and stumble through the dark forest of his fear and insecurity. In the middle of a pleasant family walk, when it seemed impossible that anything could go wrong, he would quite suddenly stop, and with that expression of tight-lipped anger on his face, that we all dreaded, announce that we were going back.

'Why, Dad?'

'Ask your mother.'

My mother, it usually transpired, had 'looked' at a man passing along on the other side of the road, or working in a field, or sitting on a gate, or driving a car. This kind of innocent glance was enough to shatter my father's self-esteem, and send him into a brooding sulky state for hours, or days, or even weeks. Eventually my mother would find a way to bring him round, but only by accepting and playing out the role of penitent, which was a very risky business, as he would only accept her penitence if she was innocent as well. He saw rivals everywhere. The man who came to build the extension onto our kitchen was, he told me, a 'naughty' man.

'What do you mean?'

'I'll tell you when you're older.'

'Why can't you tell me now?'

'It's not very nice.'

The man who took us for catechism lessons in a tall dark room in St Augustine's presbytery was also on the list of suspects. He was a big man with a large impressive moustache, a profound understanding of the catechism, and an almost total inability to communicate it to children. He was also, so my father said, not a good man.

'Bad, you mean?'

'Yes, very bad.'

'What's he done?'

'You wouldn't understand.'

'I would!'

'I'll tell you when you're older ...'

There were so many things that I was going to be told when I was older! So many little clouds of half-knowledge were massing around my understanding, shutting out the light until much later in my life.

The most painful instance of my father's insane jealousy (most painful from my point of view, that is), happened just before my tenth birthday. I arrived home one afternoon after playing some sort of tracking game through the bracken up on the common. Tired, hot and hungry, I came through the back door into the kitchen, and was about to get a drink of water and a wedge of the all-sustaining bread and marmalade, when I heard my father's raised voice coming from the other side of the dining room door. My very heartbeat seemed to fade, as it always did when I realised that 'it' was happening again. What now? I opened the door and slipped quietly into the room, thinking vaguely that I might be able to protect someone from something. My mother was shaking her head tearfully, sobbing out the words, 'It's just not true, it's just not true!'

My father, with an odd mixture of pain, anger and relish filling his face and voice, was jabbing his finger towards her and shouting, 'I saw you! I saw you with him! I looked through the window and saw you on the bed with him!'

My sympathy fluttered around the room like a nervous butterfly, uncertain where to alight, unsure where to lend the tiny weight of its concern.

'You can't have done – you really can't have done! It's not true ...!'

Despite ample evidence from the past that plain denial was an absolute waste of time, my mother continued her tearful protest, until my father, suddenly inspired, took a step forward and pointed at me.

'Adrian was with me. He saw it too! Didn't you?'

There was a wild plea in his eyes.

My mother was crying.

They were my parents. You should support your parents. My father was appealing to me to lie for him. My mother needed me to tell the truth. Someone was going to be let down, and we were all going to suffer anyway. My voice was very small as I answered.

'I wasn't with you. I didn't see anything.'

16

I don't think I looked at my father's face. I had failed him by telling the truth. I was a cold mess inside. Angry, unhappy, and of course – guilty.

As an adult, I have come to understand how profoundly my father suffered through his inability to believe in happiness, and I am now able to offer him posthumous forgiveness and feel more peaceful about the past. There is no doubt, though, that the development of my perception of God as a father was sadly distorted by the way in which he presented himself to me both as a Christian and a parent. It is fortunate that my mother was able to provide warmth and consistent care throughout my childhood, and for that I shall always be grateful.

The other great pleasure in my life, apart from eating bread and marmalade, was reading. I was an avid but nondiscriminating reader. Various aged relatives died during my childhood, leaving large and generally rather sombre collections of books to my father, who placed many of them in a big dark-brown bookcase in my bedroom, presumably to aid the process of 'doing better than he did'. I read everything. I would sit, cross-legged, on the bedroom floor, in my baggy grey flannel shirt, and my even baggier grey flannel shorts, surrounded by little stacks of novels, poetry collections and biographies. Each book was like a stone in a rock pool. Lift it up, investigate closely, and you might discover something exciting – something alive! Nor was I handicapped by snobbery. There was no such thing as a classic. I was quite happy to give someone called Joseph Conrad a fair trial, but he had to succeed on his own merits, or be replaced by a really great writer, such as W E Johns, or Richmal Crompton. I was in love with words and ideas, but it never occurred to me, until one momentous day, that something I read in a book could actually change my attitude to real people in the real world.

It was my earliest encounter with the truth, although I certainly wouldn't have called it a religious experience at the time, and it happened on the top deck of the number 81 bus which used

17

to run between Rusthall and Tunbridge Wells. The journey only took twelve minutes, but on this occasion that was long enough for a startling new truth to penetrate my ten-year-old consciousness so profoundly that it has affected almost everything I have done since that day. It was connected with something I had read that morning.

As I sat on the front seat of the big green Maidstone and District bus, a sixpenny bit and a penny clutched in my hand ready for the conductor, a phrase I had read earlier repeated itself over and over in my mind.

'Everybody is I'.

For some reason, I sensed an important inner core of meaning in the words, but I was unable to dig it out. I was frustrated and fascinated by the problem. If only the answer – the secret, had been a solid thing. I wanted to stretch out my hand and grasp it firmly – make it mine.

'Yes, son?'

So absorbed was I by the intensity of my quest for understanding, that the bus conductor's perfectly reasonable attempt to collect a fare from me seemed an unforgivable intrusion into my privacy. The friendly smile under the shiny-peaked cap wilted in the heat of a ferocious glare from this odd, skinny little boy. The poor man hastily took the two coins from my extended palm, turned the handle on his machine, and handed me a green seven-penny ticket, before returning to more congenial company on the lower deck.

I stared out through the big front windows at the road ahead. We were nearly at Toad Rock. Didn't like Toad Rock very much. Why not? Didn't know really ... Everybody is *I* ... Everybody is *I* ...

Everybody is I ... Everybody is I ...

We were passing the white frontage of the Swan Hotel now, turning slowly into the lower end of Tunbridge Wells High Street. Good old Tunbridge Wells, like a collection of huge dolls' houses.

Lovely day, lots of people about – hundreds of people in fact. Probably going to the fair on the common. Everybody is ...

Suddenly I stiffened. Body erect, hands flat on the ledge below the window, I pressed my forehead against the glass and stared in amazement at the crowds on the pavement below. The true meaning of those three simple, but puzzling words had exploded into my mind, destroying the illusion that I was the centre of the universe, and leaving me to cope, for the rest of my life, with the burden of knowledge. Every one of those people down there in the street, walking the pavements, driving cars, waiting for buses – every single one, whatever they were, whatever they looked like, whatever I thought of them, were as important to themselves as I was to myself! I shook my head, trying to clear it of this incredible notion. Everybody is I ... That funny, bent old lady with the mouth drooping on one side – she mattered, she was vital – central. The bus conductor who had interrupted my mental churning earlier; he wasn't just a bit player in my world. He was the star in his own. He had a head full of thoughts and feelings; a life inside him; he was the reason that the earth went on turning. My own father and mother, my brothers, aunts, uncles, all my friends – all were 'I'. Everybody was I, and at that moment I was somehow aware that I would probably never learn a more important lesson.

This new understanding did not transform me into a nice person. It enabled me to understand a great deal more about others, but that understanding could be used to help or to harm. In the years that followed, the latter seemed more useful than the former.

Between the ages of ten and sixteen I was desperately engaged in the task of trying to cobble together something in the way of a usable personality. Other people seemed to have one. Why shouldn't I? Somehow I had to batten down the chaos, and construct a facade that would be both acceptable and impenetrable. I certainly didn't want anyone catching a glimpse of the earnest

19

but confused little wretch that I felt myself to be. I discovered that sarcasm, skilfully used, was a means, not only of holding people at a distance, but also of acquiring a certain power. Lowest form of wit it might be, but it was also the most effective. I became an expert in the art of diminishing, belittling, and hurting with words. I blush when I recall the relish with which I applied this weapon at times, to people who can have had no idea of the yearning unhappiness that lay beneath such an alienating strategy. I had postponed happiness in order to concentrate on safety. I learned how to bob and duck and weave in my dealings with school friends and adults, though with more and more difficulty as I moved into the highly competitive world of the boys' grammar school.

Things like homework, and PE kit, and pens that worked, and tidy school uniform, were constant nightmares. I felt grubbier, less equipped in all ways, and more disorganised than any other boy in the school. I had seen other people's houses and families. They seemed almost impossibly ordered and relaxed in comparison with mine. How did they manage it? I had no idea. Our house was a place of loud, moving bodies, swirling emotions and constant television. My mother always did her best, but it was not a place where you did homework. In any case, how could I spare any attention for things like homework or schoolwork, when every ounce of my inventive and mental energy was required for basic social survival?

I was still a voracious reader, and I had considerable natural ability in the subject of English language, but by my second year at secondary school I had already slipped gloomily down into the 'D' stream, the Hades of an establishment like ours, where academic achievement was the road to heaven. My reading nowadays was a way of escape, often into the world of those very dated public-school stories that used to be published in solid thick-paged volumes with a dramatic illustration etched on the front. In these books, clean-living, square-jawed chaps who inhabited something called the Shell, or the Remove, did and said manly things in a highly organised atmosphere of Victorian morality. They had names like 'Goodman' or 'Mainworthy'. Such cads as did exist were called 'Badstone' or 'Munger', and were either reformed or expelled in the final chapter. The teachers always included a young and enthusiastic ex-blue who unobtrusively guided the hero along his path to ultimate manliness, and a God-like headmaster who combined the wisdom of Socrates with the judgement of Solomon. The trinity was completed by a mysterious moving force known generally as 'good form'. Ridiculous though it was, I yearned for such a world. It offered so many things that I had never had.

My other avenue of escape was the fantasy of stardom as a film actor. I nursed a secret conviction that I was the greatest undiscovered thespian in the country, and that it was only a matter of time before, in one of the scenarios that I spent much of my time imagining, I would be discovered by an astonished director and immediately begin a glittering career on the silver screen.

I secretly bought a book entitled *Teach Yourself Amateur Acting*, and studied it in private, so that when the great day came I should be absolutely prepared. My first part would be a leading role in a film that also starred Hayley Mills, with whom I had been deeply in love ever since the day when I sat in the indescribably delicious darkness of the Essoldo cinema, watching *Whistle down the Wind* three times in a row. It was in connection with my passionate feelings about Miss Mills that I learned the second great lesson of my life.

One day, when I was thirteen or so, I made the fatal mistake of trying to turn fantasy into reality. At that time the Mills family lived a few miles away from my home, in a little country village called Cowden. I had often pictured myself accidentally bumping into my beloved in Cowden High Street. It is a fair indication of my naivety that I usually saw this romantic encounter developing from the fact that her bicycle tyre had gone flat. Her knight in

21

shining armour would then pedal suavely on to the scene, flourishing not a sword, but a pump. She would be overwhelmed by my resourcefulness and charity, and subsequently bowled over by my natural charm, which, in my fantasy at least, was irresistible. Marriage would follow at an appropriate age. Large close-ups, glistening tears, stirring music – the lot!

One day I got tired of pretending. I wanted something real to happen for once. I had never actually been to Cowden, but on this warm, sunny, Saturday morning, I decided that the time had come. I set off on my shiny blue bicycle, tense with excitement, to make my dream come true. My belief in a satisfactory outcome to this expedition lasted for several miles, until the moment when I found myself confronted by a nameplate at the side of the road, which said simply, Cowden. I stopped my bike and, balancing on my left foot, reached over to touch the cold metal of the sign with my hand. It was real. Cowden really did exist. I straightened up again and looked around. Beyond the sign the road continued, bordered by trees, flowers and bushes. I could see the tops of one or two houses in the distance – Cowden houses. They were all real. Everything was real. By implication, then, Cowden High Street must be real, Hayley Mills must be real. She was a real person, who didn't spend her life hanging around the village street with an incapacitated bicycle, waiting for some scruffy little twit to rescue her with his pump. It was a sad moment. The world was real. As the full absurdity of my daydream dawned on me, I quietly turned by bike round and pedalled grimly back to Rusthall. Another lesson learned – hard but necessary. I would never find what I wanted in fantasy. That frightened me. Where *would* I find what I wanted?

By the time I began my fifth year at the grammar school, the whole area of education stank of dismal failure. I had never managed to acquire the work habit, and I was so far behind in all subjects except English language, that any hope of passing 'O' level exams had long since evaporated. I felt ugly, and awkward, and useless. The teachers were puzzled. I wasn't typical of the types who failed, but I was impossible to reach by then. It is also impossible to describe to someone who had not experienced it, the leaden misery of daily attendance at an establishment in which you are a legal obligation and nothing more. In all but fantasy (and that was discredited) I was worth nothing. The very school buildings themselves with their grand, mellowed, red-brick frontage seemed to mock my outer and inner disarray as I toiled through the big wrought-iron gates each morning.

I began to truant, setting off for school each morning, dressed in the distinctive grammar school uniform, and ending up walking round and round the recreation ground opposite the school, watching the old men playing bowls, or sitting with a book on the slowly revolving roundabout in the children's corner. Sometimes, at lunchtime, boys from the school would gather in a noisy group behind the bowls pavilion to smoke illicit cigarettes, often cadged from 'Jack', a highly questionable old character whose suspicious enthusiasm for the company of schoolboys was redeemed by his generosity with Kensitas cigarettes, of which he seemed to have an endless supply. Every school seemed to have its 'Jack'. Occasionally I would join this group, pretending to myself that I was normal and involved like them; that, after a morning's work in school, I was relaxing in an enjoyable, forbidden way before returning for the afternoon lessons.

When they left, the game ended, of course, and I would return to the intense solitariness of my truancy. I longed to be part of something, to be genuinely wanted by ordinary people, to be caught up in the warm casualness of relaxed friendship. Those endless months of morbidly aimless wandering while others were busy 'belonging', scarred my self-image more deeply than ever.

Eventually, and inevitably, I was 'asked to leave' by the headmaster. I felt no relief when this happened – only resentment, confusion and shame. I threw my school uniform away for ever, and stepped warily into the adult world.

Chapter 2

Tunbridge Wells in the mid-sixties was an experiential chocolate box. Every flavour of sensation was available in one form or another, and the notorious 'Disgusted of Tunbridge Wells' would need to take only a short walk through his own town to find ample cause for complaint. If you sat in a coffee bar at the lower end of the town, you were as likely to be offered marijuana as a religious tract. If you stayed long enough you would probably get both, and if you lingered even longer you might be approached by a glassy-eyed scientologist offering the chance to learn how to walk through walls in ten easy but very expensive lessons. If group violence was more to your taste, you would become either a mod, in which case you would wear a parka and ride a motor scooter, or a rocker, in which case you would need a leather jacket, long hair, and, at the very least, a regular place on the pillion of somebody's motorcycle. Membership of either of these groups effectively removed the problem of boredom at weekends and on bank holidays, which were spent planning, running from, or seeking mass conflict.

There were other possibilities. Eastern religions and philosophies were available in paperback, and once the jargon was learned, could be adopted as a way of life for a day or two. I remember experiencing some confusion over this when I walked into 'La Rue', one day. La Rue was a small cafe at the busy end of the town, where the pseudo-intelligentsia (of which I was one) met to discuss something called 'life' at interminable length, with no great profit to the proprietor who viewed with some coldness our tendency to sit in a group around one shallow glass cup of frothy coffee for hours on end. One morning I sauntered intelligently into the cafe, to find a friend called John sitting in the corner, with *I have undergone a change* written all over him. The ensuing conversation went something like this.

Me: You're early, John.

John: (*Unwilling to be drawn into small talk that might dissipate the impact of his new image*) Yes.

Me: Any fags?

John: (*Irritated by my failure to say he seemed different somehow*) No!

Me: Why are you out so early?

John: (*Dreamily*) Because the sky is blue.

Me: Pardon?

John: Because the grass is green, because birds fly, and hair grows.

Me: Right ... hair grows ... right. I'm with you now, John. (What the hell was he on about?)

SILENCE

John: (*Further irritated by my refusal to admit ignorance*) I don't see things in the same way any more.

Me: (*A generous concession*) Why not?

John: (*Triumphantly*) Because the world is round!

It turned out that John had sat up for most of the night reading a Penguin publication about Zen Buddhism, and his peculiar responses to my questions were evidences of his exciting discovery that, not only was he a Zen Buddhist now, but he always *had* been one without realising it. This made life a little difficult for him, as the book made it clear that the true adherent would never dream of actually stating crudely that he was a Zen Buddhist. Hence, the rather strange dialogue when I came into the cafe. I believe John went on to become a totally committed Marxist – for a week.

If the 'isms' failed to attract, one could always become a novelist who also wrote poetry. The attraction of this occupation in the sixties, was that it was unnecessary to actually write anything beyond the first line or two of what would undoubtedly have been a great psychological work of fiction if it had ever been finished. In addition, one might compose a few lines of totally obscure poetry, unadulterated by such dated devices as metre, rhyme, or even meaning, and designed to break the stranglehold of the old classical poets like Milton, Dryden, and other people whose works one had never read. Today, twenty years later, there are still, to my certain knowledge, two people continuing to circulate the cafes and pubs of Tunbridge Wells with exercise books and biros, who were doing exactly the same thing in 1965. Tunbridge Wells can do that to people. It can allow them to decay with such a sense of style, that they hardly notice the process until it is too late.

This was particularly so in the sixties because educationalists thought they had discovered that each human being was, potentially, a creative genius. It would have been sacrilege for any one person to criticise another's artistic efforts. The real casualties were those who never recovered from flattery.

So, the choice was mine. Which flavour would I choose? I needed something badly, but it would have to go very deep to make a real difference. My facade of ironic indifference was brittle, but effective, and it was all I had. I sensed the shallowness of all that was on offer, but it didn't surprise me. Everybody is I. Did all these others carry around inside them the same tight ball of tearful chaos that I did? At one point my disguise included a violently checked jacket, a pair of dark glasses that I wore at all times and in all weathers, and a black billiard ball which I repeatedly threw up and caught with my right hand. Nobody was going to get inside me! I must have looked, to borrow a powerful expression of my son's, a real 'super-nurd'.

There were three good and important things in my life at this point. The first, my mother, had always been there, although on reflection I can see that my appreciation and treatment of her had been variable. Often, during this difficult period, I would arrive home very late at night to find that my father had switched off the electricity at the mains. This meant that the one light-bulb which travelled from room to room as it was needed, was useless to me. The dark house was doom-laden at one o'clock in the morning, but as I groped my way upstairs – still wearing the dark glasses – I knew that, nine times out of ten, my mother would have left beside my bed a little pile of sandwiches – usually Marmite – and a large glass of milk. People say they are curious about heaven. I have tasted heaven. It consists of reading escapist literature by candlelight while eating Marmite sandwiches and drinking cold milk, in a dark house in a dark world.

The second good thing was a real live girlfriend called Anthea. She was a talented, kind girl, whose parents were predictably aghast to find that the apple of their eye had trawled in an apparent lunatic, whose taste in clothes and obsession with dark glasses and billiard balls must have suggested that placement in a locked institution was imminent.

Anthea and I were together for four years, and I owe her a great deal. She was the first person outside my family to dispel my personal myth that I was unlovable, and she put up with a lot of testing in the process. I remember her with great affection.

The third important thing was my acquisition of three friends. The first, John Hall, had attended one of those traditional public schools I was so fond of reading about, though his description of life in his particular establishment bore little relation to fictional accounts. John's natural courtesy and generosity thawed me, often allowing the vulnerable little boy of six years ago to risk a brief excursion into the outside world. John is now an Anglican priest in the north of England, and still my closest friend. The other two friends were a married couple who lived in a rented cottage in the depths of the Sussex countryside, near Wadhurst. Murray and Vivien Staplehurst accepted me so unreservedly that I really began to feel – while I was with them at any rate – that life might be worth living after all. They switched me on with their approval, affection and appreciation of my sense of humour and fascinated me with their eccentricity and larger-than-life-ness. I value their friendship now, as then.

Every Sunday, the Anglican Church of St John's in Tunbridge Wells organised a coffee-bar evening in the upper room of a building called Byng Hall, next door to The Red Lion on one side, and my ex-grammar school on the other. In charge was a young and enthusiastic curate named Clive Sampson. He arrived after evensong each Sunday, accompanied by a small group of clean-looking teenagers to unlock the front door of the hall and admit the little knot of non-church attenders who usually gathered outside. I had got into the habit of coming along each week largely because there was very little else to do in Tunbridge Wells on a Sunday evening. The coffee was very cheap, and there were other, less material attractions. I sensed that, in a way I didn't quite understand, I was nibbling at someone's bait. Something in the studied casualness of the non-mini-skirted Christian girls, and the short haired, jerseyed Christian boys suggested that they were all expecting something to happen in, for, or to me, one of these days. It soon became clear that they were waiting – and perhaps praying – for my conversion to Christianity, whatever that might mean.

I took an odd pleasure in paddling on the edge of this sea of expectation, never going in too far, but never withdrawing completely. The only formal religious content of these evenings was a three minute talk or 'epilogue' near the end, but I rather enjoyed the sport of 'cornering the curate'. Every week I would have a different question to ask, a fresh objection to make, or a new argument to introduce. Clive battled manfully with the problems, clearly feeling a little inadequate as he sorted out the whole question of universal suffering for me, and explained, on behalf of God, how predestination and free will are, actually, not incompatible at all. He half dreaded, half enjoyed these mind-stretching encounters. For me the whole thing had very little to do with God, any more than the Roman Catholic chapel had when I was a child. I enjoyed the discussions – I enjoyed seeing Clive out of his depth sometimes – but mainly I was just a sucker for being wanted. They let me talk and they seemed to want me in a slightly predatory sort of way. It was possible to relax and enjoy being large and different among these people who, though the same age as me, had skinnier arms and more innocent and organised lives.

Poor old Clive became aware after a number of weeks that talking me into any kind of Christian belief had about as much chance of success as striking a match on jelly. He had used all the illustrations, explanations, revelations and exhortations that he could think of. He was right out of '-ations'. The day came when his patience faded. His intellect stomped off in disgust, leaving his heart free to say something at last.

'I just love him!' he blurted out, smacking the palm of his hand down on the formica-topped coffee bar. 'I love him! That's all – I just love Jesus!'

This crashing service ace, coming at the end of a long succession of easily returned schoolgirl lobs, caught me totally wrong-footed. He'd broken the rules, hadn't he? Who said we were going to talk about things that really mattered to us? Because there was no doubt at all that Clive reacted to this Jesus from the gut. He'd taken a long time to say so, but it was a fact, and I was impressed. Not convinced, but definitely impressed, even a little shaken perhaps. Underneath Clive's words – and I knew all about words – lay a passionate feeling, or emotion, about someone who didn't exist, except as an historical figure.

Here we are, then, at a danger point. I can feel the temptation to embroider this incident and my reaction to it. I know how to do it. I would like to say that my spirit sensed the presence of the Lord. It didn't. I would like to say that from that moment I felt God calling me to him. I didn't. I would like to say all sorts of things that are not quite true. They might encourage people, but God wants the truth, and the truth is a funny, ragged old thing.

One instinct that Clive's outburst did arouse in me was curiosity. I was puzzled by the strength of his feelings and the process by which he had acquired them. Not that I equated strength of feeling with truth or goodness, necessarily. The Inquisition and the Nazi party were poor adverts for enthusiasm, to name but two. Clive had never burned anyone at the stake, or invaded Poland, as far as I knew, but, perhaps because of my father, I was very wary of emotion. I decided to maintain my air of indifference, and investigate as casually as I could.

I went to church. St John's was a very satisfactorily churchy-looking sort of church. Grey stone, and towers, and pointed arches, and dark wood and things. It was a heavy, comfortable, motherly sort of building, presided over by the Reverend Donald Edison, one of the sweetest-natured men I have known. Clive was his curate. I began to go to the service known as Evensong. This began at 6.30, and ended at 7.30, a long time for a devoted cigarette smoker like me, but I usually stuck it out for the hour. Soon I was settled into the new pattern. Tea at Anthea's house about five o'clock, down to the church for Evensong at half past six, and along the road to Byng Hall for the coffee bar at half past seven. The whole thing had a very pleasantly civilised feel about it. It was an oasis of order and freshness in the desert of unemployed gloom that filled the rest of the week. I remember my particular pleasure in the knowledge that Anthea's mother always ensured that Sunday tea included one of those beautifully labelled china pots of Patum Peperium – Gentleman's Relish. It was there for me.

The preacher at the evening service would usually be either Donald Edison or Clive Sampson, with the occasional visiting speaker.

One day a man called Denis Shepherd, from one of the London churches, came to speak to the evening congregation. He was a tall, broad man, with a quiet manner and an air of inner strength. As far as I can recall he had been in the Merchant Navy for some years before being ordained into the Anglican Church. I was still very much a spectator, and I would have rejected with scorn the suggestion that what this man said was going to bring real tears to my eyes, and, for better or worse, change the whole course of my life.

The talk he gave was about the brief conversation between Jesus, as he hung dying on the cross, and the two lawbreakers who were crucified on either side of him, an event which is recorded only in the Gospel of Luke. The preacher read the relevant passage before beginning his talk.

One of the criminals hanging there abused him. 'Are you not the Christ?' he said. 'Save yourself and us as well.' But the other spoke up and rebuked him. 'Have you no fear of God at all?' he said. 'You got the same sentence as he did, but in our case we deserved it: we are paying for what we did. But this man has done nothing wrong. Jesus,' he said, 'remember me when you come into your kingdom.' 'Indeed, I promise you,' he replied, 'today you will be with me in paradise.'

The Reverend Shepherd went on to speak in more detail about the kind of interaction that must have occurred between these dirty, blood-streaked individuals as they hung side by side waiting for the relief of death. He spoke particularly about the man who had recognised something special in Jesus. He was a man who, to all intents and purposes, was finished. His life was over, and a wretched, useless life it had been. Any dreams of last minute reprieve had been shattered by the first of the executioner's nails, as it crunched through bone, sinew and flesh, impaling him to the rough wooden surface of his cross. It was the end of all reasonable hope. The dialogue between this fellow and Jesus was very uncomplicated. Presumably, it arose from what each saw in the other as they shared the same kind of physical agony. What did the criminal see in Jesus? Nobody knows for sure, but it was probably some kind of natural authority blended with deep compassion.

He obviously looked like someone who, despite his present circumstances, was going somewhere – an 'in-charge' sort of person, a grown-up. He must have known a bit about Jesus already, the conversation shows that: but perhaps he had never looked closely at him before, or believed it was possible to reach the heights of virtue that must surely be required from followers of such an uncompromisingly moral character. Whatever else he did or did not see, though, one thing is clear. He recognised a sudden, breath-taking opportunity to make everything all right. Morally naked as he was, there was no hope of convincing the Galilean that he deserved anything, nor was there time to live-a-better-life for a while in the hope of investing a little in his divine bank account. Perhaps what was happening was that the child in this hardened law-breaker, the part of him that still wanted to believe in something or someone, was yearning for the warmth and comfort that all children must have. In the eyes of the man beside him, he saw an invitation to be loved and wanted, not because of, nor despite, anything, but simply because that is what children need. Jesus' eyes, as they looked into the lost and dejected face of his neighbour, were full of the love of his father. They were saying, 'I don't care what you've done. I don't care what you are. I don't care what others say about you. I don't even care what you think of yourself. You're coming with me. Don't worry, everything's going to be all right.'

As I sat next to Anthea at the back of the crowded church, the preacher's words seemed to be meant specially for me. I felt like a child too. The puzzled little boy who had wanted so much to stop his mummy and daddy arguing so that they would be happy together, but had failed, not only at that, but at almost everything else since, wanted to shout out his hurt across the heads of the congregation, through the preacher who seemed a sort of conduit to God, and thence up to heaven itself.

'What about me? I'm lost too! I'm lonely and ragged inside. I've tried and tried, but I just don't know how to be like ordinary people. What about me? Do you love me like you loved that man on the cross? Will you be a father to me, whatever I am and whatever I say or do? Can I safely show you how hurt and wretched I am?'

Would Jesus look at me from the cross with those same loving eyes and say 'Don't worry, everything's okay. I know all about you, Adrian. It doesn't matter what's happened up to now. I'll look after you. I know you never wanted to be hurtful or sarcastic. I know how much you wanted to do well. I know you're not the person you wanted to be. It doesn't matter – I do understand.'

Suddenly my eyes were full of tears. How I wanted that kind of acceptance, the chance to start again and be real, to relax the constant strain that the maintenance of my artificial personality imposed on me. This man was saying that Jesus offered all these things in the twentieth century – right now. As I stood for the final hymn, my hands supporting my weight on the pew in front of me, I managed to control the tears, and after the blessing we joined the stream of people flowing down the centre aisle towards the big front doors where the preacher waited to shake hands with people as they left. Just before we reached him, Anthea and I looked at each other. Without speaking we knew that both of us had been affected by what we had just heard. As I shook hands with Denis Shepherd a few seconds later, I found myself saying quietly, 'Could we see you afterwards? We want to become Christians.'

Later, when the congregation had dispersed and all was quiet, we met him in a room at the back of the church and told him that we wanted to do 'whatever you did' in order to get 'whatever you got'. He seemed to understand this strange request, and suggested that we should say a prayer in which we asked Jesus into our hearts as Lord and Saviour. I didn't know what that meant, but I wasn't going to let mere technicalities put me off when real happiness was available. We found it hard to frame a prayer properly, so, in the end he prayed for us, while we joined in silently in our minds, and said 'amen' with him at the end. The prayer was short, but it included terms and concepts that, while appearing quite straightforward at the time, awe me nowadays with their depth and mystery.

'Heavenly Father, we know that we have sinned against you, like all mankind, by turning away from you. We thank you that Jesus died on the cross to pay for our sins and to offer a way back to you. We ask that Jesus will come and live in our hearts by the power of your Holy Spirit, and that we may be able to love and serve you for the rest of our lives, and be with you in heaven forever when we die. We ask this in the name of the Lord Jesus Christ, Amen.'

I didn't feel anything as I prayed this prayer – neither then nor immediately afterwards, but I had prayed it. My mind had said 'Yes' and I was a Christian.

There were many exciting Christian paperbacks on sale in the sixties. There are still, of course, but at that time it was something new. These books were so full of miraculous signs and wonders, that they made everyday life seem very drab and dull in comparison. After my conversion I, in common with many others, devoured this kind of literature in much the same way that large mammals are obliged to eat constantly in order to stay alive. They usually chronicled the background, conversion and subsequent spiritual adventures of a particular individual – often American. They made you gasp and weep and hope that, in time, God could use you in a similar way. Each new book that was published seemed to emphasise a different aspect of the Christian life, or a more reliable way to ensure that you had easy access to the divine machinery, and a working knowledge of its controls.

'Praise God in all adversity' said one. 'Don't be afraid to be angry and honest with God' said another.

'People who don't speak in tongues are not really Christians' claimed one writer. 'You don't need to speak in tongues to be a Christian' answered somebody else.

'God is working in the established church.' 'God had rejected the established church.'

All claimed to be right, all offered evidence to support their particular claim, and most included, somewhere on the front or back cover, the seductive phrase 'This is a true story'. I now know that there is a significant difference between a list of consecutive factual events, and an account in which things like atmosphere, interpretation and illustration have been woven – often very attractively – around those events. I try to do it myself. 'Truth' can be a very difficult thing to pin down. At the time, though, I was happy to collude with the writers of these books, which meant that I discovered the 'real answer', on average, about twice a week.

Many people were genuinely and lastingly helped, especially by such classics as *The Cross and the Switchblade*, but I fear that for me and many others, each new spiritual volume was like one more shot in the arm for an addict. It reassured for a time, and gave the world a rather tinny dazzle, but it didn't last for long.

One thing that nearly all these books had in common was the suggestion that conversion meant the end of the bad times, and the beginning of the good times. Much recent Christian literature, thankfully, avoids this grotesque and dangerous over-simplification, and is as honest as Jesus was, but at that time I got it firmly into my head that conversion equalled happy-ever-after, and there was little in the presentation of evangelical Christianity at the time to dispel this illusion. I had been converted. Go on then, God. Do something. Change me. Organise me. I've said the prayer. Away you go!

It wasn't working.

Soon after the day of our conversion, Anthea and I had been sent, through the post, a list of prayer meetings, Bible studies, and youth activities that were scheduled for the coming month. This list utterly dismayed me, and for some weeks I didn't go near the church. I felt confused and hurt. On the Sunday evening when Denis Shepherd had spoken, I had been deeply moved and attracted by the possibility of acceptance and love from this man – God, Jesus. It had been an encounter between two personalities, and it had seemed to promise change. What had a typed list of activities to do with that? My resentment was on a hair trigger, and the flimsy piece of formality that I held in my hand was enough to fire it full-blast at a church which seemed to think that 'putting me on the register' would help in some way. God had offered me bread to eat because he saw that I was hungry. Now I was being told that what this amounted to was a course of cookery lessons. What had I expected? I don't know. I was full of bitterness and anger, quite unable to think rationally. I felt like the army recruit who, having responded to the charm of the recruiting officer, finds that things change drastically after signing on the dotted line.

In hindsight I can see the extent to which vanity played a part in my response. Like most people who despise themselves in private, I found it very difficult to be an also-ran in public. Perhaps I thought that the whole of Christendom should have rejoiced mightily to find such a valuable asset added to its numbers. Perhaps, in a local sense, it should have done. We who call ourselves Christians should be constantly aware that when someone responds to a call from God, we may have access to the particular kind of bread that was promised in that encounter. Let's give it. Let's ignore our prissy concern that we may be feeding someone's vanity. Let's be extravagant and let God sort the rest out.

Whatever the rights and wrongs of the situation, by the time I did go back to the church, a month or so later, I had reassembled my defences, and was ready to take on my old role of guilty performer in the new context of the Young People's Fellowship, and the Christian community of St John's Church. I learned the ropes and the language (what someone recently called 'Christianese') quite quickly. On one level I enjoyed being a part of the group, and yet being different – more 'of the world', but on another I still felt alienated and unreal. In the middle of meetings and services it was possible to feel good, to shout 'Praise the Lord!' with the others, and even feel that I meant it, but the nights were black. God never came home with me. I would return from a lively bout of rejoicing to find that, on my own, there was only fear, fear that there was no God; fear even that in some peculiar way I only existed when other people were present. My own consciousness was embarrassingly there with me, watching as some other 'I' wrestled with panic and doubt. I had never heard of holograms then, but that was what I felt like – substantial only as a projection of the beliefs, attitudes and responses of others. But how could I tell anyone this? I was a Christian. I was converted. If things weren't going right; if I wasn't experiencing the love, joy and peace that God *always* brought into the hearts of believers, there were only three possible reasons that I could think of.

1. There was no God. I had made a mistake.
2. I had done, or failed to do, something that was crucially important.
3. After taking a closer look, God had said, 'No thanks very much', and decided I wasn't up to scratch.

I didn't want to believe the first, hoped vaguely that it might be the second, and secretly believed and dreaded that it was actually the third. Sometimes, I read the parable of the sower, in which some of the seed falls on stony ground, and after springing up quickly, withers away in the sun because it has no real roots. Was that me? And were all these mild, tidily dressed young people, who didn't smoke and were working for exams or preparing to go to university or college, the seed that fell on rich soil and produced a crop, some a hundredfold, some sixty, some thirty? I felt they must be. No doubt they all woke each morning and had the much discussed and strongly advocated 'quiet time' with God. I didn't. I said I did, but I didn't, any more than I had done my homework while at school.

In fact, the whole experience became a kind of parallel of schooldays. My uniform was evangelical language and behaviour – as scruffy and ill-fitting as ever – and the headmaster was God, a distant being who was kind to those who succeeded, and eventually expelled the ones who didn't, or couldn't. What had happened to the Jesus who said he would look after me, and accept me whatever I was? I sang about him, discussed him, tried to talk to him. Where the heck was he? If there seems to be a lot of anger in these words, that's because there is. Even as I write, the memory of that feeling of angry disappointment floods into my mind and momentarily obscures the peace that I have now.

Now, of course, gentle reader, (I used to read a lot of Victorian literature as a child) I can see, as you can, that this scruffy, mixed up and over defended teenager was confusing God with middle class evangelical Christianity and that as long as I was trying to be like other people who were very different to me, I stood little chance of feeling that I was getting somewhere. Also, I recognise that my trusting mechanism had rusted with disuse, and was bound to require consistent applications of the oil of love, over a long period, before it ground into action again. Add to this my distorted perception of fatherhood and adult relationships, and it really is not difficult to account for the mess I found myself in. But I was by no means the only casualty. My heart goes out to all those others, who, in the sixties were attracted by Jesus, and tried unsuccessfully thereafter, to find him in the security of groups and jargon. In the group that I joined there was at least a handful of people who, because of difficult, painful backgrounds needed a special kind of love and discipline, but gave up in the end because the strain of copying was too great. They are at a particular disadvantage because, whereas most of the other attractions of the period – drugs or eastern philosophies or whatever – could be dropped without guilt, the abandonment of Christianity, as it was presented then and still is in many places, often left a shadow of guilt and failure darkening a corner of the spirit, that was not easily removed. This was intensified by the fact – puzzling and hurtful at the time – that whereas people in the church accepted you totally before conversion, they tended to find any deviation from the norm very annoying or unacceptable after you had 'crossed the line'.

So, the escape into reality that I had so longed for was simply not happening. Why *did* God disappear when I was on my own? Why was I still having to wear the masks that prevented people from coming close to me? Why, oh why was it all such a strain? I just didn't know.

Chapter 3

I arrived in Bristol after dark, clutching two badly fastened, string-reinforced suitcases, with not the slightest idea of where I would stay, or how I would look after myself. The city seemed terrifyingly large as I trudged out of the coach station, to find myself on one of those featureless roads that run dumbly behind large buildings. It was a viciously unwelcoming spot, and I was near to tears for a moment, as I put my bags down and tried to decide what to do next.

I suppose it was something of a miracle that I was there at all. Nearly three years had passed since I officially left school. After two or three disastrous attempts to enter the world of employment I had managed, on the strength of my ability with language, to enrol at the West Kent College of Further Education for a combined GCE and foundation drama course. Such a course could not have been better suited to one who, like me, was able to produce occasional flashes of brilliance in English Literature classes and drama exercises, this temporarily blinding tutors to the fact that I was doing next to no work at all.

A close friend, Hugh Card, wrote to me recently about those days.

'We met in 1967, at a college Christian Union meeting. I was an engineering student. You were on a drama course. I noticed your size and untidiness. You sat at a table, dropping cigarette ash on the yellow formica, taking up more space than seemed reasonable. You talked rather than listened. As you explained your ideas, bits of paper spread across the table and on to the floor. An Agatha Christie fell out of your pocket. You were the untidiest Christian I'd met.'

For two years I enjoyed a feeling of relative significance in this setting, especially as the second year was spent in the comfortable knowledge that I had secured a place on the Bristol Old Vic Theatre School acting course, to commence in the autumn of 1967.

I left the college, finally, with a B pass at 'A' level in English Literature, which delighted and (secretly) amazed me, and a scraped pass in French 'O' level, which left me with the ability to converse in the present tense with close members of the family on such useful and diverse topics as writing implements and dining rooms, but very little else. Now, I was about to pursue that old fantasy of stardom in the acting world, and I had a real place on a real course at a real and reputable theatre school, over a hundred miles away in the city of Bristol. If only I had been better prepared. For some reason I never got round to arranging a place to stay when I arrived. It was so easy to rationalise my disorganisation. I called it 'walking in faith'. Christians didn't need to trouble themselves with such trivial matters as booking accommodation in advance. God would provide.

Now, as I stood dismally next to my luggage in the darkness of a strange city, I wasn't so sure. There was one chance, though. A friend in Tunbridge Wells had told me about a church in the Redlands area of the city. She knew the vicar well. He was, she said, a wonderful Christian. If ever I needed anything I should go to him. He would help.

'Right!' I said to myself, picking up my cases, 'Redlands it is.'

After many enquiries, and a fairly lengthy walk, I found myself, at last, outside the front door of a house situated to one side of the church my friend had named. On a polished wooden name-plate beside the door, I could just make out the reassuring words 'The Vicarage'. I was very tired by now, and aching with hunger, but these basic needs were as nothing compared to my desperate desire to make real contact with someone in this alien world. Ever one for the dramatic moment, I planned my lines carefully before raising my hand to the brass knocker in front of me. After all, this might be the beginning of chapter one in my own best-selling Christian saga one day.

The door was opened by a nicely-dressed lady, probably in her fifties, who peered doubtfully out at the tall dark figure standing between what must have looked in silhouette, like two over-stuffed cardboard boxes.

'Yes?' she said, rather nervously.

'I'm starting at the theatre school this term,' said I, 'and I've just arrived from Tunbridge Wells tonight.'

'Yes?' she sounded even more nervous than before.

Time for my punchline.

'I've got nowhere to stay and the only person I know in Bristol is Jesus.'

Now she looked positively terrified.

'My husband's out at the moment, I'm afraid ... I don't know ...'

Something crumpled in me. Never mind my Christian saga, I just wanted a little mothering. My voice broke a little as I spoke.

'A friend suggested I should come if I needed help ...' I named the friend.

'Oh, yes, I know.' It obviously didn't make any difference. 'I'm afraid that my husband won't be back for some time.' The door was closing, she was drawing back. 'Try again later, perhaps ...' The latch clicked into place. She was gone.

What had gone wrong? Wrong script? Wrong house? Wrong city? Wrong world? I was desolated. My last emotional and physical reserves had been spent in reaching that front door. All the old horror of not belonging flooded into my heart as I picked up my luggage and trailed off into the darkness. The magic words hadn't done the trick. Much later that night I did finally find somewhere to stay, but the moment immediately after the door shut on that autumn night in 1967 remained as a nightmare memory for years. Christians, God, Jesus – no one kept their promises.

I was, of course, totally self-absorbed at the time, otherwise

I might have understood that middle-aged ladies on their own late at night are, quite reasonably, unwilling to admit very large religious maniacs with great armfuls of murder weapons in cardboard boxes. I'm sure that the lady concerned was as charitable as the next person, and, in one sense, she has affected me positively. Since that night I have never turned anyone away from my door.

I had not realised that it was possible to be as lonely as I was during my first term at Bristol. I used to lie on my bed in the lodgings I had found, alternately pleading and raving in the direction of this God who seemed to exist only within the confines of St John's Church, Tunbridge Wells.

Not surprisingly, perhaps, the year that followed was not a successful one in terms of the acting course. There was no doubt that I had talent, but my application and self-discipline were very poor. I soon realised that I lacked the kind of consistency required from students of what is a very tough and demanding profession. Once again, the reality trampled all over the dream. I stumbled through the days and weeks in my usual ragged fashion, still clutching my large Bible like a talisman in the most inappropriate situations, hoping I suppose that God would eventually flesh out the bones of the identity that I still thought the Christian faith might offer me.

Now some of those who have been following the story closely so far, will be aware, and are probably dying to point out to me, that 'Old God', as Bishop Peter Ball sometimes affectionately refers to him, had been putting in some pretty useful work on my behalf for some time, and getting no credit whatsoever for it. From the year before my conversion there were no less than five people who were offering me the kind of love and acceptance that God had seemed to promise on the night when Denis Shepherd spoke in the church. Whether they knew this or not, whether they liked it or not, it was so. My mother, Murray and Vivien, John and Anthea, all were keeping God's promise, and in their own way contributing to the process of breaking up the stony ground in my heart to create the kind of rich soil that would make real growth possible in the future. I didn't know this at the time, of course, but how well I understand it now. Later, in my work with children I met so many disturbed youngsters for whom security was just a rumour put about by social workers. They could be surrounded by love, and not see it. Their conviction that the world did not want them was not a belief. It was knowledge. They could not simply be talked into happiness, nor could they be bribed or lured into feeling 'all right'. Often, all that one could do was to go on loving them, practically as well as emotionally, sometimes for years without much, if any, response. They could be aggressive, rejecting, sentimental and apathetic by turns. I once sat with a fifteen-year-old boy sobbing on my lap after he had broken all my windows.

During that excruciatingly lonely period in Bristol, my head was so full of myself, scripture, spiritual gifts, charismatic speakers and Christianese gobbledegook, that I probably wouldn't have recognised Jesus if he'd jumped out in front of me on the pavement and performed amazing miracles before my eyes. Much less was I able to see the quietly persistent love of God in the eyes and arms and voices of those who cared about me.

Blinking God! I'd have broken all his windows if I'd known where they were. Then, perhaps, he would have let *me* sob on *his* lap!

It was in Bristol, in that year of failure at the theatre school, that God gave me the most valuable gift of all. Bridget Ormerod was a fellow student. Like me, she was capable of great mood-swings, but she had a kindness and sense of humour that I found irresistible. Her surname, she told me, meant 'snake in the clearing', which suggested a sort of unconcealed evil. How inappropriate for someone who has brought nothing but care and kindness into people's lives for as long as I have known her.

We spent all our time together after the first term, sometimes spending the period from midnight to dawn in the all night cafe down in the Cumberland Basin, a place where the river and the main road met and crossed by means of a pivoting concrete bridge. The whole scene was lit up at night like a stage set, this appealing greatly to the sense of drama we had in common. It was a blissful time. After a long period of non-belief, Bridget had recently had a conversion experience of her own, and, for a while I enjoyed the novel experience of feeling that God and the world and I belonged to each other, and to Bridget of course. I was in love. We were in love. We felt like two children whom God was leading by the hand into a future that seemed much more promising than I had dared to hope. Perhaps God was all right after all? Fingers crossed.

The immediate question was what to do next. We would get married. We were quite sure about that. We were also quite sure that our future did not lie in the theatre. Eventually, we decided that, although we knew very little about it, we wanted to work in child-care of some kind. Indeed we believed that this was what God was leading us to do. After one or two false starts, and a brief but very enjoyable period as domestic workers at Burrswood, the Christian Healing Home near Tunbridge Wells, we started work as housefather and housemother in a County Council boarding school for maladjusted boys, in the little town of Dursley in Gloucestershire. The school provided places for fifty teenage boys with educational and emotional problems. We occupied single staff flats at opposite ends of the building, which was set in the beautiful green-sculpted Gloucestershire countryside. We were to be married in the following year. On the day we started work it was difficult to see how anything could go very wrong.

At last I seemed to be secure enough to let my childhood insight that 'Everybody is I' work for the benefit of other people. I suppose I envisaged the children I would work with as little, neglected, empty pots, into which I, a combination of Danny Kaye and Doctor Barnardo would pour care, affection and sympathy until they were full and overflowing. They would be pathetically grateful.

I cannot recall any single child being willing to take part in this touching scenario, and after only one day's work with the boys, I drastically adapted my fantasy to one in which a child, any child, was willing to talk pleasantly for five whole minutes to a painfully inept and lonely house-parent.

Within a few weeks my dignity was in shreds. All the techniques and ploys that had just about kept me afloat in the sea of adult interaction were virtually useless against the tidal wave of raw feeling that emanated from these hurt and needy children. With the uncannily accurate insight that is born out of disappointment and failure, they saw through my assumed air of calm confidence and provoked me into responses that frightened me in their violence and intensity. One boy in particular, was a past master in the art of finding my psychological raw spot, and twisting his metaphorical finger into it with relish. He had been alternately beaten and rejected by his policeman father, and he set out to prove that I, tall and dark like his dad, would do the same. His lengthy campaign of aggression and cringing apology worked in the end. In the centre of the football field one day, I knew that my frustration and humiliation were about to find expression. I would either burst into tears or hit him. As we faced each other at that moment the only real difference between us was one of size. I hit him very hard, twice. He had revealed me for what I was; a very immature adult with far too much chaos of my own to be able to cope with his. I couldn't face that at the time, though. I needed so much to be a person who loved children. The guilt and confusion I felt over this and other occasions when I lost control, remained unexamined and unresolved, and were to result in profound problems later in my life.

That first year of work was a nightmare of demolished dignity, lost battles and periodic retreats into the bottom of my wardrobe, where the enclosed darkness offered temporary respite from this world that seemed determined to prove to me yet again, that it was horribly real. Thank goodness I had Bridget. God seemed to have gone on holiday.

The second year was a little easier, but it was marked by an event of considerable significance: the death of my father. The news came by telephone one evening, as Bridget and I, married by now, were preparing to take ten of the most difficult boys away for a hostelling holiday. My mother said that the cancer which had been diagnosed two years earlier had finally killed my father. I didn't really know how to react, and the holiday, which we decided should go ahead as planned, was actually a rather welcome distraction. The constant activity required in the job I was doing enabled me to postpone the uncomfortable task of looking at my feelings for some time. When I did finally risk a peep round the wall of my busy-ness, I discovered that I was deeply unhappy. I was unhappy for a specific reason. My father's death had not been unexpected. We had known for some time that his illness was terminal, so whenever I journeyed from Gloucestershire to Tunbridge Wells to visit my parents' home, I made sure that we 'got on' well. I felt sorry for him in his diminished, crumpled state, all the old jealousies and insecurities seeming so trivial now that he depended on my mother like a helpless child. Also, if I am honest, I was deliberately trying to put together a reasonable collection of positive memories, ready to pile up like sandbags against the inevitable attack of guilt after his death.

But my immediate unhappiness was not about anything that had happened during his life, but about what was happening *now*. Had the plump prayer book worked? Had the Roman Catholic Church worked? Had God worked? Where was my father now? I wanted to know the answer to that question more that I wanted anything else. I remembered moments from the distant past when, frustrated beyond measure by the unbridgeable gap between what he was and what his religion said he should be, he had knelt on the floor pounding a chair with his fist, and shouting through

47

clenched teeth, 'Oh, Christ, help me! Oh, Christ, help me!' Had Christ heard him, or was it all just a cruel, meaningless game?

By now, my father would know – if there was anything to know – all about heaven and hell. I had only the vaguest notion of what terms like that might mean, but I asked God about it again and again.

'Tell me ... please tell me. Where is he?'

I began to think that I would never find peace, until, one night, I had a dream.

There were two parts to the dream. In the first part, I didn't feel as if I was dreaming at all. Perhaps I wasn't. The period just before sleep can be an odd mixture of conscious thought, and unbidden, dream-like images. Awake or asleep – it doesn't really matter. I saw the face of Jesus, just above mine, as I lay in my bed in the darkness. It was a face that smiled, and the smile was one that comforted and reassured. It was there for a few seconds, and then it was gone, like a light being turned out. Don't ask me how I knew that it was Jesus' face. I just knew.

The second part of the dream was quite definitely just that – a dream. It began with a muffled knocking sound, someone was knocking on wood with their knuckles, trying to attract attention. Gradually, I became aware that the noise was coming from my left, and, turning slowly in that direction, I saw a coffin. As I stared at the brown wooden container, I knew with the absolute certainty that is peculiar to dreams, that my father was inside, alive, and anxious to be released from the darkness. With that knowledge came the realisation that someone was standing quietly on my other side, waiting to speak to me. He was a traveller, a man from Tibet, the country I have always associated with hidden knowledge and mysticism. He had travelled a long way, he said, to bring me an important message.

I can hear his words as clearly today as I heard them that night, fourteen years ago.

'There is a rumour that your father has been resurrected.'

That was all; the dream ended with those words. In the morning I remembered the details, but it wasn't until later in the day that I connected the dream message with my constant requests to God for information. As soon as that connection was made, I felt peaceful about my father's whereabouts, although I reckoned that at most, I had been given a divine 'hint'.

This experience is of course a very good example of the kind of incident that can be wrapped in the cotton-wool of spiritual jargon and exhibited from time to time in one's personal museum of 'things that show there is a God'. Thus, in the past, I might, and probably have, described the events of that night in the following way.

'I was lying awake – absolutely wide awake – when the Lord manifested himself to me, and ministered to me through his spirit in great power, with a mighty blessing. I was then shown a vision as of a coffin, and a great knocking came from within. A messenger of the Lord then appeared, and brought wonderful news that my father was gloriously resurrected. From that moment my soul was at peace, and I knew that my prayers were indeed marvellously answered.'

Notice that Tibet has disappeared altogether, and the whole thing is much tidier and more presentable. No, I seemed to see Jesus smiling at me; a man in a dream hinted that my father might be okay; the next day I was no longer troubled; I had been asking God for reassurance. These were the things that happened and they were enough.

Bridget and I worked at the boarding school for three years, and although there was some success and satisfaction, some good relationships made, and some painful partings at the end, it was an overpowering relief to walk down the drive and out through the gates for the last time. As we sat surrounded by cases in the little Dursley bus station I reflected on my amazing capacity for nostalgia.

'If,' I said to Bridget, 'you ever hear me say that I wish we could go back to the good old days in Gloucestershire, just remind me that at this moment I KNOW that's not the way it was!'

She promised she would, and has, of course, had to do so on a number of occasions since.

From Gloucestershire we moved to Bromley, in Kent, where I had been offered a place at a teaching college. In those days, the main qualification for promotion in the child-care world was a teaching certificate, and despite having been reduced to my lowest common denominators by the children at Cam House School, I wanted to continue in that kind of work. I also wanted to have a higher education qualification just for the sake of having it. Bridget had obtained a degree at Bristol University before starting at the theatre school, and, although very humble, was annoyingly bright. So – little Adrian had to have a badge to wear, just like her! I got my badge in the end, a not very impressive B.Ed degree, but by then it didn't seem to matter so much. During the three year course, our first son, Matthew, was born. I was totally enchanted with this little scrap of humanity. He was an enduring novelty, a source of endless fascination and pleasure. I loved his uncompromising, openly expressed need for us, his parents. Every sound he made, every new expression or movement was vitally interesting. Dear Matthew was, and still very much is, another link in the chain of God's loving concern for me. So too are a number of folk who were members of the local church youth club which we helped to run. They are all grown up now (they claim), but are still our very close friends, including Madeleine Dawson, who later became as regular a contributor to Company as her teaching commitments allowed.

St Augustine's, the church we attended in Bromley was one of the best kinds of Anglican assembly. By this I mean that the general ethos was more reminiscent of a family than either a morgue or an obstacle race. At the centre of the congregation was a minority of people who had a genuine faith, and a profound regard for God, while the majority came in a wide variety of temperamental and spiritual shapes and sizes. It was a very warm and caring community, and the first church in which Bridget and I felt genuinely close to, and part of, a worshipping body. The various dramatic productions and youth services that we helped with are among our warmest memories.

Despite all these positive aspects of life in Bromley, however, I still agonised over my relationship with God. I found myself doubting to the point of total disbelief. Okay, things were good at home, and very good socially at church; college was a strain from beginning to end, but I didn't have to be there much. Generally speaking, things were good. We were sharing the house of the curate, who was none other than my best friend from Tunbridge Wells, John Hall. Together we played bad but enjoyable golf once a week on the municipal course, and renewed our old practice of sitting up until the early hours from time to time, talking about everything under the sun.

I was happily married. Matthew was a constant joy. What more could I ask?

I wanted God. I still wanted that God who had made all those promises back in St John's Church when I was sixteen. In what form did I want him? I wasn't sure. I just knew that there was a knot of pain and anger in me that would never be untied (no matter how many good things happened) until I *knew* that God loved me in the way I had always wanted to be loved by a father since I was just a small child. And, as I still didn't know that, maybe there was no God after all.

It is supremely ironic that when, towards the end of our stay in Bromley, I did at last experience reality in my contact with God, I was so frightened by what he wanted me to do that I turned my back on him and 'did a Jonah'.

I had been reading an extract from the writings of Meister Eckhart, a German mystic of the Middle Ages. Particularly interesting to me was his view that repentance was a happy thing. God, he said, was overjoyed when people wanted to change their lives for the better, and more than ready to forget and forgive if it meant that a real friendship could be established. The parable of the prodigal son says exactly the same thing, of course, but perhaps now, I was more ready to accept this truth. Eckhart's words inspired me. I developed a sort of meditation technique, which had an amazingly releasing effect. I would imagine that I was standing in a mist or cloud, surrounded by all the bad or negative things in my life. I would then make a pile of these things – they were easy to stack – and stand on the top of the pile, as tall as I could. The stack was always high enough to allow my head to rise above the level of the mist into the clean, clear, light of the sun. God, in some indefinable way, was in that light. Neither he nor I could see the disreputable heap of baggage under my feet, in the mist, and neither of us cared. It was just good to be in the light, and it made all the difference. Prayer started to feel like conversation, like friendship. It was so new and unusual that I felt slightly hysterical about the whole thing, but it was real, and that was what mattered. Then, one evening as I sat alone in the sitting room at home, a thought 'punched' me in the brain. I can think of no other way to describe it, nor do I care to classify it too precisely. The words were few, but the meaning was clear.

'You must love Jason.'

Clear though the injunction was, I was still rather puzzled. The person in question (his name was not Jason) certainly didn't give the impression of needing my particular care or affection. He was strong, competent, one of those large, hand-carved, independent Christian types. Why should I need to specially love him, and what would it involve? The next day, Jason drove in from Central London where he ran a drug rehabilitation centre. He wanted to confide in me, he said. After my experience of the night before I was all ears, as you can imagine. A real job to do for God at last? He wanted to talk about a dark and difficult area in his private life, something that contrasted starkly with his public image as a professional worker and a Christian. For some weeks we met at frequent intervals. Our meetings did not feel very productive. He talked and I listened, or made feeble attempts to offer advice. His situation grew more complicated, the burden on me seemed increasingly onerous. I was out of my depth and floundering helplessly. I hated the thought that, now, when things in general seemed so much better, I might be about to fail yet again. I wanted to retreat into safety, and just at that time I was presented with a way that seemed to offer just the opportunity I needed. Since the completion of my college course I had applied for a post in a regional assessment centre in the midlands. Now, after a rather alarming interview in the big grey city of Birmingham, I was offered a job as housemaster in a unit of twenty-four delinquent boys. At the same time Jason suggested that I should join him in the work he was doing in London.

'You must love Jason.'

We went to Birmingham.

My new-found relationship with God was too fragile to withstand this deliberate evasion. I know now that, in fact, God being the way he is, he would have been quite ready to heave a sigh, forgive me unreservedly for letting him down, and start again in Birmingham, but I was not prepared to forgive myself, and that was that.

The following five years were dominated by the work I was doing in Birmingham, Norwich and finally Hailsham in East Sussex. Shift work with disturbed children split my existence into two parts – periods when I was working, and periods when I was waiting to go to work. Free time was not free of the shadow of the shift to come, unless it was lengthy enough for stretched nerves to relax, and clouds of worry to disperse. There never seemed to be time to stop and reflect on the strange tension-ridden life that I was leading. I learned to cope in the world of residential child-care. I was even able to appear fairly consistently calm and strong, compassionate and caring. I probably helped many children in the process, but every encounter was a role play involving the selection of a suitable personality from the stock that I had accumulated. The growing inner chaos was pushed deep and well controlled.

Meanwhile I was assembling my own little residential unit at home. Joseph was born in 1978, and David in 1980. It was not until 1982 that we moved off campus to share a house with a young teacher friend. For six years the sounds, sights and tensions of the work situation had infected our attempts to relax.

Holidays away were refreshing, but there is something soul-destroying about returning, and being accosted outside your front door by an excited child who passes on, with relish, the news that Fred has run away, Gloria has slashed her wrists, and there is an epidemic of pubic lice. Instant involvement – instant tension. The family frequently had to make do with the fag-end of my good will at the end of a shift, or after the second or third 'sleep-in' in one week. As a family, we were all paying a very high price for the maintenance of my public role. The nervous and emotional expenditure required for a lengthy working period was often so great that there was little time left for my wife and children, who needed their own share of my time and affection.

All my old doubts about God had reappeared during these years. I tried to rationalise the business of Jason and my abandonment of him. Sometimes I prayed. Occasionally I seemed to sense God trying to get close to me, but generally speaking I was in a spiritual desert, and, although I didn't fully realise it at the time, the growing tension of my work environment was running parallel with a steadily intensifying anger towards this being who either didn't exist, or didn't like me. Back to square one! When people asked me what I believed, I dragged out the old unwieldy package of evangelical cliches, but my heart was not in it.

Then, at the beginning of 1981, Bridget and I were involved in a new group that called itself The Hailsham Christian Fellowship. It was relaxed, informal and refreshing. Both of us experienced a lightening of our spirits as we became part of this little community of Christians from a variety of church backgrounds. Perhaps, through this group, I would find God again and all would be well.

Later in the year, Bridget and I wrote and produced a Christian revue for the fellowship, which was performed on the local secondary school stage to an audience consisting mainly of Christians from the local churches. It was called 'A Place For You', and was specially intended to reassure those Christians for whom Christian living had seemed like a long slog through ankle-deep mud. At that time the fellowship was a welcome refuge for such people. The production had a valuable unifying function for the fellowship, most of whom were involved in the project in one way or another. For us it was like rebirth.

We felt that God really was with us in the writing and rehearsal of the revue, and that, at last, we were coming out of the desert, and taking a few tentative steps into the promised land. It was a truly satisfying experience, and it left Bridget and me with a warm sense of belonging to this group of people whose lives were becoming so intertwined as the weeks went by. I had recently helped to establish a new unit for older children in the children's centre where I worked, and found myself enjoying work much more. Overall, things were looking good, and although God and I still had a lot to settle, at least I was keen to hear what he had to say again.

It was at this point, when both Bridget and I felt more confident and stable than we had done for years, that a friend phoned me to ask if I had noticed a small article in the local paper about the new television company that was due to take over from Southern Television in the new year. The company was to be called TVS, and the article described how Angus Wright, producer of religious programmes, was looking for six ordinary people to take part in a new kind of late-night religious programme.

'Why not write to him?' said my friend.

'All right,' I said. 'I will.'

Chapter 4

At various times, and in various parts of the country, I had found myself watching the late-night epilogue programme broadcast by the BBC, or the local independent television company. Occasionally they were interesting, but generally speaking I was not very impressed. They seemed to take one of two forms.

In the first, a single individual addressed the viewer with unstumbling ease, on subjects that were more or less religious in content. This kind of neatly packaged homily had a rather adverse effect on me. The speaker was heavily protected by the preparedness of his talk, and the fact that nobody was able to interrupt, or argue with what he was saying. At its best this kind of approach seemed harmless, but at its worst it could be positively intimidating. The impression often given was that the worthy person whose eyes followed you round the room as you collected the cocoa cups, had succeeded in tying up all the loose ends in his own understanding of the Christian faith, and was a living example of the way in which spiritual and psychological tidiness could be achieved. For people watching at home, whose lives were difficult and ragged at the edges, this was not always an inspiring example. If they had felt inadequate and confused before, they were likely to feel even more so now. The same thing happens, of course, in many churches, where there is a clear, if unspoken injunction to leave your 'shadow' by the door on your way in, before getting down to singing about how happy you are. There seems to be little room for people who desperately want to say, like Job, that life is wild and tragic and they don't like it, so isn't it a good thing that God can be trusted.

The second kind of programme took the form of a one-to-one interview between a questioner, who was either religiously connected in some way or just suitably genial, and a guest, who would probably appear each night for a week, to answer questions about his or her life and work. The background set was always very simple, the participants usually emerging from near darkness at the beginning of the programme, and disappearing into it again at the end. Occasionally, these encounters had life in them, but most of the programmes that I saw looked like two people trying to reproduce a real conversation that they had enjoyed the night before. Worthy, but dull, they reflected the generally poor presentation of the Christian faith that we have all become used to.

Angus Wright was interested in trying a new approach, which, as far as possible, would allow the viewer to feel involved with what was happening on the screen. Instead of one or two people delivering over-prepared lines to the camera or each other, there would be three or four folk seated around a kitchen table, in a proper kitchen set, having a genuinely unscripted conversation about real happenings and events in their lives. Hopefully, the viewer would, as it were, take a seat around the table and become involved with the lives and views of the participants in as real a way as possible, bearing in mind the obvious limitations of television. The programme would provide a familiar and consistent way to end the viewing day for those in the TVS region who for one reason or another were awake and still watching at that time of night. It would offer company, and it was this basic aim which suggested that the new programme should be called, simply, 'Company'.

Although it was years since Bridget and I had left theatre school, and abandoned the idea of acting as a profession, we had never lost our passion for everything to do with performance. At work, at church, and with the youth club in Bromley, we had never really been happier than when we were caught up in the rich complexity of 'putting on a show'. We both find the stage – any stage – tremendously exciting, whether we are working behind the scenes, or actually taking part in a performance. When I wrote to Angus after my friend's phone call, the performer in me certainly hoped that we might actually be able to take part in this new project, but it seemed more likely that he would simply thank me for contributing my ideas, and that would be that. When he wrote back, suggesting that an associate producer, Frances Tulloch, should visit us for a discussion, Bridget and I were quite ridiculously excited. I can understand that it might be difficult to see why the prospect of appearing on a tiny programme that wouldn't start until most people had gone to bed should give us such pleasure. I suppose that, at the time, it seemed like a sort of confirmation that things were looking up. Life was changing for the better. The fellowship that we had joined, the revue, a general easing of tension at work, and now this. It was as if God was saying 'Right! You've done your time, now you can relax for a while.' Yes, you're right. I still didn't understand God at all!

After our meeting with Frances, who subsequently took over production responsibility for Company, we were invited to take part in an audition, to be held in Frances' club in London. We were still very excited, but also very, very nervous.

Travelling in the same carriage as us on the train to London that day was Lionel Blair, who was appearing in Eastbourne for the season. We reflected ruefully on the ease with which he would have handled the ordeal that lay before us, and which was causing us such nervous apprehension as we clutched our cardboard cups of British Rail coffee, and passed through all stations to Victoria. I'm not quite sure what we expected of our first step into the world of television, something a lot less gentle and civilised, I suspect. For the audition, Frances had obtained the services of a charming old gentleman and his equally charming wife, who usually hired out themselves and their simple video equipment for the purpose of recording Christian meetings and events. Angus

Wright turned out to be a tall, thoughtful man, with a slightly distracted air, but a very pleasant manner. He was rather like a serious Derek Nimmo. Finally, we were introduced to Maurice Harper who was to direct Company. Maurice is a complex, attractive Irishman, who is still waiting for the world to deal him a really good hand. We were to become very fond of him.

The atmosphere was relaxed and warm as we took turns sitting in front of the single TV camera, but the five minute talks that we had been asked to prepare must have come over to our small audience as very tense and perspiring affairs. We were just learning how to breathe again when Maurice told us he was keen to see how we came over in conversation.

'Can you just talk?' he asked.

'Yes,' answered Adrian.

'No,' answered Bridget simultaneously.

Maurice ran a hand through his hair, a gesture that was to become familiar. He has always been able to subdue an oath when necessary. He subdued one now.

'Can't you discuss something that you both feel strongly about?'

We looked at each other.

'Well,' I replied tentatively, 'there is a problem we had a while ago when we did a church service. This lad. He was a bit of a nuisance – not turning up for rehearsals, that sort of thing. We weren't sure whether to get someone else or not. So we ...'

'Fine, fine!' said Maurice. 'Sit at that table. Away you go!'

So away we went, having a discussion that was two months out of date, in a big, strange room, watched by a group of people we had only just met, terribly aware that every word we said, every over-sincere expression on our faces, was being recorded by the expressionless eye of the camera and the microphone on its stand between us.

The general reaction to our efforts seemed quite positive, but as we sat, exhausted, on the southbound train an hour later, we still didn't know the outcome of the audition. The days passed, and we heard nothing. Then, one day when I was out at work, Frances rang and talked to Bridget.

I came home from work that day in my usual, slightly manic state, and flopped wearily onto the settee hoping that a cup of tea and the newspaper might somehow waft themselves in my direction. Bridget, the most likely wafting agent, was sitting very still on the edge of her seat, and something about the quality of her stillness made me forget work and tiredness and cups of tea. Something was wrong. The children? I felt a cold shiver pass through me that I always experienced when I thought something bad might have happened to the boys. Bridget spoke.

'Frances rang.'

Not the children then. Why did Bridget sound so troubled? At the worst Frances could only have rung to say that we had failed the audition. Upsetting, but hardly tragic.

'Yes ... and?'

'Well ...'

This was getting silly. I got up, grabbed an upright chair from its place by the wall, carried it over to where Bridget was perched on the edge of her armchair, and sat as close to her as I could. She didn't seem able to let her eyes meet mine.

'Bridget, what's the matter? What did Frances say?'

She raised her head and looked at me at last, eyes wide with apprehension.

'She said they want to use me for Company, but not you.' Her face was creased with pain. 'Oh, Adrian, I don't want to do it if you don't do it. You wrote the letter and I thought ...'

Poor Bridget. She really and truly was more concerned with how I felt, than anything else. So, how *did* I feel? I felt as though I'd been banged on the head with a very heavy object. Drat God! It was happening all over again. Not wanted. Not accepted. Not good enough. Why not? Deep inside me the little boy collapsed in tears as his daddy let him down yet again.

Meanwhile, I was aware of Bridget's eyes searching my face for the slightest sign of hurt or upset. She has since told me that if she had detected the merest indication of what I was really feeling, she would have decided, on the spot, to ring Frances and say that she did not want to be included in the Company team.

Usually, I could not have concealed my feelings anyway. Like many husbands I am nothing more than a big baby at times, and if I get upset I make sure those around me know about it, or at the very least I carefully let them notice that I am concealing my feelings. But this was different. In the split second following Bridget's last speech I knew that the manner and content of my reply would either free her to pursue this interesting and novel activity, or prevent it altogether. It was not right or fair that it should be so, but it was a fact.

'Thank goodness for that. I thought it was something really awful for a moment.' I knew it sounded convincing.

'You mean you don't mind?' Bridget was puzzled, still wary.

I had myself completely under control now.

'In an odd sort of way, it's a relief,' I lied. 'Let's have a cup of tea. What about taking the children up along the old railway track for a picnic ... ?'

It was the only truly heroic thing I'd ever done, but it didn't give me very much satisfaction at the time. I was used to engineering rewards for my virtue, but in this case I knew that I just had to keep my mouth shut, and suffer. Ironically, if I had not responded as I did, it is possible that neither of us would have been involved with the programme. As it was, only a few weeks passed before I was also asked to join the Company team, and I could relax from the strain of pretending to be genial but unconcerned about being excluded from Bridget's new activity.

The first Company participants were not actually as 'ordinary' as the original concept had envisaged. There was, for instance, Peter Ball, the Anglican Bishop of Lewes, already quite a celebrity in the south-east and elsewhere. Bob Gordon was a distinguished lecturer in Old Testament studies, and about to join Colin Urquhart as a co-elder at the Hyde Christian community near Haywards Heath. Ken Gardner was an Anglican priest from the parish of St Philip and St Jacob, Waldeslade, near Gillingham, and Ann-Marie Stewart was a Franciscan nun who had left her convent after twenty years to start a new form of Franciscan life in Canterbury. Ann-Marie supported herself by taking on cleaning jobs in the mornings, while devoting the rest of the day to prayer and the occasional preaching or teaching engagement. Next to this line-up of religious experts, Bridget and I were very conscious of being 'token ordinary ones'. I was an expert in spiritual confusion, and Bridget was an expert in living with someone who was spiritually confused, but that was about all.

For a time, it was a little intimidating. The TVS world seemed to be full of incredibly expensive machinery and highly trained technicians. The atmosphere in the new studio at Gillingham was one of great enthusiasm. We were in at the beginning of, not only a new programme, but a new television company. Everyone seemed to be on their toes. We were amazed at the number of people that seemed to be necessary for the making of such a humble programme. Whenever a technical problem occurred, they seemed to come out of the woodwork in their droves, each one an expert in something or other. Cameras, lights, sound, make-up, props, wardrobe; there seemed no end to the specialised knowledge required to make this five minute programme in a small corner of the vast ex-cinema studio. So what were *we* doing there? What qualified us to sit with experts, surrounded by experts, saying things that thousands of southerners from Maldon in Essex to Dorchester in the West would hear every night? Not, I hasten to add, that our fellow participants in any way deliberately made us feel inadequate. Bob was aggressively confident on behalf of all of us, Ken was always warm and self-effacing, Ann-Marie was, by her own admission and despite wide experience of public speaking, quite paralysed by nerves for the first few weeks, and Peter – well, more about

Peter later. Helpful and friendly though everyone was, the question remained for Bridget and me: what right did two ordinary people have, to talk about Christianity in front of thousands of viewers, when so many others were better informed, and certainly more consistent in the way they lived out their faith? The answer was, of course, none at all, and in realising this we realised what our contribution should be. If we could manage to be honest and open about the things, good and bad, that happened to us, and resist the temptation to make excuses for God by papering over the cracks in our lives, then we might offer hope and reassurance to people whose lives were just as frayed at the edges.

In theory, ours sounds a humble role, but in fact, we weren't really feeling very humble at all. We just *loved* the palaver of production meetings and make-up and work in the studio. It all smacked of the 'telly'. We were on the 'telly'! We developed a sort of compensatory nonchalance about the whole thing, which probably deceived nobody, least of all ourselves. That feeling of novelty and rich excitement did not last very long, and perhaps it was rather silly, but I think it was a good and necessary thing. It made us feel like children again, and that is always a healthy experience for Christians.

Some of those early programmes must have been awful. I wouldn't be able to count the number of times that Maurice, sometimes running *both* hands through his hair, would threaten to strangle the next person who started a sentence with the words 'As a Christian ...'. Then there was our tendency to be terribly, terribly polite to each other while the cameras were on us. There is nothing wrong with politeness, of course, but quite often the relaxed and strongly animated discussion which followed the programme, would have been far more interesting to the viewer than the cosy, religious head-nodding exercise that had just appeared on the screen. We were in danger (and it has remained a danger) of doing exactly what the old-style epilogue programmes had done, only more expensively. Added to this were our two great fears. We were afraid of silence, and we were afraid that a programme might finish without the opportunity for us to contribute our particular little nugget of insight or wisdom to the conversation. I filled many a silence with absolute blithering nonsense in those days, and probably still do at times. I also remember sitting at that kitchen table, waiting for a gap – any kind of gap – in the conversation, so that I could thrust my little set-speech into the proceedings, regardless of context. With a little ingenuity it was possible to force a connection of some kind. Thus, the following conversation might have taken place:

Ann-Marie: One of the most interesting things I ever saw, happened on a Monday, which is always a rather bad day for me.

Adrian: (Spotting a minute opening) Oddly enough, I was going to talk about something that happened on a Wednesday, which, as you know, is only two days after Monday. You see, my mother …

Bridget: (Determined not to be left out) Don't you think God is as much a mother as he is a father?

Adrian and Ann-Marie: (Both seething inwardly, but unwilling to display impatience in front of 50,000 people) Yes, yes, he probably is. How interesting …!

A slight exaggeration of course, but all these problems had to be faced. We discovered over the months that it *was* possible to be in conflict without throttling each other, and that a silence, if it was a natural one, was not only *not* to be feared, but could be more meaningful than a great deal of conversation.

The secret seemed to lie in two areas: honesty and listening. If the words we said came from the heart, and we really listened and responded to what others were saying, then it didn't matter whether we talked about potty-training or predestination. It would be real. As Angus has repeatedly said from the outset, people will only want to watch if something is *happening* on the screen. We are all still guilty of the same mistakes from time to time, but, one hopes, less often.

When Company first started, Bridget and I were naive enough to believe that the kitchen set, although obviously an aid to creating an appropriate atmosphere, was not something that would be much noticed by viewers. It was a rather basic kitchen as kitchens go, rather reminiscent of the fifties and not at all likely to attract attention. On the table at which we sat there might be a vase of flowers or a bowl of fruit, but generally speaking there was little that seemed interesting enough to distract viewers from our 'scintillating' conversation. We were wrong. One day, as we completed the purchase of a can of paint in a local shop, the lady who had served us cleared her throat in an 'I'm going to say something' sort of way, as we turned to go. She laid a hand on my wife's arm, and spoke earnestly.

'I do hope you don't mind me asking ...' Her expression was very serious. Bridget smiled encouragingly. 'Only – you see, my husband and I have been watching your programme all this week and – well, we've got a question that we both want to ask. Would you mind?'

We were flattered. It was in the early days, and it felt good to be recognised in public. Now, here was this nice lady who'd listened, with her husband, to everything we'd said for a whole week, and wanted help with a problem. Some difficulty in their Christian lives no doubt. She and her husband saw us as people who might have some answers.

'If we can help, then of course ...' Bridget's sincere tones matched the earnestness of the questioner.

'Only – it's been troubling us all week ...'

'Yes?' Bridget was patience itself.

The lady leaned forward. She spoke even more confidentially than before.

'The fruit in that bowl ... is it real?'

Later on, contact with viewers, through correspondence and in person was very important to us, especially in the very black days that were to come two and a half years after Company began, but at first, being recognised in the street was a strange and sometimes disconcerting experience.

One Saturday, Bridget lost her purse, containing most of our holiday savings, just drawn from the bank. Panic-stricken, she rushed around the town dragging our two pre-school children behind her. Her face smudged with tears as she searched in vain for the missing money, she was reaching a fine pitch of hysteria, when a voice at her shoulder said, 'Excuse me, but haven't I seen you on telly?' Bridget is a very modest lady, but not even the most inflated super-Christian TV image would have survived that moment. I ought to add that the purse was found and later returned to us by a very honest gentleman who stumbled over it on his way home from work.

Then there was the lady who flung her arms round my neck and kissed me on the cheek as I queued outside a cinema with eight-year-old Matthew. She fixed me with the intense gaze of the semi-inebriate, and spoke with deep, throbbing sincerity.

'Are you and Bridget as happy in real life as you are on television?'

As she departed unsteadily along the pavement without waiting for an answer, Matthew looked from me to her and back to me in wonderment.

'Gosh, Daddy,' he said. 'You don't 'alf make friends quickly, don't you?'

Sometimes, when we made programmes separately, one of us would mention that we had been going through an irritable, argumentative patch. I was standing in a supermarket queue, one day, when a voice came from somewhere behind my left shoulder.

'Sorry to hear you and your wife had a row.'

It was a lady I had never seen before. Quickly, my mind made the necessary connection. Presumably Bridget had described our recent 'bad patch' to the south of England, late last night. What had she said? What did this lady in the queue know, that I didn't? I resisted the temptation to ask, and reflected on the fact that, while honesty on television might be the best policy, it could produce some very uncomfortable moments. Nevertheless, it became clearer than ever that it was just this willingness to be open about the darker side of our lives that would enable not just Bridget and me, but the Company team generally, as it changed and grew, to relate closely to viewers who needed to know that they were not alone in their experience of failure and difficulty.

Chapter 5

So what did we talk about evening after evening? Well, for a while we tried to solve most of the world's problems in double quick time. Death on Monday, forgiveness on Tuesday, suffering on Wednesday – we sorted them all out in five minutes or so each. Sometimes it was possible to have something approaching a reasonable discussion on these vast subjects in such a risibly short time, but I think we realised fairly early on that unless the things we said were grounded in experience we wouldn't sound very convincing.

Sometimes, for instance, we would pick up on the headline news of the day, and unless we had some specialist knowledge in a specific area, it was better to produce a kind of personal, uninformed response that the majority of viewers could identify with. Essentially, we were having a 'chat' rather than a discussion, and when friends chat they will probably talk about what they've been doing, making a passing comment on the day's news, and perhaps exchange gossip or 'have a laugh'. It is not easy to reproduce this kind of informality under laboratory conditions, as it were.

Apart from the specific area of child-care, the only thing I really knew about was 'being me', so for some time my contribution tended to be rather anecdotal. I suppose this was very fitting really, as my relationship with God had been rather anecdotal over the years. I enjoyed telling stories, and they did at least have the virtue of being true. There was the story, for instance, of the lorry driver and the rose.

It happened when I was hitch-hiking some years ago. I was in the cab of a huge lorry, somewhere on the M4 heading west.

I've always loved hitch-hiking. It's a wonderful blend of adventure and legitimate inactivity. G. K. Chesterton said that he knew few things more satisfying than the experience of being stranded at a railway station. I know what he meant. The flavour of accidental solitude is tastier than Marmite, and I've experienced it most while standing on the side of the road waiting for a lift. I relish the fact that only God and I know where I am. Add to this the knowledge that every lift means contact with an unknown and quite unique human being, and you have the perfect occupation for someone with my twin vices of laziness and curiosity.

On this particular day I'd been dropped off on one of the motorway exits, and I had to wait some time on the corresponding slip road for another lift. It was late afternoon when a very large lorry squealed to a halt beside me. The driver leaned across and pushed the passenger door open.

'You'd better get in, mate. You'll never get a lift standin' there.'

I smiled as I hauled myself up to the cab. People said this to me so often, that I quite frequently waited at 'impossible' spots, knowing that some kind person would pick me up in the end.

As the huge vehicle rumbled on to the motorway, my new companion and I began the pigeon-holing process that always preceded real conversation. Once he'd established that I was well-spoken, slightly naive, and not at all threatening, the man behind the wheel leaned towards me and spoke in the tone of one who has made an important decision.

'I'm goin' to tell you somethin' I've never told anyone before!'

He paused, flicking a glance around the cab as though checking for eavesdroppers.

'I wrote this effin' poem.'

He shot a look at me then went on, apparently reassured by my quiet interest.

'I saw this rose, see? In an effin' park. I was just sittin' there, and I looked at this effin' rose, and I thought, "Blow me! Look at that!" So I wrote this poem, didn't I?'

His vulnerability attracted and frightened me. His was a fragile trust.

'Have you said it to anybody?' I asked.

'You must be jokin'! If I told my mates I'd written a blinkin' poem I'd never 'ear the last of it. Just see me goin' down the local and sayin', "Oy, I've written a poem about an effin' rose." I don't think so!'

'Could I hear it?'

After some inward struggle he bawled the poem out over the noise of the engine. When he'd finished I said something appreciative, and the journey continued for some time without further conversation.

As I gazed sightlessly through the wide windscreen in front of me, I wondered what God would think about all this. After a few minutes I had to turn my face to the glass beside me. I didn't want the driver to see the tears in my eyes. I felt that I knew what God must think. All the way down the motorway and into the setting sun he probably wept with me for all the people who have poems in them, and can't believe that anyone else wants to hear them.

That story was especially poignant for me, perhaps, as I have always enjoyed expressing my feelings through poetry, some of which I have shared with Company viewers. One poem, in particular, seemed to sum up the tension that was my legacy from an uneasy childhood. Sending these words out through the camera lens had an oddly cleansing effect.

When I was a small boy in a small school,
With endless legs,
And ears that widely proclaimed a head full of
    emergencies,
When I clung by bleeding fingertips to thirty-three plus
    nine,
And cognitive dissonance was a hard sum,

There were only two crimes.
The first was shouting in the corridors,
The second was to be a fool.
And when the bell, the blessed bell,
Let me fling my body home,
I thought I might, at least, one day,
Aspire to rule in hell,
But now I never hear the bell,
And part of me will always be
A fool,
Screaming in some sacred corridor.

A less poetic but no less meaningful account, concerned the way in which I coped – or rather, didn't cope – with the first day of my new job in Sussex, after moving down from Norfolk.

It doesn't matter how experienced you are in residential child-care, it's always nerve-racking to confront a new and horribly unfamiliar group of children and staff, especially in the intense atmosphere of a large children's centre. I was due to start at 2.30. By half-past one I'd run out of distractions, courage, faith and saliva. I wanted Armageddon to happen within the hour. Then, a decision, a solution of sorts, crawled into my mind. If I really shifted – if I took the short cut along the old railway line and across the school playing-field, I could get to the Britannia Arms in time to pour at least three pints of bitter into my stomach. That should drown the butterflies; poor little beggars – they wouldn't stand a chance. I hurried out of the house wearing the inevitable load of guilt like a haversack on my back. I had not had much to say to God for some time, but I knew what he'd think of my dash to the pub. Eyebrows raised, fingers drumming on a cloud. I challenged him 'bravely'.

'There's nothing you can do about it, God. I'm going for a drink and that's that. I want a drink, I need a drink, I'm going to have a drink. And if you don't like it, you'll have to stop me!'

As I sped along the footpath between bushes and trees, I offered a couple of suggestions to the deity.

'What about muggers, God? Why don't you get someone to leap from behind a tree and knock me out? Or maybe a dramatic soil subsidence. I could just disappear into a crack in the ground. Is that what you're going to do?'

I laughed rather wildly as I crossed the sports ground and jogged up the hill towards the town. I really wasn't very proud of what I was doing. Here was the main road at last. On the other side the pub; the beer.

'Last chance, God. Road accident? Needn't be anything serious. Broken limb perhaps?'

I negotiated the busy road without incident, and walked into the saloon bar of the Britannia. I ordered a pint. I watched it being pulled; I licked my lips. I put my hand out and took the brimming glass. As I drew it carefully towards me I felt in my jacket pocket with my other hand for some money.

'Hard luck, God! Cheers!'

Suddenly, I froze. Panic – horror – no money! I'd changed my jacket. I hadn't a penny. The barman didn't know me from Adam.

'I'm sorry – I haven't got any money,' I said pathetically.

'In that case, we haven't got any beer,' replied the man – clearly an Old Testament type, and he reached over and took my pint back from me.

I didn't start laughing until I was halfway back to the Centre. I was still laughing inwardly as I went into work at half-past two.

It was rather like – being drunk.

After telling this story one night, I discovered that we had a hitherto unsuspected audience of publicans. As I visited pubs in and around the area over the next couple of weeks, I found that landlords and their wives were intrigued by the details of the account. Which pub was it? What kind of beer was it? They usually watched Company, they said, because once all the clearing up was done, it was nearly midnight anyway, and by the time they

72

were able to put their feet up, our few minutes of chat was about all that was left of the evening's viewing.

It was also a good example of how openness can be a releasing agent. Having revealed that I was a Christian with a healthy liking for beer, and an unhealthy tendency to use it as a prop sometimes, it seemed easier for others to be frank about their own vices or failings. Although, at the time, I didn't know the answers to such problems, it did seem to me that it was better for people to feel free to talk about these things, rather than be paralysed by feelings of guilt. A similar effect was produced by Bridget's lively descriptions of times when everything went disastrously wrong, just as she particularly wanted to look like a calm, confident wife and mother. Those who knew what it meant to wilt under the disapproving stare of 'mothers-whose-children-behave-well' whilst wrestling unsuccessfully with their own rebellious crew, found it refreshingly easy to identify with these graphic tales.

Of course, me being me, it wasn't long before I began to see myself as God's gift to the late night box-watchers, put at that table to offer hope to an army of insomniacs. What I didn't realise was that God intended to sort *me* out over the next three years, and the first step in his campaign, using my participation in Company as a lever, was to do something that I had been trying to do for years. He found a way for me to give up smoking.

I was a dedicated smoker, and had been for sixteen years. In most of the photographs taken since I was sixteen, I was holding a packet of cigarettes and a box of matches in one hand, and a book in the other. Cigarettes were the only uncomplicated comforts I knew, little friends who were always available, never answered back, and didn't object to being trodden on. By the time I was thirty-three I was smoking at least sixty cigarettes a day; one every twenty minutes; one thousand pounds worth every year. I smoked when I got into bed, and I smoked before I got up in the morning. I lit up as I walked out of the door, and again as I waited for the bus. I smoked before, during and after a bath. Often I would leave a church service or an important meeting halfway through, ostensibly to visit the toilet, but actually to snatch a few reassuring drags before returning to the smokeless zone. Most delicious of all – oh ecstasy! – I smoked after a meal.

My smoking was conducted with a curious underlying intensity. I protected my addiction fiercely, realising, perhaps, that I was using it as a weapon in the battle to postpone real involvement with a world that was never quite satisfactory. At the same time, I had always felt guilty about being a smoker. It was one of the things a Christian *ought* to feel guilty about, wasn't it?

Nowadays, I believe that God is, in fact, quite nice, but for years I retained the image of something between a headmaster and a bank manager, before whom I played the role of a naughty boy with an overdraft. Now that I no longer smoke, I am quite sure that smoking, in itself, is no more of a sin than anything else, but I was a slave to the habit, and it was costing a fortune. I performed every spiritual gymnastic in the book. I made decisions at meetings, I went forward at rallies, I repented and pleaded and argued with the rigidly austere God that my heart had created. The only thing these experiences had in common was the pleasure with which I lit up the cigarette that invariably followed each decision to give up. Money, health, guilt – nothing was a strong enough motive to stop. For a couple of years now, I hadn't bothered to try.

Then, one day, as Bridget wrestled grimly with our dilapidated top-loading washing machine, something happened. She burst into tears of frustration as the appliance forced her, yet again, into a losing submission. She said just ten words.

'If you didn't smoke, I could have a new machine!'

She had never complained before. I walked round to the electricity showrooms and bought a washing machine on hire purchase. I calculated that if I cut down my daily ration of cigarettes to twenty, the money saved would cover the repayments. I decided to smoke one cigarette each hour, on the hour. I lived for the moment when, as my youngest son put it, the big hand was on the twelve. Each hour lasted several months. Each cigarette seemed to last a few seconds. My family hid. After a month of this, I knew that the moment of final decision had come. It was now or never. Give up altogether or go back to sixty a day. I decided to give up. The difference this time, was that I knew how to put a much more effective armlock on myself than at any time in the past. A few days later I talked at the Company table about how I no longer smoked. My heart sank as I burned my boats so finally. Relatively small though the Company audience might be, I knew that it was large enough for me to be 'leapt on' by regular viewers if they saw me smoking in the street. But it was my pride that would do the trick in the end. I had said I no longer smoked, and I hadn't the humility to fail. So much for sharing weakness!

The next few months were horrific. Each morning I woke, to remember, with a stab of horror, that I'd given up. I saw little point in getting up – in working – in doing anything. Like someone who has been bereaved, and that's how I felt, I could not be consoled. I resigned myself to suffering. Prayer? God? Don't ask!

Then, one afternoon, six months later, I could stand it no longer. By then I had moved over to work in the secure unit for violent and absconding children, and for once, everyone else was out. On the desk in front of me as I sat in the small staff office, lay a single cigarette, white and alluring, firm with tobacco – beautiful. It had been a hard day. I was tense and nervous. I had had enough. Company or no Company, pride or no pride, I was going to smoke that cigarette. I hunted feverishly through the desk drawer where the lighter was usually kept. As I searched, a small, feeble voice at the back of my mind repeated the same desperate prayer over and over again.

'Don't let it be there – don't let it be there ...'

It *was* there. The cigarette was in my mouth. I flicked the lighter. It didn't work. I flicked it again. It still didn't work. The stupid thing was out of petrol. I wanted that cigarette ...!

Of course! Matches! Some of the children kept matches in the little pigeon-holes set against the wall on my right. I leaned over and started to pull out the contents of the little square wooden boxes.

'Don't let there be any ... please don't let there be any ...'

There were no matches in the pigeon-holes. Not a single, solitary match. Never mind. I was going to smoke that cigarette. The bin! The rubbish bin! You always found the odd live match among the rubbish. I had no dignity left. I emptied the metal container onto the floor and scrabbled through the messy heap of papers, orange peel, and general stickiness.

'Please, don't let ...'

Nothing! No live matches. I got up and almost ran down the corridor, out of the unit and down towards the kitchen that supplied meals for the entire children's centre. I knew I could get a light there. I stopped on the threshold of the large, busy kitchen, and looked around. On my right a gas flame burned brightly beneath the water heater. In front of me a huge, yellow box of matches sat fatly on a shelf. To my left, one of the cooks worked over the stoves. She was a smoker. I knew that she carried cigarettes and a lighter in her apron pocket. I took a step forward, then stopped. Quite suddenly, the madness left me. I slipped the crumpled cigarette into my side pocket, and trailed wearily back to the unit. Since that day I have not smoked a cigarette, but it was a year before it became easy.

So why was it so difficult? Why couldn't the desire to smoke have been taken away by some sort of divine surgery? That certainly seems to happen to some people. Why not me? I think there were three things I needed to learn.

First, there is no real sacrifice without suffering. I had known that, but only in my head.

Secondly, when you have reached the end of your own resources, God does help – even if it involves 'fixing' lighters and removing matches. Sometimes a miracle is just the tiny puff of wind that makes it possible to go on toiling at the oars.

Thirdly, it allowed me to believe in change. It is not an exaggeration to say that, in my view, if weak-willed old me can give up smoking, then anybody can do almost anything.

So, stage one in the divine plan was completed. One of my most deeply rooted defence systems had been removed, and if it hadn't been for my 'declaration' on Company, it just wouldn't have been possible.

But that was only the beginning. From the start of my involvement with Company, I was meeting people who forced me to re-examine and overhaul my whole understanding of spirituality, Christianity and organised religion. The first and certainly one of the most influential of these was Peter Ball, the Bishop of Lewes.

Chapter 6

I could sit and watch that man all day.'

As I sat behind the cameras in Studio two watching the three Company participants chatting quietly as they waited for the programme to begin, I became aware that the technician sitting next to me was gazing with a peculiar intensity at the still figure in the monk's habit, seated at the end of the kitchen table.

'What do you mean?' I knew what he meant.

'Well ...' He leaned back in his chair slightly embarrassed by his own remark.

'It's like sitting on the edge of a lake. He doesn't even have to talk. It's just sort of relaxing to watch him.'

I knew exactly what he meant. Since the day when I first met him in February 1982, I had been intrigued and fascinated by the phenomenon that was Peter Ball, the Bishop of Lewes. I had never known a bishop before, and I had a vague and totally uninformed prejudice against ambitious prelates – princes of the church – that sort of thing. So too, I was soon to discover, had Peter Ball. I think I was fortunate in that I had never heard of him before we met as Company colleagues. When he drew up in his rather battered blue car outside our house in Hailsham, to drive Bridget and me up to the TVS studio in Maidstone, I felt under no obligation to be impressed or overawed by this man who, I later learned, is regarded by many as one of the wisest and most godly men in the Christian church. This was just as well, as his first words to me were, 'Hello Adrian, have a Mars bar.'

As I climbed into the front passenger seat, I registered various obvious pieces of information. Middle aged, healthy looking but tired, dressed in a full length dark grey habit, rather charming boyish smile, perhaps a hint of toughness in the eyes. As we travelled northwards towards Maidstone, the three of us chatted very easily together. Peter didn't seem much like a prince of the church. He seemed more like a normal, but oddly happy human being who had somehow managed to achieve maturity without losing the excitement and playfulness of childhood.

'I expected you to talk about God all the time,' said I, rather crassly, as he negotiated the very busy Tunbridge High Street.

'You being a bishop I mean ...'

Peter's smile lit up the car.

'People do seem to think that I ought to have a view on God all the time, and of course I have, but I do find it difficult when people assume that God is my sort of hobby. They talk to me about religion in the same way that you would talk to a philatelist about stamps, or a photographer about developing or something. Basically, they are not seeing me as a real human being.'

I was sure Peter meant what he was saying but his manner belied his words. I sensed that he had spent many many hours indulging the belief of others that he should talk to them about God.

Bridget leaned forward and spoke.

'But why is that, Peter? Why don't people want you to be a real human being?'

'Ah, well ...' Peter became serious. 'I think, Bridget, the problem is that we have got this attitude in the church at the moment, that the good Christians are those that spend a lot of time with religion. That's a load of junk! In fact there's too much religion.'

Listening to Peter was beginning to feel like a beautiful but unexpected cool shower on an oppressively hot day. As we turned onto the Hadlow road and headed out across the Kent countryside, the world seemed to me a slightly better place than usual.

'When you say "religion" ...?'

'I mean religious exercises. The more time you spend in

church, the more Bible studies you go to, the more prayer meetings you attend, the better Christian you'll be. That's a load of junk. We're here for the transfiguration of the world, not to form a little cosy club of Christians who are all constantly involved in religious exercises. Of course we must pray – of course we must worship; those are at the centre of our lives, but then we need to live as fully as we can in a sort of joyful unselfishness, caring about people, and transfiguring ordinary life. We hope that we can touch everything and see it sparkle.'

Oddly enough, I didn't find Peter's use of the pronouns 'we' and 'our' discomforting or guilt-inducing. I couldn't honestly say that prayer and worship were at the centre of my life, and as for things sparkling when I touched them, well – they didn't seem to. Joyful unselfishness? Not a lot!

The curious thing was, though, that there seemed to be a power in Peter's words and presence that made me feel I could become all the things he had described; something that caused me to think that perhaps I wasn't such a bad chap after all.

This was quite new for me. Most of my Christian experience seemed to have emphasised the vast gap between the perfection of God and my own sin-ridden, worm-like existence. Often there had seemed to be some kind of ban on feeling 'liked' by God. It was all right to be loved, because that was *despite* everything you were. The atmosphere around Peter, however, contained a sort of rich encouragement that gave permission to relax and be warmed by something that is better described as fondness than anything else. This principle has held good with many people I have met since then. The nearer they are to God, the better they make you feel, without in any way suggesting that you should minimise or ignore your faults or weaknesses. I find this very encouraging. Presumably, God himself is the source and ultimate example of this quality. God is nice, and he likes me. What a thought!

When we arrived at the Gillingham Studio, we were able to witness the 'sparkling' principle, as Peter greeted cameramen, make-up ladies and security men in a way that suggested each one was vitally important to him. As he moved around the large studio building, he seemed to carry his own shining atmosphere with him. Later, in the course of the Company programme, I asked him about this.

'Peter, do you enjoy meeting people – all of them ...?'

He patted his flat hand gently on the table and nodded slowly.

'I do, Adrian. I honestly do enjoy people enormously. I am absolutely scintillating with excitement when I meet anyone; but it can cause problems.'

Bridget and I must have both looked puzzled.

'Well, you see, there are only two things that I am really any good at. One is squash, and the other is making people feel that they are special to me, and of course they are; but I meet so many people and you simply can't give yourself totally to everyone all the time. It gets very complicated, and I think sometimes it's dangerous because people get very angry when I don't telephone them or write letters ...'

He shook his head in dismay at the thought.

'Obviously,' said Bridget, 'they see something in you that's different, like I do; but you've only got twenty-four hours in your day, like everyone else. Do you think that what they're actually seeing in you, is Jesus?'

Peter's face shone again.

'I do hope so, I do hope so. I'm sure it doesn't happen all the time with me, but I wish it happened every minute of the day. We've all got a personality, and I believe that it can be transfigured by Jesus. We each must be a tiny little diamond in the kaleidoscope of the glory which is Jesus.'

Suddenly I felt personally involved in what was being said. The lights and the cameras drifted away from my awareness as I asked another question.

'The thing is, Peter, that diamonds are valuable, and one of the problems a lot of Christians have, is how to go on being valuable when they know what kind of people they really are. How should they go about learning to appreciate their value in God's eyes?'

I tried to sound detached, and interested in an academic sort of way. It wasn't easy, as I was actually hungry for his reply. Peter thought for a moment, his brows knitted. Then his face cleared.

'You see, the church has gone round saying that all humility means is that you think yourself a load of junk, a load of "garbage" as the Americans call it. In Lent, for instance, we all have to regard ourselves as garbage cans for forty days. We need to realise that, actually, God is totally fascinated by us. He took five thousand million years to, in a sense, evolve and create us. That's quite a long time even in terms of eternity – it's a second or two, isn't it? He is absolutely entranced by us. I love it! When I kneel down to pray in the morning, I don't say to begin with, "God, you're really great, you're wonderful." What I do feel at that moment, is that I am coming home. I know that he *is* really great, but I am coming home, and he is saying, "Oh, it's great to have you!" I don't understand it. You see – I know that I am very, very sinful, but I know something else as well ...'

I was too much of an expert in controlling my emotions to actually cry, but I could feel tears swimming in my eyes as Peter's gentle voice continued, warmly enthusiastic about this God that I had difficulty in recognising.

'You see ... I know that if I was to go out today and commit the foulest crime possible with every single person in the village where I live, and then went to prison as a result, then repented, and said sincerely to God, "God, I am so very, very sorry", he would say ... well, what do you think he would say?'

We were like little children listening to a bedtime story. We shook our heads, wide-eyed.

'He would say, "Great! This prison is full of people who you can love with me, and I love you, even more than I did before!" So I would get on with loving where I was, and a whole new world would happen in that prison. God is all right! I really do believe that with all my heart, and I can't really understand why everyone doesn't.'

'God is absolutely real to you?' A statement of fact rather than a question. Peter leaned back, his hands disappearing into the sleeves of his habit as he folded his arms.

'Ever since I can remember, Adrian, I have never known a time when God has not been the realest presence in the world to me, more real even than human, touchable presences.'

'So when … I mean …'

Bridget paused, her hands outstretched as though testing for rain, while she searched for the right words.

'You wouldn't say then, that you have had what is usually called a conversion experience in the evangelical church? A point where you asked Jesus into your life, and then the Holy Spirit came into your life, and then you started to walk the Christian path – that sort of experience?'

'No.' Peter continued carefully. 'Not one in which I would be able to say, as evangelicals do say sometimes, "Before it I wasn't a real Christian and after it I was.' I find that way round diffi-cult. I mean, I haven't any doubt that these are real experiences, given to them by Jesus Christ, and when I hear about it I rejoice. I haven't any inhibitions about it; but I believe that rather than me inviting Jesus into my life, Jesus is actually, very sweetly, taking me into his life. There have been very special times of course. I remember when I first realised that I hadn't got to try to "make-it" with God. There he was, and he accepted me totally. There was nothing I could do to work for my own salvation. I was just totally assured by him. It was a great *release* to know that I never needed to earn approval with God. I could totally relax. That was a big experience.'

After the programme had finished, we drank coffee in the canteen up on the first floor. I was beginning to see why people wanted to talk to Peter about God. Guilty as all the rest, I took up the conversation where it had ended a few minutes ago.

'Peter, why do you think people get so screwed up about whether God loves them or not? What goes wrong?' Another casual, disinterested question! Peter stirred his coffee rather absentmindedly as he replied.

'God doesn't just *love* us. He loves us extravagantly. I want to use the word extravagantly because people sometimes use the phrase "God loves us" in a way that puts me off entirely. Sometimes it sounds like a sort of pressurised love. "He loves yer, an' he's gonna get yer!" Or, he loves you and you are going to become someone totally not yourself. These testimonies you hear sometimes ...'

He grinned wickedly.

'Sometimes I think people were far more attractive in their old unredeemed state. No – I want to use the word "extravagantly", because that's how God loves. After all, that's how lovers love, isn't it? They don't love moderately, or if they do there's not much point in getting married.'

He finished stirring at last, and took a sip of coffee, then replaced the cup on its saucer and beamed at us.

'Extravagantly – profusely – outrageously – that's how God loves us!'

It was extraordinary. After that first meeting I seemed to hear about Peter Ball everywhere. So many people seemed to have seen him or been confirmed by him, or been changed by something he said, or simply impressed by an encounter with him. The interesting thing was that these were not just Church of England worshippers. He seemed to have appeal for a wide variety of folk, including non-believers, who were attracted by his informal style and the sheer sparkle of the man. He related easily to people of all classes, and to a wide selection of church denominations, including the extreme evangelical ones, where even those who weren't quite sure if Mother Teresa was 'saved' or not, couldn't help but sense in him the spirit of a very loving God. Peter himself, clearly did not enjoy some of these occasions. I have never known a man in whom nervousness and effectiveness were so strongly present together, as in Peter when he addressed the monthly 'Growmore' meeting at the Congress Theatre in Eastbourne one Sunday evening. After the worship session, consisting largely of choruses led from the front, Peter, who finds that type of worship a little difficult, grey in habit and face, plodded from the back of the hall to the front to deliver an address remarkable for its humour, humility and insight, in contrast to the obvious feelings of woeful inadequacy in the speaker.

Impressed as I was by this unusual person, I wanted to find out what fuelled or energised him. How had he become the man he was? How did he remain the man he was? Was it the result of some kind of religious trick, or had God decided to smile on Peter for a particular reason? One day I visited Peter at his home in Littlington, a little Sussex village tucked away in the Downs, not far from the famous Long Man of Wilmington. There, in the homely sitting room of the rectory he talked about himself and his work.

Peter told me that he had been a monk for more than twenty years, as has his twin brother, Michael, who is the Bishop of Jarrow. Eight years ago, somewhat against his personal inclinations, Peter was installed as the suffragan Bishop of Lewes, and is now based at the old rectory in Littlington. Here he lives with a group of young people who are participants in the scheme that he devised to enable school leavers to spend two months at the rectory in work and spiritual training, followed by ten months in the community in teams of two or three, actively occupied in such areas as youth and voluntary work, while supporting themselves by part-time paid work.

Clearly, Peter's years as a monk under vows of poverty, chastity and obedience must have had a lot to do with the quality and steadfastness of his present life, but I wanted to know what kept him going now that he was a monk who was also a bishop, closely involved with all aspects of the real world. How did he cope with it? Peter settled back in the comfortable settee opposite me and talked about his daily routine.

'The first thing that happens each day, is my alarm clock going off at 4.15 am ...'

He noticed my wince of horror.

'We get through a lot of alarm clocks in the monastic life, because the temptation is to throw them straight out of the window. But usually I manage to get up and the first thing I do is to make an act of devotion, saying, "Lord, this is the *best* day there's ever going to be in my life", and I mean it too, although I don't always say it with conviction ...'

Peter chuckled reflectively.

'I want it to be – I really do. Every day I ask God that I shall go out to love and praise him with all my whole being, and over the last thirty years I must have managed that for ... oh, at least five minutes.'

I was still wrestling inwardly with the idea of rising at 4.15 every morning.

'So, that takes you to – let's say, 4.30 am. I still don't see why you need to be up quite so early.'

Peter's eyebrows rose.

'Oh, well, the next thing I do is rush downstairs, do one or two ordinary things, then take the dog for a walk. That's the most beautiful part of the day really, walking down the lanes in the early morning. The shapes in the winter, the freshness in the summer. Then, usually at about a quarter to five, I hurry down to our little chapel in the cellar for about an hour and three-quarters of – hopefully – uninterrupted prayer or meditation, whatever you like to call it. I hope it is adoration. God embraces me in that time. I think he is always very pleased to see me.'

I was silent for a moment, thinking of my own fragmentary, undisciplined prayer life. By 6.30 each morning, Peter had already spent at least two hours being with, and being embraced by God. That was before the day got going. I sighed rather ruefully.

'Right, so what happens at 6.30?'

'We say ordinary morning prayer ...'

Good heavens. More prayer!

' ... then we hold our daily celebration of the eucharist and then it's time for breakfast.'

Breakfast – common ground at last. I had breakfast too!

'We have our very simple breakfast in silence, always in silence, because the devil likes to get at people after they have prayed, especially at the beginning of the day, in order to spoil the rest of the day. The silence means that you can only *think* a person is horrid rather than say it.'

'Is it all right to think it?'

'Well, it's only half a sin.' Peter burst into laughter at the expression on my face. Still smiling he went on.

'After breakfast we wash up, and then we clean the house from top to bottom every day, and we do it with a feeling of absolute urgency because we are on the border line between heaven and hell, where we believe we have been called to be the mouthpiece of creation in a big way. Every Christian is, but in the monastic life perhaps more so. In Christian prayer and service we are at the centre of life. Not the periphery as many think.

'We are here to stand between the world and the devil, to fight him before he corrupts and destroys, and sometimes it's a real old struggle against his infernal majesty.'

I was out of my depth. Breakfast, cleaning and the devil?

'Why is the cleaning so important, Peter?'

'In all things, Adrian, we aim to do a perfect job. Each one of us must be super-Harpic round every bend. You see, the Lord is here. His spirit is with us, and we know that we want to do it as perfectly as we can because the king of kings arrives every minute of the day – even in you, the king of kings has arrived.'

'Even in me?'

Through the sitting room window I could just see the top of the Downs in the distance. For some reason I found Peter's comment, light though it was, profoundly comforting. Even in me, the king of kings had arrived ...

I wanted to pursue Peter's comment about not being on the periphery of life.

'How can a monk be at the centre of life?'

Peter suddenly looked very serious.

'Adrian, I have got to say honestly, and I mean it most sincerely, I am not a holy man, but if you spend hours and hours with God, you may very well see things more clearly and with more real knowledge than the person who lives on what I would call the periphery. That's why people go to holy men for help even if they've been shut up in a monastery for twenty years, because they sense that here is a chap who lives in the middle of life, and is able to, for instance, discern right and wrong, in a quite different way. Why, I've known people go to a monk who has been closed away for years just to ask him what kind of petrol they should use.'

'And would he have known the answer to that?'

Peter smiled. 'I don't know about that, but there is no doubt that one does get communications about things.'

I was intrigued. I tried not to sound too interested.

'Like ... ?'

His voice was very quiet as he replied.

'On two occasions when I have been talking to someone, I have known that they were going to die.'

'Really?' I said foolishly, and probably a little nervously.

'Oh, yes, I could see death around them. I remember one chap – he wasn't particularly ill – I went back to the brothers and said, "He'll be dead in six months", and he was. I saw death around him.'

'And this is part of seeing the world from the centre?'

'Yes – and I recall another time.'

Peter sat forward as he suddenly remembered.

'There was a lady. Doreen was her name and she was very pregnant. One night I woke up at a quarter to twelve, and something – "within me or without me, I know not which" as Paul

88

would say – said I should get out of bed and pray for Mrs Flag because she was just having her child. So out I got. Later, I heard that her baby had been born at just that time.'

'Was that in the form of a thought that came into your head, or ...?'

He clasped his hand thoughtfully.

'To quote Paul again, "In the flesh, or put of the flesh, I know not." But I do know that there wasn't any doubt about it.'

What a meal some Christians would have made out of these experiences. It didn't seem to bother Peter whether they were labelled or classified. They were just a natural feature of this vision from the centre that he was talking about. I wondered how Peter viewed the way in which other churches dealt with spiritual gifts.

'You hear a lot nowadays about things like prophecy and speaking in tongues. Word of knowledge is another gift that seems to be "in vogue" as it were. How do you feel about these things, Peter? The idea that God can zoom in on a service and say, "I've got a message for Fred, and this is it ..." '

For the first time I felt the bishop was not altogether easy in his reply. His words were slow and carefully considered.

'Yes ... I am happy. Paul makes it quite plain that everything must be done decently and in order and it's very difficult to get this balance. The Catholic Church, on the whole, has made the liturgy so frameworked and stereo-typed, that it's actually very difficult to get these bits of informality in. On the other hand, some of the evangelicals have made it such a "hats in the air affair", that it's difficult for people to be able to concentrate on God, on giving themselves to him in sacrament, and in his word. It's very difficult to get it right. On the whole I think we need eucharistic worship and we need informal worship, but we probably ought to keep them distinct.'

It was a very careful reply.

'And the gifts themselves ...?'

'I am sure that there are people who have gifts of knowledge or prophecy. I've been to a lot of churches where it happens ...'

His voice took on a more definite note.

'What worries me about prophecy is that it always seems to be jejune.'

I didn't know what he meant.

'Well, here we are, living in a world which could be on the edge of a nuclear war, where the wealth of the West is absolutely gross compared with the starving world, and you don't hear people saying any of the real strong stuff which I believe we should expect from prophets. It amazes me. Most of the prophecies I hear are saying that God is love and he loves you a lot. Well, of course he does, but is that what prophecy is for?' He paused, gazing into the distance, then smiled and relaxed back into his chair with a bump, his feet see-sawing into the air as he landed.

'I like tongues! I like to hear people singing in tongues. I've always said that if you have a special friend then there are two things which you must be able to do. You must be able to be silent with them and you must be able to talk nonsense with them ...'

I laughed, remembering how, when John Hall and I met, we often talked complete but enjoyable rubbish for hours on end.

' ... and the nonsense is not nonsense. It's because the love is so big, it bubbles out, and tongues is that freedom of bubbling out in love. It's lovely, you just go on and on.'

There was a short pause as I watched this bishop giggling with his legs in the air. No one who got up at 4.15 every morning had the right to be this happy.

'Have you ever doubted the existence of God, Peter?' He became quiet and serious again.

'Not doubts about the existence of God, no. Times when holding on was very difficult though, times when there was a great temptation to disobey, or seemingly disobey God.' Peter became very still, his voice so low that I had to lean forward to make sure I didn't miss what he said.

'I very much wanted to be married once ... when I was about twenty-three. And God seemed to be saying, "Become a monk." I remember the whole time over that Christmas – they were very very black days.

'The balance was so fine. I only had to pick up a pen, and in thirty seconds write to this girl and say, "OK, it's on again. When shall we meet?" Just a thirty second job it would have been, and it would have made all the difference between two totally different lives.' There was an expression of wonder on his face.

'When I think of Jesus calling Matthew "as he passed by". Amazing isn't it? Fifteen seconds to decide. Jesus looked over his shoulder and said, "Hi, Matthew. Come on – follow me!" Then he just walked on. He probably didn't even look behind him to see whether this geezer was coming.... Amazing!'

'Who made that choice about your future? Was it you, or was it God?'

'We made it between us, I think – together ...'

He raised his voice in mock anger.

'He suggested it and I agreed, and I've got a bone to pick with him about it too!'

Suddenly he was laughing helplessly.

'I'm not a resentful creature,' he said, his mirth subsiding, 'but I get close to it.'

'So you've come to terms with celibacy then, Peter?' I queried.

He looked at me for a moment, his eyes twinkling.

'Adrian, as I've already told you, God loves me extravagantly. I'm not just a celibate. I'm an extravagant celibate!'

Peter often returned, and still does return to the twin themes of extravagance and transfiguration. He is fond of quoting the story of Jesus feeding the five thousand, and points out that twelve basketsful of food were collected after the meal. A sign, he says, of God's extravagant giving.

He maintains that the church has a responsibility to transfigure the community instead of just forming a holy huddle once a week. For instance, he says, local churches should be as interested in producing a good football team, as in organising a good Bible study group. He is an inspiration to many, a puzzle to some.

As for me, he was the initiator of my understanding that Christianity is not about *systems* and God, but about individual people, and the relationship they build through raw, prolonged contact with a creator who is genuinely and warmly interested in them. Peter is a man who has real discipline, a real prayer life and a real joy. He is one of the small group of people I know, who has gained his experience of God from God.

Unfortunately, Peter was involved with Company for a relatively short time before pressure of work and other responsibilities made it impossible for him to continue, other than for very occasional guest appearances. Three years later I was still meeting people who remembered things that he said in those early programmes. Peter is just the same today. Whatever he touches seems to sparkle. He even makes me fizz a bit.

Chapter 7

One of the problems about saying that you're a Christian through a public medium like television, is that people have an awkward tendency to believe you, and neat organised expressions of faith seem to wilt rather, in the heat of real human need.

My friend and colleague, Ian, was really going through it. His father, who over the years had been loving parent, first-choice fishing companion and close friend, was dead. Cancer. For the last few months, Ian and I had worked together in a locked treatment unit, dealing with violent or chronically absconding teenagers from all over East Sussex. I had grown very fond of Ian; a warm, vulnerable, complex character, for whom pipe-smoking was a rich and absorbing activity, well suited to a nature that swung from deep contentment to heavy depression. He had a great talent for expressing affection, and real gifts with difficult and distressed children. I hurt for him when I saw his grief. I wished there was something I could do or say to help. There was something; but when I learned what it was, I felt quite frightened.

It appeared that in the seven months since Company had first come on the air, Ian's mother, Mrs Figg, had seen Bridget and me on a number of occasions as she sat up late watching the television, and was able to identify with much of what we said. Ian and I had only rarely talked about such things, but he asked me if I would deliver the address on the day of his father's cremation. He wanted me to do it, he said, first because I was his friend, and secondly, because, although I was a Christian I wasn't very religious. (I think this was intended to be a compliment, though it made me think at the time.) I agreed of course, but it was from that moment that I began to feel uneasy. I'd given talks before, but never on occasions like this. It was all very well to sit in that little island of light in the TV studio throwing out my views on God, left, right and centre, but this was going to be a real human event, full of pain and tears and the fear of death. What did I really know about God? What, for that matter, did I know about Ian's dad? Was he a Christian? If not, what would I say? Something vague but comforting perhaps. That would be the easy option; but would it be right? Or should I scratch the old evangelical itch, preach the 'hard line' gospel, and let people make their own minds up? It seemed to me that in a peculiar way I was neither humble nor arrogant enough to say very much at all.

As the day of the cremation drew nearer I felt more and more troubled. On the day before the service, I travelled down to Brighton to meet Ian's mum and stay the night with Ian and his wife, Sue.

Mrs Figg was nearly broken by her husband's death. I took her hand as we sat side by side on the settee in her sadly cheerful little sitting room.

'Tell me about Frank,' I said firmly. 'I want to know what he was really like.'

'He was the first person who really loved me,' she replied.

She told me that as a child she'd had a very strict religious upbringing. A lot of ritual, a lot of meetings, a great deal of church attendance and no love at all – no softness. Then, as a young adult she met Frank. He was the first person to offer her real affection and warmth. They fell in love and were married. Frank, a carpenter by trade, had always been popular at work and in the local community, especially as he had a great gift for settling arguments and disputes. She pointed to photographs of the smart, pleasant-featured man who had meant so much to her, and wept a little. She said that Frank would not have described himself as a Christian, and Ian, who had been listening quietly while his mother spoke, added that he might well have resented anyone attempting to stick that label on him after his death. I sighed inwardly. It wasn't going to be easy ...

That night, I lay awake on my bed in Ian and Sue's spare room, gazing up at the ceiling and wishing that God would write the end of my talk for me. On the little table beside me lay the sheet of paper on which I'd jotted down headings and notes for tomorrow's address. But I couldn't write the ending. Lying there in the darkness I realised what a jumble of half-formed beliefs, feelings and thoughts still made up what I so easily described as my Christian faith. I just didn't know what I could say to all those people tomorrow without compromising God, or Frank, or myself or ... I was still asking God for ideas when I fell asleep.

Sleep is a strange thing. The mind seems to go on working while the body takes a few hours off. In my case, the 'night shift' often seems more efficient and effective than the daytime one. Or perhaps God is more easily able to introduce ideas and suggestions when I am less defended and aggressively conscious. Whatever the reason, when I woke the next morning I *knew* how to end that address. The words were printed clearly on a sort of mental ticker-tape; all I had to do was transfer them to the sheet of paper beside me.

I was still nervous about the unfamiliar task awaiting me, but the central truth, the kernel of the event, was in my grasp, and as I stood in front of the mirror that morning, knotting, unknotting and reknotting the necktie that always seemed to half throttle me on these formal occasions, I knew that everything would be all right. My natural nervousness was not helped, however, by an absurd interval just outside the chapel of rest, when the undertaker asked where the minister was, as it was he who would lead the procession into the building. We had all spent a few minutes gazing around tensely, waiting for him to appear, when it suddenly occurred to someone – clearly brighter than the rest of us – that I was the minister on this occasion. Sweating slightly with embarrassment, I led the mourners into the cool interior of the chapel and after a hymn and a prayer, I began speaking to the fifty or so people who seemed to completely fill the available space. For a few minutes I spoke about the things I had learned about Frank from his wife and son. How very much they loved him, how he had many friends, how much he would be missed, how significant it was that Ian, in his thirties, would still rather go fishing with his old dad than with anyone else. I didn't have to make any of it up. It was all true. As I neared the end of the address, I lowered my notes to the table beside me. The last paragraph was still printed in my mind – I didn't need to read it. I spoke directly to Ian and his mum as they sat opposite me like two lost children, hands interlinked, eyes wet with tears.

'I am not sure what Frank thought about Jesus,' I said, 'but I am sure about one thing. They'll have met by now. And I'd guess that Jesus looked straight into his eyes, and smiled, and said, "Frank, you brought love into someone's loveless world, you were a peace-maker, and you were a carpenter. That's three things we've got in common. I reckon we've got plenty to talk about."'

On the following Wednesday night I described this event to Company viewers, pointing out how vulnerable I had felt when Ian first asked me to take the service. I had feared failure of some kind, failure to deliver the Christian 'goods', failure to make the event memorable and meaningful, failure, as well, if I'm honest, to impress. It occurred to me after the programme was finished that I was still playing games about honesty and openness. I had often said to people that I was quite happy to lay myself open at the Company table; to be truly vulnerable; but was I really? Later, as I settled comfortably back into my seat on the southbound train from Victoria, I frowned through the murky glass of the window and conducted an inner dialogue with myself.

'What do you mean when you say I'm not vulnerable on Company? I've just told goodness knows how many people about my rotten selfish feelings when Ian asked me to ...'

'Ah yes. So you have. Did you tell Ian that at the time?'

'Well, no – but ...'

'And isn't it a fact that you rather enjoy running yourself down about things that have already happened? It makes you feel good, and it protects you from real criticism.'

'Well ...'

'Doesn't it?'

'I suppose so – but, look. What about the way I've talked about the arguments and problems Bridget and I sometimes have. They're real enough.'

My internal inquisitor chuckled. 'Oh, yes. I know what you mean. You mean when you and she sit there full of confidence and looking crackers about each other, and talk about the terrible problems you have.'

'But we do have problems! Surely it must be worthwhile to talk about things like that.'

'Oh, yes. I've no doubt it is. But that's not what we're talking about. We're talking about your claim that you're vulnerable sometimes. Let me ask you a question.'

'Yes?'

'Has it ever really cost you anything, mentally or emotionally to say the things you say round the kitchen table?'

East Croydon flashed by. I sighed.

'No – it hasn't.'

'Aren't you actually determined not to show your real feelings to anybody, let alone television cameras?'

I inadvertently vocalised the irritable 'Yes!' with which I answered this question, slightly shocking a precise looking elderly lady on the other side of the carriage. Perhaps she thought that I was practising being positive.

The next day I described this conversation to Bridget, and we decided to raise the question of 'being vulnerable' with the rest of the Company participants as soon as possible. We had our opportunity very shortly after this when the whole team, including Frances, Angus and Maurice met to discuss all aspects of the programme and its development so far. By now the team had changed and grown significantly. Peter Ball was no longer with us, but we had a 'replacement' bishop in the form of George Reindorp, a very sprightly seventy year old, who had recently retired as the Bishop of Salisbury. He was now looking forward to an active retirement with his doctor wife, Alix. Other newcomers included Steve Flashman, an unusual combination of Baptist minister and highly talented rock musician, Robert Pearce, who worked for Christian Aid, Shirly Allan, an actress living in the Maidstone area, and Ann Warren, already well known as a Christian writer and broadcaster. At an appropriate point in the agenda Bridget brought up the subject of openness and vulnerability, and there was a general discussion about the advantages and difficulties of the expression of genuine feelings on television. It was finally agreed that the programme could only benefit from real communication, especially as the whole team had recently fallen into the trap of merely expressing agreement about rather unexciting truths. We all solemnly nodded our heads and vowed to be *really* vulnerable in the future. I, of course, nodded my head with all the rest, as one does in large meetings of that kind but I seriously doubted that, after all my years of being so well defended, I would really be able to open up. Less than two years later I was to be surprised by the extent to which I did reveal myself at my very lowest, but back at the beginning of 1983 it was George Reindorp who took the first step, when he told viewers about a tragic event that had happened many years earlier.

George Reindorp seems to have been in training all his life to become a grandfather. After only one encounter with this slim, white haired, vivacious character, Bridget and I knew that here was a man in whom children would delight, and there are few higher compliments than that. George, in his own way – and although it's not the same way as Peter Ball it is just as valuable – was able to make events and people sparkle with his infectious brightness and impish sense of humour. When I first knew

George however, although I thought him very charming and competent, I also, rather arrogantly, suspected that he was more Anglican than Christian. He appeared to have responses and comments about all aspects of the Christian faith neatly labelled and filed in his mind for easy reference when required. Indeed, it appeared to me that, in his scheme of things, the Church of England was God's outer office, scrupulously tidied and cleaned, and presided over by highly organised receptionists like George, who were employed to ensure that things ran smoothly; not to create problems where there were none, by asking unnecessary questions or exploring alternative ways of operating.

In my great wisdom I decided that George had never really been exposed to suffering and was effectively cushioned from real life by the privileges of high office in the church. Little did I know that George had already experienced one major tragedy in his life.

One night, soon after we had first met, George and I enjoyed an evening meal together at a hotel in Rochester, prior to a Company programme the following day. We ate and drank well, talked quite a lot (George is very good company), and then moved over to more comfortable seats for coffee. It was then that he told me about the death, in 1947, of his beloved baby daughter, Veronica Jane.

George was a parish priest at the time. He had married Alix in South Africa during the war and they were now living in Vincent Square near Victoria, with their small son Julian, in a house only three doors away from the flat which he later occupied in his retirement. Life seemed very full and good then. George was more than ready to tackle parish work after a long and eventful period as a navy chaplain during the war years. His was a large parish, including twelve thousand tenement dwellers, as well as the idle or industrious rich. There was ample scope for the use and development of those delicate skills of communication which he is able to use like a magician at times. George has always maintained that if David Jenkins, the controversial Bishop of Durham, had been able to experience life as a parish priest earlier in his life, the knowledge and understanding of ordinary people thus gained, would have balanced his academic training, and perhaps resulted in a more careful and caring expression of his views on events such as the virgin birth and the resurrection. George felt, as a working vicar, that it was necessary to get really involved with such issues as the flower-arranging rota, and the debate about whose turn it was to clean the pews, for it was in these apparently trivial, day-to-day concerns that one could meet and learn about people, and perhaps earn the right to stand six feet above contradiction to preach to them. He is the same today. Somehow he learns about the personal lives and problems of many people who others hardly notice. Often as we have walked through the TVS building together, he has called out a cheery greeting to a cleaner or cafeteria assistant and added a query about the health or progress of a friend or child or parent.

In addition to the stimulation of his work, George was deeply in love with his blue-eyed, attractive wife, who as well as being a successful doctor was an ideal clergyman's wife, although she never allowed herself to occupy a stereotyped role.

Her only fault in George's eyes was her inability to give up cigarettes. He estimated that she smoked 'half a curate a year'. In all other ways though, she was perfect for him, being – by his own admission – less self-centred, and more controlled than he ever was.

Their joy was made complete by the arrival of a second child, Veronica Jane, a beautiful baby girl, in 1947. George adored her. Four hundred people were present for the christening of this special 'Parish Baby', none prouder than little Julian who thought his tiny sister quite wonderful.

Up to now, George had chatted lightly and easily as he recalled those first, pleasant, post-war years, but now a pattern of pain, like a much-used map, spread over his face, and he stared past my shoulder into the far distance as he spoke quietly about the death of his daughter.

'She was lying in her pram, just as she often did. I was in the drawing-room talking to another clergyman, when the door suddenly opened, and Alix came in. She's a very unexcitable person, and she simply said, "Get a doctor quickly!", which struck me as being a very odd thing, because of course she's a doctor herself. Anyway, I went and got a doctor who lived close by. I knew by then that there was something wrong with Veronica Jane, but I took it for granted that everything was going to be all right. They both went upstairs, and after hanging around in the hall for a while I followed them ...'

George's eyes misted slightly as he went on.

'When I first saw her I thought she was moving. I realised later that she wasn't really. It was just the effect of the artificial respiration they were doing on her. Alix knew in fact, as soon as she picked her up, that the little one was dead. Alix wept. I was just stunned. I cry a lot about all sorts of things, but that was ... I don't know ...'

He shook his head slowly from side to side, reliving the shock of that moment.

'She was a blue-baby you see. Nowadays, of course, they could have done something, but then ... well ...'

Dear George. As I looked at him I felt ashamed. I thought I knew about people, but I knew nothing. Never suffered? I thought of my own children and experienced just a hint of the pain that the death of any one of them would cause Bridget and me, and their brothers, of course.

'What about Julian, George? How did he cope?'

He smiled and relaxed into the warmth of the memory.

'Veronica Jane went on being very real to Julian. I remember he had a little friend round to play with him one day, about three months after the death. They disappeared up to the bedroom, and a little later we heard Julian screaming at his friend, so we rushed upstairs and it turned out that this other boy had picked up a little woolly toy, and Julian was screaming, "You can't have that! You can't have that! It belongs to Veronica Jane!" In the mind of that little five-year-old, you see, she was still very much alive. And, in fact, very much later, when we had had three more children, I recall somebody saying to Alix and me one day, "How many children do you have?", and when I replied that we had four, Julian, who was of course much older then, interrupted quickly and said, "No! Five! You're forgetting Veronica Jane!" And he was right of course.'

'And how about you? Was she still there for you?'

George took a folded sheet of paper from his inside jacket pocket, unfolded it and passed it across to me.

'When she died we were devastated, naturally, and for a while I found it difficult to see where God fitted into what had happened. Then a dear friend – a saint really – wrote this to me.' He pointed at the paper in my hand. 'That's a copy of the letter. It brought peace to me, and since then it's been amazingly helpful to lots of others to whom I've given copies.'

I read the letter.

'It was with great sorrow that I heard today of the death of your child. The religion of Christ was always sincere and clear-sighted. He refused to obscure the fact that tragedy was tragedy; and wept at the grave of Lazarus. It must therefore be in the circumference of His love that we recognise our torn hearts when we part with a child who has held all that was best in us in fee.

'The fact that He could weep over the death of a loved one when He knew that in so short a time He was going to supply the answer which made hope the sequel to every tragedy, even the tragedy of sin, surely shows that here in time and space, grief and hope can come to us side by side.

'Thus I pray it may be with you and your wife.

'It has been given to me to see our progress to God as a road divided in the middle by a low wall, which we call death.

Whatever our age or stage of development, or relationship with other human beings, there is no real change involved in crossing the low wall. We simply continue in a parallel course with those who loved us in our development and relationship. I do not believe that God has altered one whit your responsibility or service for your child.

'I do believe that she will grow side by side with you, in spirit, as she would have done on earth; and that your prayer and love will serve her development as they would have done on earth. There is nothing static about the other life.

'The difficulty is that our spiritual sight is so little developed compared with our earthly sight. We cannot watch the development and growth as we could on earth. Yet much can be done by faith, by the realisation that what we hope is true, and that we can train our minds and imaginations to think in terms of truths, even if they are pictured in earthly forms. The companionship which was given you, you still have. The growth to which you look forward will still be yours to watch over and care for.

'You will be much in my prayers at this time. What I have written I know to be true and I pray that you may be enabled to live in that truth and to find the answer to your tragedy.'

When I had finished reading, I refolded the paper and handed it back to George.

'Thank you,' I said. 'Thank you for telling me about what happened to your daughter and for letting me see that.' I paused.

'Are you going to talk about Veronica Jane on the programme tomorrow, George?'

'Yes,' he replied brightly, 'I thought I would. It may help others who have lost someone they love very much.'

The following evening George repeated the story of Veronica Jane as we sat around the kitchen table in the Gillingham studio. It clearly cost him a lot to go through the whole thing again, and I felt glad that there was a cushion of thirty-five years between him and the tragedy. There was an unusual stillness about the studio as the programme came to an end. Those working on the studio floor and in the control room had been deeply moved by George's story, and so, presumably, had viewers at home. It had been an event rather than a performance. Bishop Reindorp had undoubtedly pioneered the vulnerability that we all thought to be necessary, but suppose, I reflected, one wanted to talk about a tragedy that was happening in the present, and not thirty-five years ago. Would that be possible, or even desirable? Not very many weeks later we had a chance to find out, when George talked in a Company programme about the second major disaster in his life. This time we were quite unprepared for what he said, and it was not an incident from the past. It was happening to him right now.

We didn't associate George with tragedy. It was fun preparing and making programmes with him. He had a fund of stories that were very amusing and always well told. What was more, he never seemed to mind being stopped in the middle of his attempts to repeat them for the second or third time. His ability to switch from being avuncular to being like an excited small boy was very endearing and enriched our gatherings greatly, especially when we all felt rather limp and formless. George stacked untidy bits of the world very neatly when necessary. We indulged in a little playful sniping at times. I noticed that George had developed a very effective conversational ploy which he used in argument or debate. He would state his point of view with great force and panache, then, thrusting his chin aggressively towards the person he was addressing, say, in a tone implying that any attempt to put forward an alternative view would indicate advanced mental decay, 'Don't you agree?' I kindly pointed this out to George who was as grateful as one might expect, but I did notice that he modified the query thereafter to 'Do you agree?', which does at least have the virtue of sounding like a real question. He bided his time, awaiting an opportunity for revenge. It came one day when I started a Saturday night programme by describing a thought that had occurred to me while I sat in the local pub on the previous evening.

'I was well into my second pint,' said I, 'when I really saw what Jesus meant when ...'

George's sense of humour was so tickled by the idea of divine revelations beginning to occur at the two pint mark that he never allowed me to forget those few words.

'You know, Adrian,' he said one day. 'You're very fortunate. Most people have to drink all evening before they start to see things.' He paused, then stuck his chin out, his eyes glinted. 'Don't you agree?'

It was so enjoyable working with George, and he seemed such a happy man that the revelation of his great sadness was a real shock. We had decided to make a programme about the year that had just finished, and although we hadn't discussed the content in detail, Bridget and I assumed that most of the conversation would be about events that had made news in 1982; politics, sport, significant social change – that sort of thing. George was due to start the ball rolling, and sure enough, when the floor manager cued him he began to speak. But it wasn't what we'd expected.

'The most important thing to happen in my year never got into the newspapers or onto television,' he said. 'As you know, my wife Alix and I were hoping to retire into the country when I finished full-time work, but it is not going to happen now because Alix is suffering from Pik's disease, and she's going to move into a nursing home.' George's voice broke slightly as he went on. 'The thing is, you see, that the disease involves progressive deterioration of the brain, so ... so she will need to be there for the rest of her life.'

Bridget and I sat in stunned silence, temporarily incapable of taking in what he was saying. We had never met his wife, but we had heard so much about her. Alix. The girl with the vivid blue eyes; the lover of flowers, the marvellous mother, wife and friend, full of inner sympathy and strength, the hostess who had entertained a thousand people a year, George's 'thought-mate', and an eye to catch across the room when someone said something ridiculous and you wanted to share your secret laughter with the only other person who would really understand ... She was not to be with George in his final years.

He went on to describe how Alix had become more and more withdrawn over a long period until it became clear at last that something was terribly wrong. When the illness was diagnosed, George's first concerns were practical ones. Where would she live for the rest of her life? Fortunately (George said that it was like Christian losing his burden in *Pilgrim's Progress*), someone presented him with an anonymous gift at this point, and through the generosity of that unknown person it was possible to arrange first-class care for Alix for an indefinite period. The next, and greatest task facing George was learning to live alone and face his retirement years without the steady, loving support of his wife.

'It's not the big things, you understand. You've had a good day – you've maybe had a bad day. You go home and she says, "How did it go?", and you say what happened and who said what, and she says, "How do you feel about it ...?" That's what you miss, that sort of ordinary, comfortable chat. And then you miss having someone to hold in your arms; and quite apart from that, you were such good friends ... such good friends.'

At the close of the programme, Bridget and I and Frances, the producer, were in tears. But behind my tears all the old anger flared up again. I found myself saying silently to God, 'Well? Explain that one then!'

Over the following weeks, George came to terms with his situation quite remarkably, although a basic level of sadness remained of course. He seemed to have gained a new understanding of God's love for him as a son and a friend, quite apart from the official and ceremonial relationship that had existed over the years.

I probably had more difficulty accepting what had happened

than George did. Perhaps this wasn't so surprising when one considered the fact that he had been pursuing a clear path of duty for more than half a century, and had good reason to trust God. Much later, over lunch one day in his Vincent Square flat, I told George how I had felt on hearing about Alix, and asked him the question I had wanted to ask at the time.

'Where is God in this, George? Has he allowed it? Has he got a point to make in it? What's going on?'

'I did ask a lot of questions like that,' he replied slowly. 'You go all through the possibilities. Is it because I have to learn something? Is God saying, "You've talked a lot about faith, now – what about it?" You ask yourself all those questions.'

For a few moments he studied the end of his fork, then laid it gently down on the table.

'In the end I simply have to say the same as old Polycarp, the Bishop of Smyrna, who was a holy man – rather different from me! They said to him, "Now, we really don't want to have to put you to death, so be a good chap and throw a few grains of incense on the altar for the emperor just to make it all right, then he'll let you live." And he said, "Lo, these eighty and six years have I served God. Shall I cast him off in my old age?" Well, now, God has been marvellous to me. We've got wonderful children and we're a very happy family. We've got nine and four-eighths grandchildren! So, although at first I did ask all those questions, and I still don't really understand it, I know that in it somewhere – God knows where – and I mean that literally, God IS, and I hold on to those words from scripture: "God has prepared for those who love him, such good things as pass man's understanding, that we loving thee *above all* things ..." I've said that – talked about it a thousand times. I have to go on trusting.' He stopped for a second. 'Good heavens. It sounds as though I'm saying it's so *easy*. I get very very lonely still, especially as Alix is so out of character now, and when I do visit her each week, she quite often seems to lack interest in me, and draws the visit to a close after a very short time. It's hard sometimes when I go down there, longing to see her and then ...' George straightened his cutlery neatly on his plate.

'Do you believe that you'll meet Alix, as she was, in another place, after death perhaps?'

There was more passion and certainty in George's voice when he replied, than I think I had ever heard before.

'Oh, Adrian ...' For a moment he was lost for words. 'Somehow – if Christ is what I'm convinced he is, and believe and know him in my heart to be, so far as my little mind can take it in, I'm absolutely certain that all will be well. Shall we see again those whom we love? Yes! What will they be like? We do not know! When I wake up after thy likeness I shall be satisfied!'

Each sentence that George quoted, sounded like a girder that strengthened him. I realised that these words had a meaning for him that brought far more than intellectual reassurance.

'A bond of love like the one between Alix and me could never be completely shattered,' he continued. 'My God is not capable of such a capricious whim. We shall somehow be together again, not as husband and wife but in some other, better way. For the present I can only live a day at a time, but for what I've had, I give thanks.'

I had one more question. 'If Jesus was sitting here in this chair beside you now, and you wanted to say one thing to him about all this, what would it be?'

Through the big front window of George's sitting room we could see on the other side of the road, two of the masters from the famous nearby public school, hitting golf balls across the school sports field. One of them gave his ball a mighty crack, and I watched it sail into the blue, and disappear, to land somewhere on the far side of the grassy expanse. George's voice, as he spoke, was very gentle.

'I think I'd say, "For the past – thank you *very* much." Why?'

The 'Why?' was not a demand, just a simple question. George

trusted God. I knew that now. And could it be, I wondered, the reason he had been able to be vulnerable on Company, was that he was accustomed to being vulnerable to God? An interesting question.

And what about me? Would I ever be able to let people see *me* broken and bruised? Never!

Chapter 8

Peter Ball, George Reindorp, and other Company regulars and guests all shed their own particular light on the truth. Father Tony Cashman, for instance, brought my understanding of the Roman Catholic faith right up-to-date when he described how spiritual gifts such as tongues and prophecy are increasingly common among Catholic Christians nowadays. Robert Pearce, a regional secretary for Christian Aid, has broadened my understanding of international issues, especially when describing his trips abroad and his personal reaction to the sight of people in acute need. I particularly enjoyed meeting Mother Frances, an Anglican nun who runs Helen House in Oxford, the only children's hospice in the country. She was a delightful mixture of strength and freedom, with a sense of humour that seemed, somehow, to invigorate the air around her. Another welcome guest was the Roman Catholic Bishop of Arundel, Cormac Murphy O'Connor, an ex-rugby player and a man with a deep commitment to the building of bridges from denomination to denomination. I'm sure Cormac won't forget Bridget and me in a hurry. After we had made our programmes on that Tuesday, he kindly offered to give us a lift home to Hailsham on his way to Arundel. Unfortunately my navigating skills deserted me when we were about halfway home, and we wandered through endless Sussex lanes for what seemed an eternity. We did get home in the end, and Cormac was very patient!

When Vishal Mangalwadi joined us as a guest, I was determined to get his name right first time. Vishal works on behalf of the poor people in his part of India, and has suffered imprisonment and violence because of his quiet determination to be a true follower of Christ in that situation. As the run-up to the first programme began, I repeated Vishal's mouthful of a second name over and over in my mind, to make sure it came out smoothly. 'Mangalwadi – Mangalwadi – Mangal ...' The floor-manager cued me and I spoke confidently to camera three.

'Hello. It's nice to have a special guest with us tonight, and it's ...' My mouth opened and shut like a fish. I'd forgotten his *first* name!

All of these people were Christians of one variety or another, of course, but the time came when Frances announced that there was to be a new member of the team who was not a Christian, but a Jewish rabbi. His name was Hugo Gryn.

Hugo turned out to be a bundle of fizzing activity, a short, physically dynamic, clean-shaven man with a crackling sense of humour, enormous energy, and a gravelly voice with an attractive combination of transatlantic and Central European accents. Like me in the past, he smokes incessantly, and with something akin to dedication, as though each fresh cigarette wards off the resolution of some fearful issue. With others he is rarely still, always watchful, studying and learning from eyes, adapting a little here and there in his responses, still employing, perhaps, in a modified form, the survival skills he learned in the harsh schools of Auschwitz and other camps during the war. Highly educated, multi-talented, a fascinating speaker and supreme teller of stories, Hugo is a congregational rabbi in the West London Synagogue, which has a full membership of thousands, and is a constituent of the Reform Synagogues of Great Britain. He seems to have been to most places and met most people. He is always on the move around the city, the country, the world. A skilful user of the media, he is familiar with both television and radio broad-casting, and he has brought a new dimension of interest and entertainment to many many Company discussions. Hugo always 'delivers'. He is not a man who would find it easy to be at a loss, and I have only very occasionally seen him display anything but buzzing competence. I don't think Hugo believes that many people would be interested in his sadness when it occurs, and, as he said to me once, when he does get hurt, he tends to go inside himself, rather than turn to others.

I had often wondered, before meeting Hugo, where all the Jewish jokes came from. I now believe that, even if he doesn't make them all up, Hugo is largely responsible for giving them currency. Whenever we meet nowadays, I look forward with relish to the latest story. I don't interrupt, but I recall that, when I first met him, I stopped a joke after half a sentence.

'These two Jews were on a bus ...'

I interrupted pompously. 'Do they have to be Jews, Hugo?' What a wonderful non-racist person I was.

Hugo's expressive face twisted into concentrated thought, then relaxed, one eyebrow raised humorously. 'Okay, I'll start again. There were these two Chinamen on their way to a Barmitzvah ...'

I collapsed.

A story that was much appreciated by Company viewers was Hugo's account of the elderly Jew who desperately wanted to win the weekly lottery that was organised in his community. This man stood before the open ark in the synagogue and called out with a loud voice.

'God! Let me win the lottery this week. I need the money. Please let me win!'

To his dismay there was no reply, and someone else won the cash that week. On the following week he came back to the synagogue, and stood before the ark once more, beating his breast and calling out in an even louder voice.

'Oh, God! You must hear me! I've been a good Jew all my life. I've done what you've told me to do. I've been in the synagogue every week. Now I'm asking you to help me. Please! Please, let me win the lottery this week!'

112

Again there was only silence, and again the prize-money went to another man a couple of days later.

The next week he prostrated himself before the open ark, pleading and begging God to answer his prayer, and let him win the lottery, just once. After a few minutes of this, he lay exhausted and speechless on the floor of the synagogue. Suddenly a voice came from the open ark. It was the voice of God.

'Look, meet me halfway, will you? Buy a ticket!'

My mother, well into her sixties by the time Hugo joined Company, and a very reliable barometer for the programme generally, took a real shine to the rabbi. She thought him kind, good-looking and original; very high praise from her.

On a more serious level, I wondered how we would handle the gap between Hugo's beliefs and those of the rest of the team. Most of us were Christians of one denominational shade or another. He was a Jew. Should we confront? Should we compromise? Should we ignore the differences and talk about something else? Generally speaking, discussions tended to be very polite and non-controversial when we did talk about our contrasting faiths. Hugo was asked on one occasion to say something about the enormous variety of faiths that exist in the world. Were they all misguided, or perhaps, all true in their own way? Hugo subscribed to the latter view. Just as a crystal will throw out different facets of the same light, so, he maintained, each religion or like-minded group receives a facet of the single, central truth, which is God.

It was a good answer, and a diplomatic answer, but I couldn't make up my mind when I saw that programme, whether Hugo really did believe what he was saying. What would I have said if I had been involved in that discussion? I would have been polite I expect. I'd have nodded, and said, 'How interesting'. What did I believe? Did I go for the crystal idea? Or did I believe that, unless they turned to Jesus, all Jews would be rejected from God's presence on the day of judgement? I imagined Hugo and me walking side by side into the presence of God. I tried to picture myself

113

being accepted and the rabbi rejected. My mind wouldn't do it – the other way round, perhaps, but not that way. I could sense a piece of the love of God in Hugo – nothing to do with his religion. It was just there. God would surely welcome home that piece of himself. Who was I to judge after all? There was little to show for my faith. Hugo's had survived experiences that I could only guess at. What did I know about suffering, compared with this man who had not long been a teenager when he first entered a Nazi death camp, and saw his younger brother taken away to be executed because he had no useful function for the Germans? Why was Hugo not only still a believing Jew, but a rabbi, after coming through experiences that might be thought to deny rather than affirm the existence of a loving God? There was never enough time or an appropriate opportunity to explore these areas with Hugo during the Company broadcasts, but I really wanted to know the answer to that question in particular. Also, what was the difference between Hugo and George in relation to the way they coped with personal tragedy? Or Peter Ball for that matter, who had given up the warmth and fulfilment of marriage and family life for the sake of serving the same God as Hugo. Why did they all continue to follow him whatever happened? The only way to ask Hugo these questions was to actually book time with him. His diary was always packed, but he named a date and on that day, a strangely significant one as I learned later, I met him at his London office.

Hugo was oddly ill at ease that morning, partly because he had been following what was, even for him, a very rigorous and demanding schedule, but also for another reason which I was to learn as we talked. People were clamouring for his attention in person and via the phone up to and beyond the point where we finally sat down. He fumbled with the telephone as he replaced it on its rest at last, half-dropping then retrieving it, glancing up quickly to see if I had noticed his uncharacteristic clumsiness.

Finally he was settled, with the inevitable cigarette safely lit, leaning back in his chair and narrowing his eyes as the smoke rose in front of his face like a thin grey screen.

I had with me a book called *Returning*, a collection of exercises in repentance by past and present Jewish writers and poets. One poem in particular had moved me more than anything I had read for a very long time. I knew Hugo was familiar with it, because he had chaired the RSGB Prayer Book Committee which had assisted Jonathon Magonet, its editor in his compilation of the anthology. I read the poem out loud.

> *The house of God will never close to them that yearn,*
> *Nor will the wicks die out that in the branches turn;*
> *And all the pathways to God's house will be*
>   *converging,*
> *In quest of nests the migrant pigeons will come surging.*
>
> *And when at close of crimson nights and frenzied days,*
> *You'll writhe in darkness and will struggle in a maze*
> *Of demons' toils, with ashes strewn upon your head,*
> *And lead-shot blood, and quicksand for your feet to*
>   *tread.*
>
> *The silent house of God will stand in silent glade.*
> *It will not chide, or blame, or scoff, will not upbraid,*
> *The door will be wide open and the light will burn,*
> *And none will beckon you and none repel with stern*
> *Rebuke. For upon the threshold Love will wait to bless*
> *And heal your bleeding wound and soothe your sore*
>   *distress....*

I finished reading and looked up. Hugo was nodding vigorously.

'Yes, I know that piece well. Actually, it's about abandonment – the kind of abandonment that we experienced in the camps. It reminds me of ... did I ever tell you about the postcards?'

I shook my head.

115

'It was in a relatively small camp in Silesia. About four thousand prisoners I think. It must have been in ...' Hugo frowned as he tried to remember, then stabbed the air with his cigarette in triumph. 'It was the summer of forty-four! We were made to work from dawn to dusk for six and a half days a week. I think it was Sunday afternoon we were allowed off, and then, absurdly, sometimes the camp orchestra would play. Can you imagine that, in the middle of death? Anyway, one day, to our great amazement we were all supplied with a postcard each, and some pencils, and told that we could write to *anyone* we liked, *anywhere*, and they would be delivered via the Red Cross.

'So, there I was, standing with my pencil and my postcard, and gradually I realised I had no one to write to. My father was there in the camp with me, but I had no idea where my mother was. The rest of the family had all died in Auschwitz. Everybody dead. Grandparents, brother, cousins, aunts, uncles, everybody from my part of the world, by that time they were already dead. I knew I had some relatives somewhere in America, but I didn't know their names, and I certainly didn't know any addresses. I really tried to think of someone, but, in the end, I was one of many who handed in a blank card. I had no one to write to, and I didn't think there was anyone in the world to whom it mattered if I wrote, or didn't write, if I lived or died. There was a sense of being totally abandoned.'

'Was that very hurtful?' Another great 'Plass' question.

'It was *so* painful. I came face to face with the fact that I didn't matter to anyone outside that camp. Thank goodness I mattered to me, because plenty of people around me soon stopped mattering to themselves, and then, well ... the suicide rate was very high.'

'But you did have your father there with you?'

Hugo stubbed out his cigarette.

'Yes, I did, and it was really because of him that I managed to avoid the excesses that many other prisoners were driven to. He

116

was a very sane, very intelligent, very good man and he kept me from doing really bizarre or shameful things. I don't mean that I was particularly good. I just had that peculiar dimension of luck in having him with me. He kept hope alive, you see. I remember he once saved the margarine ration for weeks, and he made a little bowl out of clay, and a wick from strands of cloth, just so that he could light a candle to celebrate the festival of Hannukah. "One way or another," he said, "we *are* going to celebrate!" And he got all the people together to light the Menorah.'

'Did you understand why he did that?'

Hugo threw his hands out and opened his eyes wide. 'No! I thought it was a waste of margarine. I said so. Especially as the candle didn't even light when it came to it. It just sputtered and died. But he took me on one side – I was about thirteen or fourteen then – and he said, "Understand this. You and I have gone through a lot. A long, forced march with next to no food, and once we lived for a couple of days with no water. You can live for quite a long time without food. You can even live without water for a day or two, but I am telling you that you cannot live for three minutes without *hope*. You've got to have hope!" And he was right. As long as people were taking that much trouble to make a single candle to use for a religious ceremony – well, there must be hope, even in the middle of suffering. He taught me that.'

'Did your father die in the camps?' I flinched inwardly as I waited for Hugo's reply.

'Actually, he survived the whole war, but ... you see, we ended up at this camp in Austria, a really vicious place, just a few days before the end of the war. We had been on a forced march to get there – more than half of the march died on the way – and in this camp there was not just hunger, but raging typhoid. Everybody had it. When the Americans liberated the camp on May the fifth, there were unburied corpses everywhere, and those who were alive were all sick. All those still living – and my father was living – were taken to a kind of makeshift hospital, although I'm not sure that they really knew how to treat us. And my father and I shared a bed in this place ... It was then that he died.'

'So he died after ...'

'Yes! After liberation! When they came to take him away, and I knew for sure he was dead – I wouldn't let 'em! I was hysterical – beside myself. It was the ultimate in being cheated, you see. He'd actually survived ... the sight of him being taken away was very bad. I had typhoid too, and everything seemed blurred and confused. I do know though, because they told me afterwards, that at that moment I attacked one of the German SS men that they were using as orderlies. I mean ... I really wanted to kill him. I was completely out of control. And after that ... it was just oblivion. I wasn't even able to be there when they buried him, presumably in some sort of mass grave ...'

Hugo selected another cigarette from the packet beside him, and flicked his lighter expertly. He was in control, but there had been a glimpse of a very young and desperate Jewish boy for just a moment.

'Do you know the date of his death?' I asked.

He thrust a hand towards me, palm downwards, fingers outstretched, patting the air, a characteristic gesture. 'Adrian, you're catching me on a very, very, peculiar day. After I came to, some pious Jews who had been there when my father died, gave me the date and told me not to forget that my Yahrzeit – that's the anniversary of my father's death – was the fourth day of the Hebrew month of Sivan. Whether they were right or not, I'm not sure, but that's the date I've got.'

'And that day is ... ?'

Hugo nodded energetically. 'Today!'

No wonder he had looked distracted – less together than usual. Time heals, but scars can ache terribly. Should I go on?

'So ... is this a bad day to talk about ... ?'

Hugo interrupted, leaning forward and smiling. 'Peculiar! Not bad, just peculiar.'

I took the plunge again. 'What happened to your mother, Hugo?'

'She survived. She went through Auschwitz, just as we did, and then on to another camp, where she not only survived, but helped to organise an escape group of women.'

'She wasn't with you when your father died, then?'

Hugo's response to this question was a strange, gentle, sweetly-growled 'No-o-o-o.'

'When was she freed?'

'She was released a few months earlier – in March I think, so she had already made her way back to our home town, and eventually, I made my way there as well.'

'Do you remember your first meeting with her when you got back?'

He replied vehemently. 'I remember it very, very, *very* well!' He settled back in his chair. 'I had a very complicated journey home from the camps. Transport in Europe was all over the place at the time, and you just had to travel as best you could. It was a very odd time. I went by train, I went by boat, I walked, I even stole a horse and cart with a couple of other people once, and used it for three days then abandoned it in some town. Eventually, I came to Budapest. I wasn't home yet, but I suddenly remembered that I had relatives in that city. I managed to find out where they lived and presented myself at their door.'

Hugo paused for a few moments, his hand arrested in mid-gesture, his eyes focused on the image in his mind. It didn't look like a happy memory. He went on in tones that sought to excuse the people who had opened that door to him.

'I must have looked very peculiar ... and I think they felt very ill at ease with me. They never even invited me in ...'

Hugo threw the last sentence away, but I caught it, because it triggered the memory in me of that doorway in Bristol, and the abject misery of being turned away when I most needed to be taken in. That had been bad enough. How must Hugo have felt after so many years of desperate survival, so much loss and death, when people who might have laughed and wept with him, however distantly they were related, didn't even ask him in? I didn't know how deeply that had hurt him, and for some reason I couldn't face asking him. For my own sake, I think.

I realised that Hugo was going on.

' ... and this train went and went and went until we reached a point about three or four stops from my home town in Russia. Before the war it had been in Czechoslovakia, but now the borders had changed, and suddenly I lived in Russia. No matter! Wherever it was, it was home, and I was nearly there. Anyway – the train stopped at this station a few miles from my destination, and a man got on and sat in the same carriage as me. We got into conversation, and after a while it turned out that he knew my family.

' "Did you know," he asked, "that your mother is at home?"

'Well, I didn't know, of course. It was the first time I'd heard of it. I told him so.

' "Yes!" he said. "She's there and she's fine, and she's waiting for you,... and your father. Where's your father?"

'He told me that someone had come back from the camp where my father and I ended up, just after it was liberated by the Americans, and given my mother the news that we had *both* survived. So I now knew that my mother was sitting at home waiting for me to walk through the door with my father. Well ...'

I stared at Hugo in silence, moistening dry lips with the tip of my tongue as I tried to imagine how he had felt. No fiction writer could have concocted a more tortuously dramatic situation.

'When the train stopped at my home town,' went on Hugo, 'I didn't want to get off. I said to this man, "Look, I'll just stay on for a couple more stops, and have a think about things, and then I'll come back." I was afraid to get off! But ... they wouldn't let me stay on the train. Whether they actually held the train up for a while I don't know, but somehow they persuaded me – conned me – into getting off the train, and I started to walk towards my house. Believe me, I didn't have much luggage! So, I'm walking down the road towards the house where this man said she was staying. It's a summer afternoon, and, you can imagine, I'm nervous. Then, I looked up, and there was my mother, watching me from an upstairs window as I trailed along the road towards her – alone. And when we were finally face to face, she didn't ask me anything. She looked at me and took it all in, then we embraced. And then ... you know, we have a tradition that when someone in the family dies, you sit Shivah. That means you sit on a low stool for seven days, and that's the formal mourning. But if the news of death is delayed, you still go through this ritual of mourning, but for just one hour. So my mother just looked around, found a low stool, and sat in silent mourning for an hour. At the end of the hour she got up – she still hadn't asked me anything – and she said to me, "Hugo, you're the son. You say Kaddish." That's a prayer of praise that we say, and it doesn't actually mention death at all. It starts "Magnified and hallowed be the name of God ..." So I said it. And then, when I'd finished – then, we started to talk. I didn't really understand it then, but I do now. You see, the language of religion and ritual was, if you like, the mediating influence.'

'You mean that the ritual *was*, in a sense, the conversation between you and your mother?'

Hugo nodded. 'That's right, and we didn't need anything else. It wasn't until days later that she said "Now, what exactly happened?" There was too much to say at that first meeting, so we didn't try. The most important thing, she knew anyway, just by looking at me.'

Coffee arrived. After a little clinking and stirring we were settled again.

'Why, Hugo ...' – it was the question I had wanted to ask – 'why, when you had seen so much suffering, so much misery, did you decide to become a rabbi?'

'Well, it's a good question, because, actually I always wanted to be a scientist – I *am* a scientist, I've got a degree in maths and bio-chemistry – but I agree with Emil Fakenheim when he said that Hitler mustn't be allowed a posthumous victory. He invented an eleventh commandment ...'

'Which was ...?'

Hugo wrote the words in the air with his hand. 'Thou Shalt Survive! It wasn't enough to stay alive physically. It was just as important that Jewish values, and above all, Jewish learning should be preserved. And the thing is, Adrian, that in the Jewish tradition, learning and spirituality go hand in hand. Most of us come to spirituality through learning – not the other way round. I was very lucky to have a great teacher ...' He pointed to a picture on the wall beside us. 'Leo Baeck. In the end, he and another rabbi who was coaching me, sensing that I was beginning to believe I was the only person in the world who was still seriously interested in Jewish studies said, "All right, if it's so important, then go ahead and devote yourself to Jewish learning!" So I did.'

Hugo chuckled richly. 'I was bluffed – dared into it, and I was lucky really. They stopped my bitching just like that. It just shows how important it is to fall into the right teachers' hands at the right time.'

'So you became a rabbi?'

'I became a rabbi.'

'But you didn't feel a call from God in the sense that Christian priests talk about it sometimes?'

'I might have been *sent*, but I don't think I was called.' Hugo was laughing again. 'I don't really know ... I believe that God actually rules all our destinies, so, in that very general sense, perhaps he sent me. More specific than that I wouldn't like to say. I don't quite see God picking me out and saying, "Now, Gryn, I think you ought to do so and so ..." No, it's not my notion of God.'

'But if ...'

Hugo interrupted. 'We have free will! I have it, you have it. If you abuse yours you might well diminish mine. That's where it all goes wrong. But ...' He leaned forward, one hand raised, but flat, to separate heaven from earth.' I can't blame God for *my* getting it right *or* wrong. For me, that equation just doesn't work. The things that I saw in the camps, the suffering I experienced can be wasted or not, according to how I exercise my will. I am able to know more accurately than some, perhaps, what hurts, causes pain in others. My aim is to simply *not* do that which is hurtful.' He waved his cigarette as if to attract my innermost attention. 'The Golden Rule is different in the Christian and Jewish traditions. The Christian tradition says "Do unto others as you would have them do unto you." But the Jewish tradition says "Don't do unto others what is hateful to you." There's a difference, and it's a difference that I learned through suffering.'

'And God is involved with suffering.'

'I think that God wept with the Jews in the camps. I think that God weeps with all who suffer, and I mean *with*, not just *for*!'

I was still having great difficulty in understanding Hugo's relationship with God. I felt I had grasped the importance and significance of learning and the need to preserve tradition and ritual, but there was so much in him, and in the stories he had told, that spoke of a God who did take a personal, caring interest in this person who had been 'lucky' enough to find a teacher like Leo Baeck, whose influence had changed the course of his life, and 'lucky' enough to have his father with him through the camps.

Perhaps it was just the conditioned Protestant in me, but I couldn't dismiss the strong impression that at some point in his life Hugo must have encountered God in a very close and profound way. Was it I wondered, that I simply needed to have my own image of God reinforced?

'Has God ever spoken to you, Hugo?'

'In so many words?'

I adapted hastily. 'Not necessarily, but has there ever been an occasion when God gave you a nudge, or a push?'

'Yes there was. Yes. Quite clearly.' No hesitation at all. I sat very still and listened as Hugo went on.

'It was Yom Kippur, and I was in prison, and I had a kind of bolt-hole in this place I worked in. I knew that if I worked the twelve to fourteen hours a day they demanded I wouldn't last. There just weren't enough calories coming in to keep me going. By that time I was a cunning, experienced prisoner – I knew the ways of the prison world anyway. So, I used to disappear for a few hours at a time, and just sit in this bolt-hole of mine. It was in a builder's yard. You can do things in a builder's yard. Well, it was Day of Atonement, and all the Jews in this camp knew that, and I knew it, so I got in there – into my hiding place. Well ... I didn't have a prayer book, but I remembered some of the prayers, and I ... I decided I'd pray. So I did.' Hugo's voice was a soft growl. 'Half-remembered prayers ... bits and pieces, and I ended up really crying. I just cried and cried ...'

It was a vivid picture. Hugo, already forced to be old beyond his years, sitting in the darkness, weeping for Judaism, for his family, for himself.

He went on, his voice low but very firm. 'I was convinced then, and I remain convinced to this day, that my cry was heard. I'm not saying it saved me, because that was a chance thing, but I *know* I was heard, and I in turn also heard ... understood that the ways in which we hurt each other, these are not God. Actually, that's when I became religious, in that bolt-hole that day. It never left me. I could draw a picture of that place now. It's that clear. On that day, I understood, for the first time, the reality of God; understood that he is not just an extension of me – that he is wholly "other". And, yes, I can communicate, and it's not a one-way thing ...'

'And that principle continues?'

'All the time.'

I felt surer than ever that there was something that Peter and George and Hugo had in common. Something about trusting, despite not really knowing. Something about not claiming more than was actually true ... I couldn't quite put my finger on it. I glanced up at the clock – nearly time to go. One more question.

'Hugo, you said that today might be the anniversary of your father's death. What would he think of you if he was here now?'

For a moment I witnessed a rare sight – Hugo at a loss.

'I want notice of that question!' He considered for a moment. 'Well, first of all he would be surprised that I was a rabbi, and not a scientist. He would say I have reverted – my grandfather and his father before him were both rabbis. He wouldn't be displeased about it, just surprised.' He blew a long stream of smoke towards the ceiling. 'Then I'd set out to show him he could be pleased. I think we'd get on well. I don't think he would be particularly ashamed.'

I didn't think he would either. In fact, I thought that he would probably be very proud of the way in which this son of his had kept the eleventh commandment.

Chapter 9

As 1983 got under way I was feeling rather shell-shocked. So many things had been happening in all areas of my life. I had given up smoking more than a year ago, something I had always thought impossible. Then there was the television programme which seemed to fill up a large proportion of my free time.

The bulk of my time and energy, however, was spent on the work I was doing in the newly opened locked unit at the Children's Centre in Hailsham. Planning and running this treatment facility had proved to be an intense and often stressful experience for all concerned, as we were dealing with extremely difficult teenagers in a very small and restricted environment. One child in particular was very disturbed. She had been with us for many months, a fifteen-year-old girl who, after a disastrous early life had been unable to settle for very long in any of the county establishments or foster homes that had been tried over the years. Placement after placement had failed, and now Meryl was an expert in institutional disruption, unwanted by her family, and unsuited to any but our small physically secure wing catering for no more than five children at the most. Meryl was able to wind up and manipulate adults to screaming pitch. On more than one occasion I arrived at work to find a staff member alone in the office, shaking with tension and anger after a few hours with Meryl, who seemed to feed on this kind of response.

Generally speaking there was a relatively peaceful atmosphere when she and I were together but there were times when she tested my self-control almost to breaking point with her finely judged, spiralling hysteria, and constant attention-seeking ploys. I was no longer the very immature personality who had hit out at that boy in the middle of a field ten years ago, but that was really only because I had learned more techniques and knew how to stack tension away in some inner space that, although I didn't realise it at the time, was already dangerously overpacked.

A typical incident occured one autumn afternoon, when Meryl and I were the only two people in the unit. I was ensconced in an armchair in one corner of the multifunctional dayroom while she, rather moodily, pushed snooker balls around the half-size table that stood in the centre.

Meryl desperately wanted to find foster parents who she could live with, but, predictably, the search for these 'super-humans' was taking rather a long time.

Already, that day, she and I had talked about how much progress had – or rather, had not – been made and I knew that she was feeling angry and frustrated. Poor Meryl, despite a succession of horrendous failures, always managed to whip up a froth of optimism and excitement about 'The Next Place'. Everything would be different! Oh, yes it would! She would change! Why couldn't it happen tomorrow? It wasn't usual for her to use aggressive tactics with me, but today was different. Her mind and body were aching with the strain of containing such heavy, jagged emotions, and I was the only available means of off-loading some of this intense feeling.

Sitting comfortably in my chair, absorbed in a newspaper, I was suddenly aware of Meryl's voice, filled with a sneering challenge.

'What would you do if I put this effing cue through that effing window?'

I knew how essential it was to think very quickly in these situations. Indeed, it was the extra half-second's thought that often made the difference between a successful outcome and disaster at times like this. I had been the author of enough calamities in the past to know that. In the moment after Meryl's question, the following thoughts flashed through my mind. Firstly, she was quite capable of doing what she threatened, and there was a real danger of injury, leaving aside the less important matter of damage to the building. She was on the far side of the snooker table, and therefore out of grabbing range, even if I came out of my chair like a rocket. Also she would expect me to react angrily, or nervously, or to reason with her. Any of these responses would have suited her well, offering as they did, the possibility of tension-filled dialogue, culminating in an emotional 'splurge' of some kind. I had learned to avoid predictable responses. And lastly my stomach was knotting up, as it always did when 'aggro' loomed, no matter how confident I might feel about the outcome.

The pause before my reply must have been imperceptible. As I spoke, I didn't move my eyes for even a fraction of a second from the open newspaper that I was holding.

'Just a minute.'

It was hardly a response at all. There was a short pause. Meryl must have decided that I couldn't really have heard what she said. She repeated her threat in a slightly louder voice.

'I *said*, I'm going to put this effing cue through that effing window!'

Still without looking up I answered her, trying to put into my voice the mild, abstracted irritation with which one reacts to an annoying, but trivial interruption.

'Look, Meryl, I just want to finish this little bit in the paper, then I'll be with you. Okay?'

The newsprint swam before my eyes as I waited for her next move. There was another, longer silence. When Meryl spoke finally, it was with a rather pathetic, baffled wistfulness. I wasn't keeping to the rules!

'Yeah, but I said I was going to put the effing cue through the ...'

My raised hand interrupted her. I folded the newspaper,

placed it neatly on the magazine rack beneath the coffee table, then turned deliberately in my chair to face her, crossed my legs, folded my arms and demonstrated my readiness to give her my full attention.

'Now, Meryl, I'm listening. What can I do for you?' It was the polite bank clerk with his next customer.

Meryl was a little muddled by now. She held the snooker cue up and replied quite quietly and politely, 'I'm going to put this effing cue through the window.'

'Yes ... and?'

Meryl looked blank. I was supposed to supply the 'and'. She collected herself a little. 'Well, I'm going to do it! I am!'

I nodded soberly. 'I'm sorry, Meryl. I don't quite see what you want me to do. If you've decided to break a window with that cue, then I expect that's what you'll do. You must make your own decision about whether it's a good idea, or not. I'd like to be able to help, but ...' I spread my hands in a helpless gesture. 'What can I do ...?'

Meryl raised the cue, her eyes fixed on mine. Was I bluffing? 'I am gonna do it!'

I looked up at the clock above the sink over on my left. 'Look, Meryl, I really have got to make some phone calls. I'd better go and get on with it. You stay here and decide what to do, and I'll be in the office.'

I stood up and strolled casually past the end of the snooker table, down the passage on my left, and into the little unit office a few yards along the corridor. As I passed within 'striking' distance of Meryl, I sensed her sudden increase of tension. I knew that it would happen now if it happened at all. I waited for the sound of smashing glass ... but it didn't come. Instead, the disconsolate figure of Meryl appeared in the office doorway, the long wooden cue now dangling loosely in her hand. I snatched the redundant weapon from her, and shouted loudly into her face as all the pent up emotion of the last few minutes burst out.

'Don't ever do that to me again!'

After this explosion, we sat and reviewed what had happened, looking for ways in which Meryl might have expressed her feelings more appropriately.

Meryl had many difficulties after her placement at Lansdowne but Bridget and I became very fond of her and she continued to visit and stay with us as a friend in the years that followed.

Work with children like Meryl was very stimulating and exciting – you never knew what would happen next – but it was also rather wearing.

Nowhere was the God who came, and comes down in the person of Jesus, more needed than in the lives of these children I was working with. Children like Meryl, and many others, were already emotionally crippled before they reached their first or second birthdays. Theoretical compassion was useless to them. Their experiences did not generally make for an attractive presentation and success in caring for them demanded a carefully balanced mixture of warmth and firmness. This could occasionally take extreme forms, as in the case of Miranda, another long-term resident in the secure unit, a very powerful girl, full of passion and chaos. On more than one occasion I was able to defuse the violence in her, only by putting my arms lovingly around her and whispering bloodcurdling threats into her ear at the same time. It worked because she knew I was sincere about both. I suppose – on reflection – that God operates in a similar way. The Bible has always struck me as being largely made up of God's love on the one hand, and his blood-curdling threats on the other.

Both Meryl and Miranda were victims of cruelty and mismanagement. I have always strenuously resisted the argument that says people cannot be held accountable for their crimes because of difficult childhood experiences, but there are notable exceptions, who, by the time they have struggled through and arrived wild-eyed at the age of sixteen, deserve a full apology and a pension for life.

Many people, however, do not actually commit crimes or anti-social acts as a result of early problems. They do, however, often end up with an emotional limp, an inadequacy in one area or another. Perhaps Jesus' statement that people need to be 'born again' has a special meaning for those who would welcome the opportunity to start life again and get it right this time round.

I was interested to see, as the months went by and people started to be more open, how many of the Company team had suffered as young children, and had seen, or wanted to see, God coming down into their lives to change the consequences of early trauma. Ann Warren, for instance, lost both of her parents at a very early age, and has been a refugee from her past ever since. It is her insight into her own situation, and her determination – with God's help – to overcome the darkness inside her that has enabled her to help so many others through her books and counselling. Peter Timms, the prison governor who made headlines when he left the prison service to become a Methodist minister, lived with the conviction that he was unloved for years, after his mother's early death, and formative years spent with a family who, although very caring, never really succeeded in making him feel that he belonged. Sue Flashman, one of the brightest contributors to the programme, has been very open and honest about the fear and insecurity that has dogged her all her life, and that is only now beginning to ease after much expert Christian counselling. Again, the roots of her problem lie in childhood, and any attempt to find a solution without reference to that fact would fail before it began. Frances Tulloch, Company's producer, has much in common with these folk. She also sustained a lot of inward injury as the result of her parents' broken marriage, and has had to slowly and painstakingly reassemble a shattered self-image over the years.

Does God come down and help? How does he do it? I'm sure he does it in many ways, but one of the most striking examples that I have seen is in the case of Jo Williams, my good friend and Company colleague. Of all the team, she is the one whose background most reminds me of the children I have worked with.

When Jo was 'discovered' as the newspapers put it, she was working as a cleaner in the TVS studios in Southampton and running a local scheme offering help and friendship to old, sick and desperate people. She called it Neighbourly Care and appeared one day on the TVS community services programme PO Box 13 to describe her work. Angus Wright immediately asked Jo if she would like to join the Company team and, slightly bewildered, but willing to have a go, she agreed. She became even more bewildered when the national press ran a story about her elevation from cleaner to TV star, especially as there was no question of her giving up her cleaning job to live on the 'huge' income she would receive from her television appearances. Whoever wrote that story clearly knew nothing about the kind of budget usually allowed for late-night religious programmes.

On the day Jo was due to make her first trip to the studio as a broadcaster, there was a ring on the doorbell, and on opening her front door she discovered a uniformed chauffeur standing smartly to attention beside a vast white limousine looking oddly out of place in the very ordinary little Southampton back street where she lives. With great ceremony she was ushered into the cool interior of the sleek vehicle and soon found herself gliding smoothly across the South East of England in the direction of Maidstone. Feeling very apprehensive, Jo leaned forward eventually to timidly ask her charioteer if it was 'all right to smoke'. Sensing her unease the driver abandoned his air of respectful detachment and suggested she "op in the front with 'im', an invitation which she gratefully accepted. On the outskirts of Maidstone, however, he stopped the car, and insisted that she returned to the back seat in order that her arrival should be suitably regal. As the car purred to a halt outside the big glass doors of the TVS building, Jo reached out with her hand to pull the door lever and felt her heart suddenly leap into her mouth as the driver hissed violently out of the side of his mouth, 'Don't touch that handle.' Jo, suitably chastened, sat like a pudding while the chauffeur stepped smartly out of the car, marched smoothly round to the side and released her with the dignified servility peculiar to his profession. From there, she ascended to the press-room, where interviews and photographs awaited her. That was the end of that kind of super-star treatment, but it was the beginning of something much more valuable for Jo.

Jo's very first memory is a violent one. She was three years old at the time, sitting on the kitchen table at home in the middle of being washed by her mum. An argument sprang up between her parents, increasing in intensity as the little girl, in her birthday suit, forgotten for the moment, watched and listened nervously hoping that things would soon be all right again.

Eventually, her mother picked up an alarm clock and flung it at Jo's dad. Jo doesn't remember whether it hit him or not, but she does know that following that argument, she was sent to live with an aunt in Wales for a time, completely bewildered about what was going on, and more importantly, about whose fault it was. From Wales she moved to another aunt in Portsmouth, and from there back to her mother in Southampton only to be evacuated to Bournemouth almost immediately because of the war.

When the war ended, Jo, aged nine, was at last able to come back home, and she must have hoped against hope that she would never have to leave again. About a year later, however, her hopes were dashed when, as a ten year old, she arrived home from school one day to find that her mother had left for good. On the table was a brief letter, telling her to go with her younger brother and sister to another member of the family, and a pound note, presumably for bus fares. Jo had no idea where this other person lived, so pocketing the letter and the money, she led her brother, aged six, and sister, aged nine, round to the lady next door, who took them in and called the police. When a very kindly policeman and policewoman arrived, Jo was taken to a local reception centre, where she lived for about six months as one of a group of children in the charge of a house-mother, before being transferred to a Doctor Barnardo's Home, far away in Liverpool, where she stayed until she was fifteen.

Jo's memories of life as a child 'in a home', are not good ones. She already had the idea firmly fixed in her mind that she was a 'horrible' little girl. She must be. If she had been a nice little girl her mummy would never have sent her away when she was three, or at least she would have got her back as soon as she could. And then, later on, that note on the table had been the final proof her mummy didn't want her, and in that case, how could anyone else ever want her? She was *horrible*! Her experiences in children's homes did nothing to dispel this lack of self-value. As a twelve year old, Jo used to assemble with the other children in the home every weekend to await the arrival of local people who would 'select' a child to invite to their homes for tea on the Saturday or Sunday. Each time, Jo presented herself, scrubbed pink, and wearing her very best clothes, longing to be the one who was picked for this treat. 'Let it be me!' she would say silently to herself, 'Oh, please! let it be me!' But, for some reason she never was picked. Not that she ever really expected to be. After all, what else could a horrible little girl expect?

At school there was a different kind of problem. Jo was sent off each day from her children's home, wearing the regulation issue black gymslip and stockings to mix with girls from ordinary families who seemed to have an enormous variety of clothes in all sorts of lovely colours. Noticing the curious glances directed at her sombre attire, which remained clean but unvaried as the days went by, Jo decided that something had to be said. Unwilling to confess to the shameful crime of not having a family, she invented a baby, tragically lost before birth by her mother, and explained that she wore black because she was in mourning. This very sad tale attracted quite a lot of sympathy, but two months later someone became curious about the fact that the period of mourning seemed inordinately long. Poor Jo, remembering how well the story had been received the first time, and having only the scantiest understanding of the facts of life, invented a *second* lost baby which, on this occasion, did not go down at all well. Jo laughs now when she tells this story, but it requires little imagination to see how excruciatingly embarrassing it was at the time.

At fifteen, Jo was transferred yet again, this time to Didcot in Kent, where, as a quite unreligious attender at the local Anglican church, she found herself rather fancying a good looking young curate, whose name was David Shepherd. From there she was moved to a hostel in Reigate, where she was taught housecraft, followed by yet another move to a working girls' hostel in Norwich, where she found a job selling fruit for a firm called Sexton Brothers. The effect of all these moves should not be underestimated. Each one involved breaking bonds with friends, with a distinct locality, with an environment which, even if not particularly pleasant in itself, offered the security of familiar sights and sounds from day to day. By the time she was sixteen, Jo had moved at least ten times.

One of the regular customers at the shop where Jo worked was a 'little old lady' who lived nearby. They got on very well and it wasn't long before Jo left the hostel to move in with her new friend, who became not only her foster mother, but a little later, her mother-in-law, when Jo married Netta's son, Joseph, a sailor in the Merchant Navy. Jo was blissfully happy for the first time in her life. Her husband was sixteen years older than her, and she didn't actually love him at first, but she had a home. She was wanted by nice, good people. She had married for security, and found it. Later she did fall in love with Joseph, experiencing what she calls 'tummy feelings' when he was due to return home from sea after a trip.

Joseph turned out to be a very good husband. He looked after Jo, made all the important decisions for her, and even cured her of the worst effects of her bad temper. She used to break things when she got angry. One day Joseph carried a complete china tea-set out into the garden and very calmly and methodically smashed every piece. When Jo, puzzled and aghast, asked him what he was doing, he replied quietly and reasonably that if she could do it, then so could he. She stopped breaking things.

In 1957 their daughter, Karen, was born. Jo was twenty-one and determined that Karen would not suffer the kind of neglect that she had. She admits she overdid it. Karen became a spoiled and difficult teenager. It was a problem, but Jo also had Netta and Joseph who continued to provide a place where she really belonged, where she could feel secure.

In August, 1978, Jo was in hospital having treatment for back problems. At 10.30 one night, as she lay in the ward, unable to sleep, someone brought the news that Netta had died that day. Netta was dead! Jo could hardly believe it. Thank goodness Joseph was all right. She knew he was at home feeling rather poorly, but it couldn't be anything very serious. It couldn't be! She needed him to be all right, to go on looking after her.

Less than two months later, on Sunday, October the first, Jo knew that her husband was about to die of cancer. Suddenly she was filled with overwhelming panic. She phoned the local Roman Catholic priest, and begged him to come to the house. As she waited for him to arrive she feverishly hunted out every candle, every holy statue, every religious emblem she could find and placed them on a table in the same room as the dying man. When the priest arrived at last, she dragged him into the house, up the stairs and into the bedroom, crying and screaming for him to pray for a miracle to save Joseph. They both prayed, but there was no miracle. At 2.55 on the following Sunday, Jo's husband died. His last words to his wife were simple but true. 'We've had twenty-five good years.'

The only emotion that Jo could feel was anger; deep bitter anger. She was angry with Netta for dying, angry with Netta for taking Joseph with her, angry – so very, very angry with Joseph for going with his mother when Jo needed him so desperately. The people she loved had done it all again – gone away, leaving her lost and alone. They didn't care – they'd never cared! She'd known it all along, and she was stupid to think it could ever really change. She *was* horrible! She was a horrible little girl.

Jo sat down one evening soon after Joseph's death with a half bottle of whisky and more than a hundred codeine and aspirin tablets. Carefully, she crushed the tablets between two sheets of paper and poured the powder into a tumbler. She then poured whisky into the tumbler, stirred the powder in with a spoon, and swallowed the mixture straight down. She wanted to be dead. Fortunately, her attempt to swallow such a huge quantity of tablets all at once resulted in vomiting, and instead of dying she lay unconscious and undiscovered for the next forty-eight hours. When she eventually came to, the impetus to die had diminished, and over the following month, a month in which she was virtually deaf as a result of the suicide attempt, Jo did a great deal of thinking about her situation. She realised that the only way out of her darkness and depression was through offering help and support to others, and it was out of this realisation that the Neighbourly Care Scheme was born, a scheme that resulted in enormous benefits to many sick and troubled people in the Southampton area.

Jo worked hard and found it easier to live with her own grief as she became involved with the lives and problems of others.

In 1980 she married again, somewhat on the rebound, but her new husband, Don, was a very charming and intelligent man, and it was good to feel secure again. Three weeks later, she arrived home one afternoon to find Don hopelessly drunk and very abusive. He was a chronic alcoholic. Jo was horrified: there had been no hint of the problem before their marriage. Now she was confronted with a situation that was as frightening as it was unfamiliar. There followed a dreadful year of conflict and despair. Jo, terrified by the intensity of the hatred she now felt for Don, but relieved to hear from others in the same situation that her feelings were not abnormal, decided that, for the sake of her own sanity, Don must leave.

Alone again, Jo threw herself with even greater energy into her Neighbourly Care work, and the studio cleaning job. Then, came the appearance on PO Box 13, followed by Angus' invitation, and, in a little flurry of publicity, Jo became one of the Company team.

By the time Jo joined us we had moved from the Gillingham studio to the brand new TVS building at Vinters Park near Maidstone. Here we shared a studio with the news and current affairs programme, Coast To Coast. At one end was the news desk, at the other, the Company kitchen.

Frances had managed to find a flat in the country, out at Harrietsham, where the four participants for each week were able to catch up on news, discuss programme topics for the coming week, and generally relax together. Sometimes there would be a special guest joining us for a few programmes, and he or she would usually stay at the flat with the regulars, helping out with domestic tasks like everyone else, regardless of rank or status. This was very useful as it helped to create a closeness between members of the group, which resulted in a more natural interaction in the studio itself.

We had some good evenings at the flat. Bridget and I particularly enjoyed being there when George was staying. He always entered into the occasion with tremendous zest and good humour, invariably teasing Frances about what he described as her 'posh Islington life-style', and christening her 'Black Rod' at an early stage in the proceedings. We grew very fond of many of our fellow kitchen-dwellers as we came to know them better through time spent in that informal environment. The friendships we have established with some of our colleagues will last long after Company is gone and forgotten. Certainly, we shall never want to lose contact with Jo Williams.

We liked Jo as soon as we met her, although she tells me that

I 'put the fear of God into her' when she came up to Maidstone for an audition. She remembers thinking that I was very aggressive in the programmes she had seen in the past. She soon realised that I was a softy really, and once we were able to get to know each other in the relaxed atmosphere of the Harrietsham flat, we became good friends. Jo is a very motherly type, and I must confess that I do enjoy being mothered, especially in the mornings. Jo shares with George Reindorp and Peter Timms, one supreme virtue that probably gives them the edge in the race to heaven. They all get up early in the morning to take tea to everyone else. It is a mark of my greatness that I am happy to lie in bed and let these three store up riches in heaven through this charitable act. It is a sacrifice, but I do it.

During Jo's first evening in the flat, she told us about some of the events in her past, concluding with an account of her second, disastrous marriage. Later that same evening, after our production meeting was over, and we had eaten together, she talked in more depth with Ann-Marie, who is a very sensitive listener. Ann-Marie listened quietly as Jo told her that she could never have Don back again, then promised to pray for both of them. This was quite a new idea for Jo, who had always believed that prayer was for emergencies and special occasions.

That week's programmes went well. It was clear that Jo was going to be a valuable member of the team. She was quite unselfconscious about asking the 'obvious question', unlike one or two of us who had perfected the art of looking as if we knew the answer really but were generously allowing others the chance to talk!

A few weeks later Jo received a phone call at home. It was from a hospital in Bristol. Don had jumped from a bridge in an attempt to kill himself. Obviously it was a genuine attempt; his body was wrecked by the impact of the fall and there was a strong chance that, if he lived, he would be confined to a wheelchair. Did Jo want to see him? Everything in her wanted to say 'Never!'

but she didn't. She said 'Yes.' Later, seeing him broken and help-less in his hospital bed, she felt pity for Don, but not forgive-ness. That year of misery was too clear in her memory for that. Nevertheless, she agreed that he could come home when he left hospital. The day before Don's return, Jo remembered her con-versation with Ann-Marie, and said a prayer about the future. The next day, standing on the platform at Southampton railway station, she watched Don as he alighted from the Bristol trains, and felt a wave of forgiveness and compassion flood through her, washing away – for the time being at any rate – all the anger and bitterness she had been feeling. She took Don home.

That was far from being the end of Jo's troubles. Don was still an alcoholic, and he was still drinking. Jo herself was ill much of the time, and often very depressed as the old bitterness began to creep back in and poison her efforts to find peace. In addition there were problems in Jo's relationship with her daughter who now had a lovely little boy called Joseph.

But something else was happening as well. Both inside the studio, and at the Harrietsham flat, Jo was asking a lot of search-ing questions – desperate questions, not for the sake of theologi-cal debate, but because she wanted and needed to know.

She had never read the Bible. What was it like? She read it in a modern translation and understood it for the first time.

She asked on the programme one evening why no vicars or priests had visited when Joseph died. Over the next few days she was inundated by ministers of various kinds.

What was all this about healing? Could Don walk again if she prayed for him? She did pray, and gradually he did walk again.

Did God listen to all our prayers? What about all the suf-fering? Jo wanted to know everything. They weren't unusual questions, but there was a childlike quality in the way she asked them, and in the way that she received the answers, that I frankly envied. George was wonderful with Jo, but she seemed to attract great warmth from everybody, including James Blomfield and

Roy Millard, two young men who had become very much part of the team. They developed a very soft spot for Jo – James once zooming across country from Dover to Southampton at a moment's notice when Jo hit a really bad spot.

Once, she phoned Bridget at home, when she was feeling suicidal, and said, 'Give me one reason for staying alive.' Bridget could think of nothing very logical to say, but what she did say was enough. 'I love you, Jo. As long as I love you, you just can't die.'

It was clear that Jo was beginning to see the Company team as a sort of extended family; her trips to Harrietsham and the studios were a refuge from the storms of everyday life. Whether this was desirable or appropriate, I really don't know. I think that many viewers enjoyed becoming part of this 'family' of Jo's. Over the months she had shared the whole of her life story with people at home.

There came a day when Jo had simply reached the end of her tether. The doctors had just examined Don in hospital after yet another drinking bout. Their verdict was chilling. There wasn't much of his liver left to function. He was unlikely to live for very much longer, especially as he was still drinking. Not only that, but Jo was ill herself. That was how she felt – ill, lonely and useless. That night the Company participants were Jo, myself, and Prabhu Guptara, a freelance writer and journalist and a man for whom I have a great liking and respect. Jo wept openly as she told Prabhu and myself how close she was to giving up altogether. She couldn't pray, she said. God was angry with her. I reached across the table to take her hand, and Prabhu joined his hand with ours as I prayed for Jo and Don, for their peace and health – for some deeper kind of healing in both of them. I don't think I felt much faith in my prayer being answered, but I said the words, and we all said 'Amen'. After the programme, Prabhu put his arms round Jo who was still crying, while I stood by with a heavy heart. I'd said so many prayers in my time, often for children whose lives were just like Jo's and Don's – a mess. How many of those prayers had been answered?

I shook my head and compressed my lips as I watched Jo regain her composure. I prayed again silently. 'Please, God! Please do something for Jo! For Don!'

Had he heard? Was he going to do something? I couldn't have guessed at that moment, how much was to happen to me before I knew the answers to those questions.

Chapter 10

I knew why I felt so hopeless about praying for Jo. It wasn't just the memory of children in care who had stumbled from disaster to disaster, regardless of what I did or prayed, although that was certainly part of it. It was something else – something that had happened earlier in the year, to someone I hardly knew.

Just after I was converted at the age of sixteen, I travelled to Bakewell in Derbyshire with the other young people of St John's Church, for their annual weekend house-party, organised by Clive Sampson, the curate, and featuring a very impressive guest speaker, a young Anglican curate whose name was Ross Patterson. We arrived in the conference room for our first meeting, to find that Ross had rigged up a system of strings across the top of the room to support a very large, and very vicious-looking kitchen knife in such a way that, if it should fall, the point would plunge straight into the top of his head as he stood talking to us from the platform. We liked that. After all, it *might* fall. It was a powerful visual aid in his talk about the need for salvation, and he was a good speaker, strong and humorous. He was also a good tennis player and all-round sportsman. One of those people, in fact, who seem to have a magic touch in everything they do, and a vivid illustration of the truth that not all Christian men are effete.

During the course of the weekend Ross invited as many of us as were interested to come to a mission meeting a few miles away, where his vicar who had travelled down from York for the occasion, was due to speak. I was quite intrigued. I suppose I reckoned that if Ross was only the curate, then his boss must be Patterson cubed; some kind of superman. It was with great interest, therefore that I filed into that church hall somewhere in Derbyshire to see and hear David Watson for the first time.

He wasn't like Ross. He wasn't like anybody. There was something in his speech and delivery that was quite unique. I was fascinated. Most of us keep words and sentences stacked carelessly in untidy piles in our minds ready to throw around haphazardly. There was a bespoke quality about every word and phrase that this man used. It was as if each tiny component of his speech had been carefully cut and polished by hand before being inserted into sentences that seemed to shine with a sort of translucent purity of intention. I had never heard anything like it before, and although I soon forgot the content of that particular talk, I never forgot as the years went by, the feeling that I had listened to someone who not only *believed* what he was saying, but was able to translate his thoughts into words of crystal clarity.

Over the following nineteen years, David Watson became known all over the world as one of the most effective communicators in the Christian church, through books, television appearances and missions. The unusual combination of a strong simple faith and an ability to show clear and cogent reasons for his beliefs, meant that he could appeal to people on all levels including those who might previously have felt that the Christian faith required an abandonment of intellectual integrity. Personally, I found his books much less appealing than the man himself, although they have obviously been very helpful to many many people. For me, he was a reminder, sometimes irritating, and sometimes reassuring, that there were Christians around who meant what they said for reasons other than that they had some personal emotional or psychological axe to grind.

At the beginning of 1983 it was announced that David Watson had cancer. The prognosis was poor. Unless a miracle happened he would die. All round the world people prayed for that miracle. I think some people would have jettisoned God and kept David if that had been an option. Perhaps that was the problem.

Friends from a church in America, where many healings have reportedly occurred, flew specially to England to pray for him. David spoke in interviews about how he felt a strange warmth pass through his body when they laid hands on him for healing, but neither he nor they ever claimed to *know* that he would be healed, only that God could, and might make him better.

One night we asked Company viewers to join us as we prayed, like thousands of others, for David's peace and recovery. Later on that year, in July, Frances invited him to join Bridget and myself and George Reindorp in Company for seven evenings to talk about how those prayers had, or had not been answered, and how he viewed the future.

George had met David on a number of previous occasions, but for me it was rather strange to encounter a distant memory in the flesh. I was not disappointed. There was that same clarity of expression and delivery, and a much greater depth of peace and confidence. I marvelled once again at the differences in people who followed God closely. David was very much himself, however much he might have in common with other Christians. He didn't look or behave as if he was terminally ill, and during the evening that we spent in the flat out at Harrietsham, there was no visible sign of his energy flagging.

As we left the flat on the following morning, the owners of the property, Lord and Lady Monckton, appeared from the main house, and were introduced to David, who shook hands warmly with them. As we were about to move off, Lord Monckton, who is a Roman Catholic convert and an endearingly lordish sort of Lord, took a small transparent paper packet from his pocket and held it out towards David.

'Like you to have this,' he said with a gruff cheerfulness.

David looked at the little envelope. Peering over his shoulder I could see that it contained a small square of cloth of quite unremarkable design.

'Relic of Padre Pio,' went on Lord Monckton.

I had heard of Padre Pio, an Italian priest and mystic, now dead, who was said to bear on his body the marks or wounds of the crucifixion. Others had experienced the same strange phenomenon – Saint Paul, Francis of Assisi, Dorothy Kerin and others. Presumably this little piece of cloth was a fragment of some part of the old priest's clothing.

'That's extremely kind of you,' responded David. 'Thank you very much.'

Lord Monckton smiled happily, pleased with the way his gift had been received.

'He's very active in Kent and Sussex y'know.'

I was a little taken aback by this. The Roman Catholic belief in the significance and influence of the dead on our day-to-day lives was not something that I could identify with at all. I was pretty sure that David would feel the same way. I wonder why it is that the way in which he reacted to this last comment of Lord Monckton's has been my most abiding and personally helpful memory of David. It wasn't *what* he said, it was the way that he said it.

'Really! How *very* interesting.'

Those few commonplace words conveyed an enthusiastic respect for the other man's point of view, and were not followed by one of those words like 'but', or 'however', or 'nevertheless', which usually lead quietly into total disagreement. It may seem rather trivial, but I learned something quite new at that moment about meeting people where they are, and not dragging them crudely into the arena of my own beliefs in order to club theirs to death.

We recorded seven programmes in the studio that morning, watched by Michael Harper, who was a close friend of David's and a religious adviser to TVS. Most of the programmes were indirectly or specifically connected with the illness and its effect on David's faith and family, and attitude to God. The atmosphere in the studio and the control room was one of hushed concentration as he spoke about the panic of waking at midnight, drenched with sweat, wondering if there was a God after all; of examining his faith to find out what remained when all else was shaken away, and of finally reaching the point where he wanted to go to God, but was willing to stay if necessary, instead of the other way round. He spoke of his present conviction that the best was yet to be, and grinned, like a child on Christmas Eve, when he said it.

'God's love,' he said, 'will not necessarily transform the situation – the sickness itself, but it will transform our reaction to it, and that's what really counts. I am responsible for either giving way to self-pity, which actually becomes a problem for other people as well as myself, or letting God's love and peace transfigure my reaction.'

We asked David what his central message to people would be at this stage in his life. He didn't hesitate.

'The most important thing is that people really need to *know* that God *loves* them. An awful lot of people are hurting for one reason or another. Down at the roots you find that they are not *sure* that they are loved and accepted – by anyone. To know that God loves them, that's the important thing.'

At the end, David prayed aloud.

'Father, we thank you that you have shown yourself to be a God of love. Help us, and all those in pain and need, to realise how *much* you love us, and to trust you whether we understand or not, for Jesus' sake, amen.'

As we left the studio that day, David was looking so well, and sounding so strong and optimistic that it was difficult to imagine that the cancer existed in his body, let alone that he could be dead in the near future.

Later in the year Bridget and I met David again, when we visited him and his wife Anne at their house in London with Frances Tulloch, to discuss a Sunday morning worship programme scheduled for the following spring. It was interesting to meet

Anne. She struck us as being very real, and refreshingly practical about spiritual matters. Our discussion went well, although David didn't seem as well as he had done earlier in the year. We were quite excited about the prospect of making a programme that would last for an hour instead of less than ten minutes, and I think that I had developed a rather unreal expectation about the way in which personal spiritual problems might be resolved through frequent contact with David.

When I arrived at the TVS studios one evening, early in 1984, to learn that David Watson had died, it was as though some kind of heartless trick had been played on me. I know it seems childish and selfish but I felt cheated. Of course I felt for Anne Watson and her children as well, but they were strangers to me. I just wondered why God had, apparently, snatched away the man who could have solved my problems. Rational or irrational, that was how I felt, and the little fire of anger that had always burned deep inside me, flared up dangerously as this fresh fuel was added to it.

We went ahead with 'Meeting Place', as the Palm Sunday programme was called, and we were fortunate to have David MacInnes, a close friend of David Watson's, to take over the task of leading the service, but it was not a happy occasion for any of us, including little David, our youngest son, who was also taking part in the programme, and developed German measles on the day of the recording. I don't know who was more unhappy, him or me!

The period from Easter to autumn that year, I remember as a series of manic highs and miserable lows. Everything was losing its worth before my eyes, so it didn't really matter what I did or thought, or said. I was heading for some kind of crisis, but on the way to it there were two 'moments' that were to seem very significant in the future.

The first happened as I sat in church one Sunday morning. A picture started to form in my mind of a huge lake surrounded by plots of land, each one occupied by a single person. Behind the plots that gave access to the lake were more plots, again occupied by individual people. As I explored the picture mentally, I saw that the lakeside dwellers were made up of two kinds of people. The first kind rushed to and fro from the edge of the lake to the boundary between their own plot and the one behind, carrying cups of water to their landlocked neighbours. Most of the water got spilled in the process, but they worked on frantically, doing their best. The other kind were not working frantically at all. They were simply digging steadily on their plots of land, with no apparent interest in the fate of the waterless tenants whose land adjoined theirs. One of the cup-carriers stopped, red-faced and breathless, and spoke with some annoyance to one of the diggers.

'Why don't you do as we do? Why don't you get a cup and carry water to those who have none? It is selfish to work only on your own land as you do.'

The digger leaned on his spade for a moment and smiled. 'You don't understand,' he said, 'I'm digging a trench.'

The second moment was a moment of prayer. Like most people I had always had great difficulty about talking to God. It was all right sometimes, but more often than not my prayers bounced off the ceiling and the walls like a badly hit ping-pong ball, rolling to a halt eventually at my feet. On certain rare occasions though, a particular prayer seemed to pierce the barrier between myself and God with the kind of sweet certainty that one experiences on hitting the perfect off-drive in a cricket match (equally rare in my case). This prayer was like that. Bridget and I, realising that the kind of Christianity we were living out fell very short of the picture painted by Jesus, decided to say a very risky prayer.

'Father, we know that we haven't done very well with any-thing much up to now, but we really want to go all the way with you. We realise that we don't even understand what that means, but, whatever it costs, and however much it hurts, please let it happen. Amen.'

If I could have grabbed that prayer back as it zoomed off to its heavenly destination, I think I would have done. But I couldn't, and it wasn't long before God started to answer it in an unexpected and alarming way.

Chapter 11

'The police are here.'

My head was spinning as the nurse put yet another stitch into my injured wrist, but the words penetrated my brain with needle-sharp clarity. I was going to be arrested. After years of collecting children from police stations, and countless discussions about how to avoid getting there in the first place, I was about to find out how it felt to be 'nicked'. I relaxed my head back onto the pillow, and tried again to make some sense of what was happening to me. What had the doctor put on my sick note three weeks ago? 'Severe stress reaction.' They were just words. What had really happened?

When my three sons were all 'little' children, I used to wake in the morning sometimes to find that there were five people in our king-size double bed. Matthew, long and well-built, would be draped across the foot of the bed, forcing me to take up a near-foetal position, while Joseph was usually jammed firmly into my back, thus causing me to throw my head back and create space just under my chin for little David, who, during the night, was little more than a heat-seeking device. I ended up lying in exactly the same posture as a long-jumper in mid-leap; arms stretched above my head, back arched, legs bent, the classical position for gaining maximum distance. Poor Bridget would just be a shapeless form, crushed against the far wall by this living jigsaw of human bodies. In the morning I had to painfully ease and straighten out all those parts of me that had been adapting for most of the night to the unyielding bodies of my three small but solid night visitors. Being very tall, the pain could sometimes be intense, and on occasions I would abandon my own territory and either get up very early, or seek refuge of a sort on a vacated, two-foot-six wide bunkbed in the children's room. Anything to ease my aching bones.

This is the best way I can think of to describe what was happening to me in the summer of 1984. My mind and emotions were cramped and strained by the constant need to adapt to the varying demands and expectations of people, situations and attitudes that never seemed to allow me to stretch and relax, to be unashamedly myself, whatever 'myself' turned out to be. Whether I was under more pressure than others in similar situations I don't know. I only know that the 'act', the ability to go on playing all these complex games that normal life seemed to involve, was using up all my inner resources.

Even as my faith and belief in God and myself was draining away from me, there seemed to be an increase in what was wanted from me as a social worker, as a father and husband, as a Christian, and as someone who appeared often on television talking about God as though I had something worthwhile to say.

I was tired of locking children up for a start. Ironically, in the two years that I'd worked in the secure unit, I had finally begun to accept that it was safe to relax and be genuinely concerned about the people I was caring for. I enjoyed the challenge that each child's needs presented, and I began to believe that I might be on the verge of becoming real in my dealings with them. But real people are vulnerable, and for years I had disallowed, repressed, and postponed the expression of feelings that were too deep for words. Now, I cared desperately about the fate and future of these children, and although we did have some success, it became increasingly difficult to live with the failures, especially as I, like the other staff in the unit, was turning the key on them daily. By then, Meryl had gone to a psychiatric hospital, and Miranda had gone to prison. So many children had passed through the 'sad-mad-bad' cycle even before reaching us, and all too often a custodial sentence seemed to be society's relieved response to a conveniently concrete crime. The whole exercise began to appear a vastly expensive, cynical game, and I, who had pretended so much in the past, simply could not pretend any more. At work, in the six months before I finally broke down, I had felt mounting inner hysteria, and detachment from an institution which, although excellent in comparison with other places I had known, now seemed ridiculous; a place where we supervised the disposal of social rejects and colluded with social-service higher management in playing the 'professional and caring people game'. No doubt my vision was distorted by tension and role-play fatigue, but now, as I view things more calmly and objectively I see it in the same way. There were some good people working in a system that was top-heavy with bureaucracy, and too often expedient rather than caring.

The other game that I had become very bad at was being-a-Christian-and-going-to-church. I didn't seem able to keep to the rules any more. I wanted to say that I was sad when I was sad, happy when I was happy, non-believing when God didn't seem to exist, angry when I was angry, and bad when I was bad. I wanted the freedom to be all of me, and not a little, spineless, spiritually arthritic version of myself. I wanted to break away from the awful, simpering, Christianese language that seemed to obscure and stifle passion and human-ness whenever it threatened to break through the carefully organised spontaneity of meetings, services and conversations.

I wanted to shake off the arid virtue which had taken the place of real goodness for so many years, and force a full-frontal collision with reality; to dive naked into the dark waters of the risk-infested non-religious world, from which God – if he was God – would rescue me because he loved me, and not because I strained to conform to precious group norms that depended for their maintenance on unspoken agreements that nobody would mess things up by telling the whole truth. These were not clearly specified or dignified needs at the time. They were ragged, wild longings to find the reality of God that had been promised all those years ago on a Sunday evening in St John's Church. No more systems, no more pretence, no more props. I had been conned and compromised for long enough. Let the props snap, and let God do whatever he was going to do – if he was there!

For more than thirty years a great shout had been building up in me, a shout of tearful protest that I couldn't manage, that people *didn't* seem to mean what they said, that I felt like a small person trapped in a large actor's body, that all I wanted was to collapse, and be allowed to be useless. As for God, and most of those who claimed to represent him, they – in my mind – were the arch-offenders, the 'smiling' ones who had deceived themselves just sufficiently to be able to deceive others. I hated and despised the neat middle-classness that allowed them to pose as Christians without significant effort or cost. It was my turn to do, be and say what I liked, and the rest of the false, smiling, stupid, bloody world could go hang!

One night I returned home late after going out for a drink with friends. As I walked through the front door, something snapped. I started to scream and shout, punch the walls with both hands, and sob uncontrollably. My wife, who, with a friend, wrestled through the whole thing with me for hours, tells me that I shouted the same phrases over and over again.

'I can't lock them up any more! I can't lock them up any more! I've tried to be good – I've tried to be good! I want to be me! I want to be me! I can't lock them up any more!'

And indeed I couldn't. Children, feelings, hurts from the distant past, agonies I'd never shared, bitter anger against God, the church, and everything connected with it – I couldn't lock them up any more. Down went all my defences for the first time since I was a little boy, leaving me raw and vulnerable to whatever temptations and influences might be around.

The weeks that followed were a nightmare, not only for me,

but for Bridget as well. No work, no church, no stability, no reason for me to do or not to do anything other than what was immediately stimulating or sense-dulling. The darkness had a thick, sweet attraction difficult to resist. I would disappear for hours at a time, returning home late at night, usually drunk, still wanting only to drown thought and feeling in loud, powerful rock music, or more drink. And the anger continued to rage in me, making it impossible to meet most of the people I knew, especially those who wanted to tell me I had 'stepped outside the Lord's will' and could step back in again by applying some formula or other.

There are aspects of that period that are very difficult and painful to remember. For some reason I seemed to need to abdicate completely from commitment to previous close relationships. My family, more important to me than anything else in the past, suffered and watched, and waited for some light to appear in the darkness. Every day offered new potential for disaster as I wrestled with the strangeness of a world that, in some ways I was seeing for the first time. I would stand on the pavement in the High Street, watching people as they passed to and fro, and wonder with genuine amazement how they could possibly have discovered a strong enough motive for moving in such a purposeful way. I recall sneering sceptically at the girl in the Chinese takeaway when she responded to my order in a normal, pleasant way, 'You almost sound as if you really care!' The whole world felt like the setting for a wearisome game in which everyone cheated.

One day, I arranged to meet a friend, someone who I could still communicate with, in a pub in Eastbourne. I arrived late to find that he'd gone. I boiled. Disproportionately angry and tense, I slammed out of the pub and crossed the road, intending to call Bridget from the phone box and unload some of the blackness that was building up in me. As I stepped into the kiosk, a hot wave of anger surged through me. Part of me, oddly detached, watched, hypnotised, as my fist arched towards one of the small square glass panes, and smashed through. I drew my hand back, all the anger gone now, and gazed disbelievingly at a long and sickeningly deep gash in my wrist. Oddly enough, at that moment, I felt only relief as I watched the blood drip onto the floor of the box. It was so good to see some external evidence of the gaping wounds inside. Fear followed immediately. Why had I done it? Was I really going mad? Suddenly I was very calm. In a nearby shop I got someone to call a taxi for me, and a few minutes later, I wrapped a piece of cloth round my wrist and climbed in. Before long I was in the accident and emergency ward of the local hospital.

The nurse put a final tape on the dressing, and grimaced sympathetically at me as I swung my feet onto the floor. I realised that the old, tired coping mechanism was grinding slowly into action, just as it had in so many difficult situations over the past years. But this was different. I was the one in trouble, not some desperate teenager needing me to get them out of a fix. My 'crime' was not a major one by any standards, but the situation was a completely new one for me. How was I going to handle this encounter with the law? I automatically selected and rejected options. 'Sullen and disturbed', maybe? Or perhaps 'weary and resigned' would be more effective. I finally settled on 'surprisingly calm and pleasantly co-operative'. The receptionist led me to a small side room where two young policemen were waiting. Politely, and with a hint of embarrassment (it turned out that both of them were Company viewers) they informed me that I was arrested on a charge of criminal damage, and that anything I said would be taken down and might be used in evidence against me. Later, in the bowels of the police station, I was fingerprinted, photographed, and left to sit in the corner of a small room containing nothing but a table, a bench, and a couple of posters on the wall. For some reason, this bleak little room seemed familiar. Then I remembered. This was exactly the same room in which I had found Miranda on the last occasion that I had been called to

156

collect her from a police station. I was a rank amateur in crime and violence in comparison with her, but as I sat on the same bench as she had, waiting for someone to return, I felt the sting of tears in my eyes as I realised for the first time, why she, and other children I'd known, had shown such violence in similar situations. Why were two young, pink people in blue uniforms, so obsessed with a piece of glass? Didn't they know about the last thirty years? Didn't they *want* to know? I wanted to ask them, to argue with them, to *make* them understand, because they were the visible, official representatives of punishment without passion, the hard words without the loving arms. By now, if it had been Miranda, the place would have been in uproar. I was lucky. I had been around longer, and back home I had four pairs of loving arms to balance the inclination I suddenly felt to shout and punch and kick and swear at the mechanicalness of justice. I was thirty-five; not fifteen. I held my tongue, and smiled, and wasn't charged, and went home.

Richard Wurmbrand tells of a judge, placed in the cell next to him in an underground communist prison, who spent much time asking forgiveness for the way in which he had passed sentence on so many convicted criminals without any genuine understanding of what imprisonment really meant. For any arrogance or self-righteousness that I have shown towards children in trouble in the past, I also ask pardon, realising that we all stand together in the need for mercy and compassion. God help us all.

The difficulty and despair of this time is well illustrated by two pieces of writing that have survived the turmoil somehow. The first is a poem, written at the point where I realised that the particular kind of Christianity I had tried to embrace, was more likely to prolong the agony than cure it.

Who made these poison pools
In desert lands
So sweet and cool?

A welcome lie,
The chance to die with water on my lips.
I've seen how others try to die unpoisoned in the sun,
I do not think that I can do as they have done.

The second, and far more graphic illustration is provided by an extract from a letter written by Bridget to a very close friend at the time. I include it here, with her blessing, in the hope that others who find themselves in the same position, will see that theirs is not a unique experience, nor a hopeless one.

... if anyone else asks me how he is, I think I'll scream. I don't know how he is. I don't know *him* any more. He keeps saying this is the real him, and only my memories of fourteen years keep me from believing him. He is still lovely to the children, and they, thank God, seem by their cuddles and hugs to be able to reach him in a way I can't. All I seem able to do is wait and pray, and I seem to do an awful lot of both!!! I just keep on and on at God all the time, it feels like bashing on his door until he finally answers, and every now and then I get a total feeling of peace, as if he has done just that. When Adrian is out, and I don't know where he is, I just beg and beg God to just hold on to him and keep him safe and bring him home – Whatever state he's in.

I'm living one day at a time now. I only wish everyone else could. They seem to want instant recovery, and I feel a ludicrous sense of failure when I have to say, 'He's about the same, really ...'

... Sometimes I just feel hurt and angry that it's happening. I love him so much, and it's my life he's wrecking as well as his. – I know that's horrible, and I hate myself, but I do feel it, especially when he says he's glad it happened. I wish to heck that *I* understood what's happening to us all. I can't see any future at all at the moment ...

... sometimes all I can do is hold him like a child, and I can feel the agony in him. I must try not to keep crying – it makes everything ten times worse, because he feels so guilty about what's happened – so sorry for all of us. I wish God would hurry up and *do* something, anything!...

Bridget was quite right when she said that some people wanted my instant recovery. They fell into two groups. The first was made up of those who had used *me* as a prop until now. There was almost an air of annoyance in their response to the news that I could no longer offer support. I understand that now, but it hurt me then. The second group, not large, but significant, was composed of those Christians for whom non-recovery seemed to constitute an attack on their faith.

God knows, I was a million miles from being as innocent as Job, but there was no doubt that as far as one section of the church was concerned, I was 'spoiling the game' by not recovering quickly and testifying to the healing power of God. I had shared their creed, and now I was threatening the theology of that creed by stubbornly refusing to get better, and protect their religious confidence. One or two were visibly angry, not just with me, but with others in a similar situation, who were letting the side down by being chronically unwell. Rightly or wrongly, I felt that such people had what Oswald Chambers calls 'The ban of finality' on them, the result of theology – albeit lively, active, theology – being put before God. After one or two very negative encounters of this kind, Bridget deflected approaches from people who wanted to tidy me up spiritually, not least because I had abandoned politeness, and was quite likely to say exactly what I thought in strongly unreligious terms.

On the positive side, I look back with enormous pleasure at the wide and sometimes surprising variety of folk who supported and loved and put up with me, not because they had a particular axe to grind, but simply because they cared. Some were Christians from our own church, some were from others. Some were not Christians at all. There were friends from the past and the present, one or two from work, others who, previously, I had felt I hardly knew. They had one thing in common. They gave something of themselves to me, and asked for nothing back. They were glimpses of God in the desert.

The image of the desert is particularly appropriate as, shortly after I stopped work, my perception of myself in relation to the church was crystallised in my mind by a daydream, or mental picture in which I found myself in a vast desert, standing on the edge of an oasis full of excited, cheering people. They were all facing inwards towards the centre of the oasis, and, try as I might, I just couldn't break through the tightly packed bodies, to see what was causing all this noise and activity. In the end I asked someone on the edge of the crowd to tell me what it was he was trying to see, and why everyone was pushing and shoving and jumping up and down so excitedly.

'The king!' he said. 'It's the king! He's there in the centre!'

'Have you seen him?' I asked. 'Have you actually seen him?'

'No,' he replied. 'I haven't seen him, but we all know he's there! Isn't it exciting!' And he went back to his calling and waving.

Disheartened, I turned my back on the oasis and walked slowly away into the desert. As the commotion gradually faded behind me, I became aware of a dot in the distance, which, as I came closer, seemed to be a heap of rags, piled untidily on the sand. At last, I was near enough to see that it was a man, his eyes large and dark with suffering, his clothes in tatters.

'Who are you?' I asked.

The man smiled a smile of deep, sweet sadness, and spoke softly. 'I am the king. I couldn't get in either.'

There were other glimpses of God. A friend suggested I should visit the Anglican vicar of a small, nearby country church, a man who might be regarded by many people I knew as 'unsaved', or 'uncommitted'. At one time I might have thought him so.

So why, I wondered, as he and I walked his dogs along the old disused railway track, and took shelter from the soft autumn rain under one of the tall, brick bridges, did I feel a relaxation and a peace that I had not found elsewhere?

'What do you think of God, then?' I was still rather graceless.

Frank smiled imperturbably. 'I've never met him,' he said quietly, 'but,' gesturing around him with his stick, 'if he made all this, and was the one who gave me my talents, I think I would love him if we met.'

What was all this? If we met? Was this any way for a Christian to talk? Not where I came from! And yet, on the two occasions that I walked through the countryside with this gentle, peaceful man, I sensed, even in the midst of my confusion, that Jesus walked with us, and that he and Frank were old friends.

I saw God, too, in the support of my fellow Company participants, when I arrived in Maidstone for the first programmes I had made since the night I had lost my 'props'. In many ways this attempt to continue with Company was an experiment. Just about everything else had fallen apart, and neither Bridget nor I were very confident about my ability to hold things together enough to cope with production meetings, studios and cameras. It was providential that my colleagues on this 'test run' were Hugo Gryn and Prabhu Guptara, a rabbi and a 'Hindu follower of Christ', but, more importantly, two compassionate and warm human beings who, with their own kindness and control, held me in a stable frame of mind, and enabled me to get through the meeting and programmes without too many problems. Some have thought it strange that I should have been able to go on making television programmes throughout this period. I can only say that it was the best anchor I had for a time. The flat in Harrietsham, and the kitchen table in its little pool of studio light, were familiar, safe environments, that were detached from the rest of my life, and always had been. My visits there provided an ongoing reassurance to me that I wasn't going completely round the bend, and that I was still – if only minimally – useful to someone. I soon realised though, that I could only carry on with Company if I was prepared to be honest about what was happening to me. It wasn't a welcome prospect. I had never exposed or shared pain and hurt before, and in my present fragmented condition, I couldn't be sure that I would control my emotions.

On the occasion when I did first describe what was happening to me I very nearly ended up in tears, but I managed to get through it somehow, and I was very glad I did. The response from viewers to that programme, and subsequent ones in which I talked about what was happening to me, was so warm and supportive, that it was like having a whole other family behind the cameras. Letters and messages from people 'out there' offered prayers, hugs, shared experiences, and constructive advice. It isn't easy to put into words how much the concern shown by those letters meant to me during this time.

Meanwhile, what about God? For a quite lengthy period, the answer to that question was very simple. There *was* no God, and if by any chance it turned out that I was wrong and he did exist, then I hated him with all the newly released passion in me. Other people, like George Reindorp and Peter Ball believed that he had been with them, helping and directing them, throughout their lives. Not me! With me, God had really screwed up, and I preferred the simple conclusion that he didn't exist, to the impossible task of reconciling my situation with the active concern of a loving, omnipotent presence.

Now here, as some comedian used to say, is a funny thing. I had dismissed God. He wasn't there. I was doing all sorts of things that my dry morality had woodenly prevented in the past. I was feeling and choosing and sinking and rising without any reference to any religious rule-book or its author. But, try as I might, there was one thing, or rather, one person, who I just couldn't shake off. No matter how far I penetrated the darkness, no matter how low I went, no matter how much I drank, there was Jesus.

One day, I was sitting in a pub with a man I had known in the past. He had moved away, and was back just to visit. He can't have known anything of what had happened to me, and we had met by accident that day. He was a farmer, and his name was

Bill. He'd always had the disconcerting ability to see through lies and insincerity. He was about as tactful as an avalanche, but he had a sort of rich agricultural charm, and I liked him. Bill knew that I was a Christian. When he was resident in the TVS region, he'd often watched me attempting to put the world to rights at midnight on TV. Now, there was something about the way he was gazing into his beer with knitted brows and pursed lips, that suggested he had something to say about it.

After a sudden swift gulp from his pint glass, he banged it back down beside him, rested his elbows on the table, and pointed both forefingers in the direction of my eyes, unconsciously indicating that in them he would read the truth, whatever I might say.

'You still doing that programme?'

I nodded.

'I don't understand you,' he said. 'I can't understand why a bloke like you wants to be a Christian. You always seemed quite sensible – normal. I don't see how you can believe it.'

He watched me closely – waiting. Our eyes seemed so rigidly locked together, that I had the absurd fantasy that if he leaned back quickly he would pull my eyeballs out. Had he complimented me, or was it an insult? A bloke like me? For a moment I felt the old tension grow in me, the tension that invariably preceded my regurgitation of the undigested lump of evangelicalism that I'd swallowed in my teens; a congealed mass of guilt, half-remembered scriptures, and fear, that until recently had neither nourished me, nor passed out of my system. It was different now. In the old days I would have searched for words to keep me in the good books of both Bill and God. Quoted John 3:16 perhaps, like a magic charm, to ward off real communication. I realised that, now, I could answer truthfully. I was not bound to produce either a bon mot, or the paralysed jargon that had clogged the arteries of my spirit for so long.

'I just don't see how you can be a Christian,' repeated Bill, doggedly.

'Nor do I, actually.' I seemed to hear bells ringing, people cheering.

Bill's gaze relaxed a little. He looked more puzzled than accusative now. The fingers drooped.

'I mean – what about the church? I mean – surely you can't think the church is much good the way it is – surely?'

'The church is a mess,' said I, remembering my old set speech about it depending what you meant by 'the church'. I was beginning to enjoy myself. Realising that I wasn't going to enlarge on what I'd said, Bill ploughed on.

'Some of the people who say they're Christians – don't you find it embarrassing – people thinking you're like them, I mean?'

'Yes.'

'On that programme you do – Company. That bloke who seems to think everything's evil – I mean, do you agree with that?'

'No.'

Bill had almost reached the end of his furrow.

'Some Christians,' – the fingers were up again – 'some Christians believe the whole Bible is one hundred per cent historically accurate, every word. I mean – how can they?' He paused. 'Well, is it?'

'I don't know.' I wasn't sure. I realised that I never had been sure.

Bill was leaning back in his chair, rubbing the small bald patch on top of his head, (the one that had never bothered him at all) his face contorted by the search for comprehension.

'But in that case, if that's all true ... what's left? Why *are* you a Christian? Why bother?'

My euphoria faded suddenly. Why bother, indeed? Bill didn't know it, but he'd got the question wrong. Not – *why* was I a Christian, but *was* I a Christian at all? Was anything left? I suddenly remembered a rather frightening thought that had occurred to me one day, not long before I broke down, as I sat in church watching people come in before the start of the service.

Supposing, I thought, each person came to church with a regulation black briefcase containing, in some impossible way, their personal evidence that the Christian faith was true. Every Sunday, we would nod and smile at each other, indicating our briefcases with genial confidence as if to say, 'Lots in mine, brother. No problem here!' One awful Sunday, though, the minister would announce that, today, we were all going to open our cases in front of each other, and examine this mass of evidence. One by one, in a heavy silence, the cases are opened. They are all empty ...

I had opened my 'case' in front of Bill. Was anything left in it? Could there be anything real and truthful tucked away in a dark corner somewhere? To my surprise, there was; but it was such a raw, indefensible, insubstantial piece of truth, that neither cleverness nor jargon could express it. It embarrassed me to say it, and Bill reacted as though I was some kind of spiritual flasher.

'I don't bother at the moment, Bill, but if I ever bother again, it'll be because I love Jesus. Do you want another drink?'

And it was true. Even in the deepest darkness, like the faintest of nightlights, he was there, not trying to make me do, or believe, or feel anything in particular, not even causing me to believe in God, absurd as that may sound, but simply 'being there'. It is not rational. It is a humble fact. Much later, I wrote some words to a friend's tune in an attempt to capture the essence of this experience. The title is simply 'Song to Jesus'.

> I didn't have to see you,
> In the darkness, there by the side of me,
> I knew it had to be you,
> Knew you loved the child inside of me.
> You smiled in the darkness,
> It seemed to blind and burn.
> But when my eyes were opened,
> I smiled in return.
> For you were there.

I didn't have to hear you,
In the silence, you were a part of me,
I knew that I was near you,
Knew your love was deep in the heart of me,
I knew that you were saying,
'Our happiness has grown,
For prayer is only friendship,
You never were alone,
For I was there.'

I didn't have to hold you,
Tried to trust you, trust in your care for me,
The secrets I had told you,
Hoping you would always be there for me,
So let the darkness gather,
And let the silence roll,
The love that made you suffer,
Is burning in my soul,
And you are there.

In one sense it was this constant, unbidden awareness of Jesus, that led to the activity that was instrumental in my regaining stability, and an interest in relatively normal living. I started to write; and the first thing I wrote was a series of six stories called *The Visit*. They chronicled the experiences of a fairly ordinary church member, confronted with Jesus, in person, paying an extended visit to a church of vague denomination in 1984. Not surprisingly, the stories are littered with allusions to my own experience, although the central character is quite unlike me.

Writing helped. It was a discipline and a therapy. The love of my family helped. They never stopped supporting me. Friends helped, especially perhaps, Ben Ecclestone, an elder at the Frenchgate Chapel in Eastbourne. He never preached at me once, and was – and is – refreshingly honest about his own faith and life. Company helped. It sustained a faint belief in me that I might not be totally useless. All these things contributed to a gradual process of rebuilding, or, more accurately, reassembling. I became calmer, more disciplined, readier to accept that I had to fit into the world as it was, albeit with a much freer outlook and a far greater flexibility in my view of myself and others. But I didn't know what to think about God. God, the father? He wasn't my father, and never had been. Despite the strange reality of Jesus, I still felt far removed from accepting the reality, let alone the concern of the senior member of the Trinity. Until, that is, one day when I took a very expensive taxi ride, all the way from Polegate to Haywards Heath.

Chapter 12

Damn and blast!'
I cursed loudly as the London train disappeared infuriatingly into the distance, then flopped down on to the wooden bench behind me, rubbing my bruised knee and sucking air through my teeth as the pain started to make itself felt. I'd missed the train! Only by seconds, but that made it worse somehow. Anger and frustration crashed crazily around inside me, looking for an outlet. Perhaps I could throttle the ticket inspector, sitting inoffensively over there in his little box at the top of the steps. As long as the jury at my trial was made up of twelve people who had at some time in their lives missed a train by a hair's-breadth, I had no doubt that they would bring in a verdict of justifiable homicide. As I passed him on my way out of the station, my imagined victim nearly hastened his own end by calling out genially, 'Missed it then?'

'Yes,' I replied, baring my teeth, 'that sums it up nicely.'

As I limped off down the steps, he called after me, encouragingly, 'Never mind, there'll be another one along in an hour.'

In an hour? That was no good. I was supposed to be in Haywards Heath by four o'clock, and I'd just missed the last train that could get me there in time. As I stood outside the station, still fuming inwardly, it seemed to me that someone or something was doing everything in its power to stop me reaching my destination that day. Well, whoever it was, they seemed to have succeeded. I wasn't going to make it. I leaned against the wall, gloomily watching people arriving and departing from the taxi rank on the station forecourt, and wondered why this particular trip had come to seem so very important.

It had started a couple of weeks ago when I was thumbing through the dog-eared little volume in which Bridget and I recorded addresses and phone numbers. For some reason I had written down Michael Harper's address in Haywards Heath a long time ago, but had never had cause to contact him either by letter or phone. In fact, that meeting in the TVS studios during the recording of the David Watson Company programmes, was the only occasion on which I had met or spoken to him. Now, as my eye caught his name on the 'H' page of the little book, I remembered how impressed I had been by the depth and sensitivity that I sensed in his personality. Was it possible that he might have something to say to me that would assist, or speed up, or perhaps just encourage the process of reintegration that had already started?

Following the impulse before it had a chance to escape, I took the book over to the phone and dialled Michael's number. When I finally got through to him, all I could think of to say was, simply, 'I've had a sort of breakdown. Would you mind if I came to see you?' He responded warmly, suggesting a date and a time that happened to suit both of us. As the days passed, I looked forward to this meeting, although I had no idea just how crucial it was going to be.

The day of my trip started well. I didn't have to be at Polegate station until about ten past three, so there was plenty of time to relax and organise myself. After drawing some money from the bank after lunch for the coming weekend, I walked slowly down to the precinct in the centre of Hailsham to catch the 2.55 bus, which I knew from experience would arrive at Polegate in plenty of time for me to get the London train.

The bus arrived late. Not very late, but enough to set up a sort of nervous ticking in my stomach as we lumbered out of Hailsham and turned heavily on to the south-bound dual carriageway towards Eastbourne. The ticking increased to a frenetic whirr, as the bus breasted a slight hill and I saw the lines of stationary traffic before us. Of course – roadworks! I'd forgotten that they were taking the road up just before the Polegate turn-off. It put another five minutes on the journey, and by the time I got off near the Horse and Groom pub, I was almost whimpering with frustration. I still had quite a distance to walk – or rather sprint. I flew along the path towards the station, so panic-stricken at the thought of losing my train, that I lost my footing and fell heavily onto the ground, cracking my knee against the kerb, and shaking my innards into a jelly. With hardly a pause, I hauled myself up, and staggered onto the station, only to see my train standing tantalisingly by the platform, passengers boarding and alighting with impossible casualness. I could still make it! Unfortunately, the man at the ticket office refused to let me through without a ticket, and I had made the fatal mistake of letting him see that I was in a tearing hurry. With excruciating, deliberate slowness, he gave me my return ticket, took my money, and counted out my change. By the time I reached the platform the train was pulling out of the station, and all I could do was swear.

Now, as I watched taxis come and go on the forecourt, I felt miserable and defeated. There was nothing left but to find a telephone and let Michael know I wouldn't be coming. I knew that he had only an hour to spare, as he was going away the following morning. There would be no point in getting a later train. I trudged slowly up the road towards the centre of the town, knowing that there was a nest of phone kiosks just outside the Post Office.

As I walked, though, a wild thought occurred to me. Why shouldn't I go to Haywards Heath by taxi? Well, why not? I counted the money in my jacket pocket. There was twenty pounds exactly. Would that be enough? I didn't know, but I could find out. I hovered, undecided for a moment, imagining Bridget's reaction if she knew that I was contemplating using a sizeable chunk of our available cash for a taxi fare. I decided to take a chance. Turning round, I hurried back to the taxi rank, and asked one of the drivers if he could get to Haywards Heath by four o'clock. Yes, he thought he probably could. How much would it cost? He wasn't sure. About twenty pounds perhaps. I climbed in, and away we went.

I can remember only two things about that journey. One was the fare meter, displaying the cost of the journey as the miles rolled away beneath us. After a while I saw nothing but the red-lit numbers beneath the dash board, changing alarmingly every few minutes as another ten pence was added to the total.

The other thing was what seemed like an endless monologue by the driver on the subject of how he dealt with people who were sick in the back of his taxi.

By the time we reached Haywards Heath I felt as if I was going mad. My mind was in a surrealistic whirl of red lights and vomit. We stopped outside Michael's house. It was five minutes past four, and the meter showed eighteen pounds, fifty pence. I gave the driver the whole twenty pounds, and hurried up to the front door My feelings as I rang the front door bell were rather similar, if I'm honest, to the way I had felt all those years ago when I stopped my bicycle next to the Cowden sign, and asked myself what on earth I thought I was doing. What was I doing *now*? Was it really going to be worth all that money and effort, just to spend an hour with a man I hardly knew?

Someone who I took to be Mrs Harper answered the door, and showed me through to a study at the back of the house, where Michael sat working at a pleasantly cluttered desk. He greeted me very warmly, and seemed genuinely concerned about the difficulties I had been experiencing. His depth and gentleness had an oddly softening effect on me, but it wasn't until we prayed together at the end of the hour, that I realised why it was so necessary to be at that place, at that time, with that person. God wanted to speak to me. After praying quietly for a little while, Michael was silent for a moment. Then he spoke again.

'The Holy Spirit is showing me a picture of a field, Adrian.

The field is your life. It's going to be a bigger and more beautiful meadow one day, but at the moment it's being cleared. There are rocks and brambles and bushes that are being shifted and uprooted to make space for useful things to grow. But I'll tell you something . . .'

'Yes,' I thought, 'please *do* tell me something.'

'Nothing has been wasted – nothing! The soil underneath all these things is rich; richer than it would have been if they hadn't been there. It's going to be a *beautiful* meadow.'

As Michael opened his eyes and looked up, he must have sensed that his words had reached me on a level that had been untouched for years. I was fighting back tears as I said over and over in my mind the words that had meant most to me. 'Nothing has been wasted – *nothing* has been wasted.'

He smiled. 'Dear Adrian.' The words were from God, care of Michael Harper, and they conveyed the love of a father.

I left, and as I walked through the darkness towards the railway station, all the tears I had been holding back were released. God had spoken to me. He cared about me. He was *nice*. How did I know it had really been God speaking? I can't say, but believe me – I knew.

As a matter of history, Bridget reckoned it was a pretty good twenty pounds worth too.

That day marked the beginning of a new kind of hope, and was the first in a series of events and encounters that led me, slowly but surely, into a quite different understanding of what a relationship with God might mean. Some were quite dramatic, while others, apparently, were too trivial to be worth noticing. There was my bike, for instance.

I hadn't had a bicycle for years, not one of my own. As a kid I'd had several, including the shiny blue one on which I had set out to find and captivate Hayley Mills back in the sixties. Since my teens, though, I had hardly ridden one at all, apart from an old boneshaker belonging to John Hall, which, I seem to remember,

I lost, somewhere in Bromley. Perhaps I thought they were one of the less dignified modes of transport, I don't really know.

Now, in 1985, at the age of thirty-six, my mother was quite convinced that what I really needed was a bike. A nice big bicycle would offer more relaxation and therapy than a hundred books, or a thousand conversations, in her view. I knew better of course. Every time we spoke on the telephone, and she said for the umpteenth time, 'Have you got a bike yet?', I would smile indulgently to myself and make vague promises that I *would* get one eventually.

Then, one day as I was glancing through the local advertising journal, I noticed an ad in the 'For Sale' section.

Gent's blue bicycle for sale.
Large frame. Very good condition.
Used only six times. £50.

I think it was the 'blue' that did it. A shiny blue bike of my very own. The years fell away, and I was an excited teenager again. I'd almost forgotten what innocent excitement felt like. I rang the number at the bottom of the advert, walked round to the bank to draw the money out, and within an hour I was the proud possessor of a large Raleigh bicycle; not, admittedly, with seventy-five derailleur gears, or however many they have nowadays, but nevertheless a 'good bike'. How nostalgic the words 'Sturmey Archer' seemed as I read them on the gear-lever housing attached to the handlebars. How strange to be back in the world of tyre-levers, cotter pins, saddle bags, chain guards, brake-blocks and, of course, puncture repair outfits. How satisfying to recapture the feeling of relish when negotiating the narrow gap betwen the kerb and the lines of cars doing the rush-hour crawl, or waiting for the lights to change. But most of all I just liked riding around like a kid or enjoying the whiz and swoosh that usually rewarded a bit of grinding uphill work. I had always hated the A-to-Bness of life. Now, I could go where I liked. I could start at A, head for

M, and stop off for a while at F if it took my fancy. If I changed my mind at F, then I might forget M and pay a little visit to Q, which, as we all know, is only just down the road from R. It was lovely, and I loved it. I felt about as sophisticated as Pooh Bear on my bike, but I didn't really mind. In the course of just riding easily to and fro, I made real contact with the child inside myself, and in the process learned a simple but profound truth about contact with God. I discovered that prayer didn't have to start at A and end at B either. I learned or started to learn, that it's quite legitimate, and – dare I say – enjoyable, to meander aimlessly around, just enjoying the nearness of God, in the same way that you don't have to arrange special activities in order to enjoy being with a friend or a parent. God sat quite happily on his back door-step, watching me as I pedalled happily around in my prayers, looking up occasionally to smile at him, and feel reassured by the way in which he smiled back. It was a new experience, and a very pleasant one, despite the occasions when I fell off my metaphorical bike and bawled like a kid with a bruised knee.

It's odd how different things affect different people. I talked about my bicycle in a Company programme a few weeks after I got it, and as I left the studio one of the cameramen stopped me to talk about *his* bike. Like me, he had at first felt rather foolishly adolescent just cycling to and fro, purely for the fun of it. He experienced the same nostalgic sensations of youth and innocence, and now, as he described the difficulty of confiding this to anybody without feeling a complete idiot, an expression of real pain contracted his features.

'What happens to us? Why do we lose all that? I was happier then than I am now that I reckon I know what's what.'

I knew exactly what he meant. One of the most moving aspects of parenthood is watching your children as they discover for the first time, things that have become so familiar that you hardly notice them. I had often prayed that the spirit of excited discovery would not die in my children, as it had in me for so long. When the oldest, Matthew, was five, he and I had taken a walk through the January streets one morning, to get to the park. When we came back, I tried to preserve part of that experience in the following lines.

I wish I was my son again,
The first in all the world to know,
The cornflake crunch of frosted grass,
Beside the polar paving stones,
Beneath the drip of liquid light,
From water-colour, winter suns.

Now, I was recapturing my own sense of discovery and excitement, especially in connection with natural things; flowers, skies, textures, the seasons. For some years I had been saddened by the loss of my ability to experience first-hand enjoyment of these things. A walk through a flaming autumn wood, for instance, produced only memories of the feeling I had once known of being right in the centre of a passionate, tragic symphony, full of sadness and hope. All seasons had their own character and poetry, but the spiritual vasectomy I had performed on myself a long time ago, had somehow prevented creative involvement with the world around me. It gave me real joy to discover that sense of wonder once more; to find, for instance, that I could gaze, astonished and enraptured, at a single daffodil bloom for several minutes, just absorbing the beauty of its shape and colour.

Daffodils are not flowers
They are natural neon from the dark earth,
Precious metal grown impatient,
Beaten, shaped and dipped in pools
Of ancient, sunken light.
Folded, packed and parachuted through,
To stand and dumbly trumpet out,
The twice triumphant sun.

It was my growing appreciation of natural things, and in particular perhaps, things connected with the season of autumn, that provided an almost immediate bond with a new member of the Company team, who first appeared on the programme at the turn of the year, and has since become a dear friend and valued adviser.

I know that the idea of the Christian life being a kind of journey, is an old and rather hackneyed one, but sometimes the metaphor is refreshed by encounters with fellow-explorers, who really seem to know where they are going. My new friend, Philip Illot, was one of these. My own journey had always been more of an undignified safari than an organised tour, and until now I had been hopelessly ill-equipped for the expedition. Like many Christians, I had tended to crash through the spiritual undergrowth, stubbornly clothed in my strange denominational and temperamental costume, refusing to discard the tools and weapons that seemed so essential. Now, most of my props had gone, but I was still physically fit. I still had the ability to stand and walk and move about freely. Philip had lost even that.

As a young man of eighteen, newly come into the Christian faith, and working in post-war Germany, Philip had a very strange dream one night. In his dream he was travelling across Germany in a train, when, unexpectedly the locomotive was halted by Russian soldiers who were searching for a particular man. Suddenly, Philip knew with total certainty that he was the one they wanted. Terrified, he hid by the window, hoping to be passed by. It was no use. He was aware of his fellow-passengers looking on helplessly through the windows of the train as soldiers forced him down onto a wooden cross lying on the grass. His hands and feet were nailed to the wood, and the cross was raised to a vertical position. Philip woke up screaming.

As the years passed, and he became an ordained minister in the Church of England, Philip never forgot that dream, assuming that one day in the future, he would be able to understand its meaning. He was a 'hyperactive' priest, always on the move, always busy, his life full of people and activities. There were many good, productive years, and a few very hard and difficult ones, but eventually, Philip, with his wife Margaret, and their two children, came to a parish in Bexhill, a seaside resort on the south coast, where, as usual, Philip threw himself into the life of the church, quickly earning the liking and respect of people throughout the town.

For some time Philip had been troubled by intermittent illness. At times it was so bad that he ended up in a Sunday service, lying across the altar, wondering if he was going to die there and then, and reflecting in the midst of his suffering that it wasn't a bad place to go! The symptoms continued, and became more frequent. Eventually, whilst in hospital, Philip learned that he was suffering from multiple sclerosis. He lost the use of all but his head and arms, and is now confined to a wheelchair.

That sounds like the end of a story, but it was actually the beginning of a completely new adventure in Philip's life. It was autumn when the illness was diagnosed, his favourite season. He sensed that, just as the natural world accepts change without panic or resistance in that season, so he was being called to be obedient to what was happening. To let it be. It was as though God was bringing him to a place that had been prepared from the beginning. He acquired an inner stillness that was the stillness of arrival. He was in the right place. The strange dream of many years ago seemed connected somehow with what was happening. But *why* was it happening? Philip dreamed again.

This time he dreamed that he found a key at the foot of the cross of Jesus. Choosing to pick up the key, he was then faced with a very low door, over which the word 'BEWARE' was written in large letters. Using the key, he unlocked the door and passing through in his wheelchair, discovered a vast crowd of troubled and broken people, waiting for the special kind of ministry that a man broken in body, but not in spirit, could offer. The dream is now a reality. Philip is constantly in demand as a counsellor, a speaker, and a leader of missions. What little strength he has is poured out for others, often in ordinary ministry, but sometimes with strange and amazing effects, one of which, too private to record yet gave me a greater sense of the absolute reality of God than anything I had experienced before.

For me, Philip is the smile on God's face. His joy, in the midst of what must be terrible suffering at times, is absolutely genuine, perhaps because of a different kind of intimacy with God, that can only be experienced on the other side of pain. He tells me that 'the darker side of God is brighter than the light side', a knowledge gained through long sleepless nights, when God feels as close to his heart as the darkness is to his face. For some reason I have been able to tell things to Philip that I could tell to no one else, knowing that they (and I) are safe with him. Most of all, perhaps, I love his sudden laughter. My relationships with people who lack a sense of the absurd, are necessarily limited; but there is no such limitation with Philip. Laughter erupts out of him at times, and is invariably infectious. The combination of strength, tenderness and humour is irresistible.

I asked Philip once during a Company programme, a rather idiotic question. It was the kind of question that a lot of people would like to ask, but don't, for fear of giving offence. I knew he wouldn't mind.

'Supposing,' I said, 'you could choose to have the spiritual insights and growth that you've gained since you became ill – or – you could have your health back, and walk and move normally. Which would you choose?'

True man, and true Christian, Philip smiled as though he had asked himself the same question many times, and replied firmly, 'I would, without question, choose both!'

Another whole book could, and probably will, be written about Philip's life, but the important thing for Bridget and me is our contact, not just with Philip, but also with Margaret, who has also suffered, of course. She is pure gold. We have much in common with them, and at a time when we needed people who would really understand, God gave them to us for real, no-nonsense ministry, and for a very special kind of friendship. My visit to Michael Harper, my new bike, a new appreciation of natural things, and the ministry and friendship of Philip Illot; all of these things played their part in turning me gently towards the God that is, rather than the rather unpleasant image of the deity that I had strived with for so long. I had space to explore this new direction, as I took early retirement from my employment with Social Services, and I was not being confused or distracted by regular attendance of any one church. Each day I did little more than pray and write, and hope that the relative calm I had found would last. I really was beginning to feel that peace might be possible. I felt it even more after a surprise phone call from Jo Williams one day.

'Do you realise,' she said, 'that it's a year since you and Prabhu prayed for me and Don on that programme?'

I remembered my faithless prayer, and the feeling of hopelessness that had followed it.

'Yes, Jo. Of course I remember it. Why?'

'Well, do you realise what's happened since then?'

Jo went on to describe, over the phone and later when we met in Maidstone, how that prayer had been answered. Don, close to death a year ago, had been off the drink since that time. They say, 'Once an alcoholic, always an alcoholic', but for Don to stay away from alcohol for a year was a miracle in itself. Later, Bridget and I and the three children stayed in Southampton with Jo, and had the opportunity to meet Don for the first time. We found him to be a very charming and intelligent man, with a particular talent for getting on with our children, who thought Uncle Don was 'terrific!' That is high praise, believe me! It was a heartwarming weekend for everybody.

Then there was Jo, herself. Since the night on which we had

said that prayer, something had happened to change her life. Jo decided to visit her auntie in Wales, the one she had stayed with as a very little girl all those years ago, after the big row between her mum and dad. She'd never thought of visiting her before, but now, for some reason, she and Don decided to make the long trip to Wales so that Jo could meet her mother's sister for the first time in over forty years. While they were there, Don asked a very important question.

'Was Jo difficult and horrible when she was a little girl?'

Jo's heart must have missed a beat as she waited for Auntie Vi's reply.

'No!' said the old lady without hesitation. 'No, she was a very caring little girl. When her baby cousin was ill with rheumatic fever, I remember Jo laying a nappy out on the floor, and saying that maybe if the baby stood in the middle of it, she'd get better. She was like that. Very quiet, but a really nice little girl.'

She turned to Jo. 'Don't you let people put you down, you hear? It was your mum's fault, what happened, not yours.'

In all important ways, Jo is very uncomplicated. This information from the past changed everything. All her life she had blamed herself for anything that went wrong. It was only right. What else could a horrible little girl expect? Now, suddenly she had discovered that all her guilt had been based on a lie. She hadn't been a horrible little girl. It hadn't been her fault. She was a lovely little girl – a very caring child.

Auntie Vi had said so, and she should know. In a peculiarly real way, it was like being born again.

At the end of this year, Jo's attitude to God had changed radically. As far as she was concerned, the trip to Wales had been 'set up' by God, who had been trying for a long time to show Jo how much he loved and cared about her.

'Now,' she said to me late one night over coffee in the Harriet-sham flat, 'it wouldn't matter to me deep down if nobody loved me, because I *know* that God does, and that's that!'

My faithless prayer had been answered, and so had that 'once for all' cry that Bridget and I had sent up to God in the summer of 1984. Trenches had been dug through our lives; it only remained to wait, and see the water flow.

Chapter 13

Company has now completed its fourth year. Only Ann-Marie, Bridget and myself remain from the original team. George is no longer a contributor, but is very much alive and kicking at his flat in Vincent Square. Hugo is still with us, still telling stories, entertaining and educating. Jo Williams makes the trip from Southampton to Maidstone every month or so, and Peter Ball joined us quite recently to take part in a week's broadcasting. Peter Timms is a central figure for viewers nowadays, while Roy Millard has made it a real family affair by marrying James Blomfield's sister, Jane. There are new faces, including Ruth Soetendorp. Ruth and her rabbi husband, David, have become good friends of ours, especially as I no longer feel a neurotic need to switch on my evangelising machine every time I meet someone from a different faith. That man in the wheelchair still appears from time to time, and every now and then Bridget and I spend a very enjoyable half-day with Philip and Margaret at their house in Bexhill. Frances Tulloch, the major architect of Company, continues to produce the programme with the assistance of her hardworking secretary, Wynn Steer, who is beloved by all of us for her patience and good-humour. Angus Wright has now left TVS, and, at the time of writing, no one has been appointed to take his place.

Bridget and I calculate that between us, we have sat at the table in the Company kitchen on at least seven hundred separate occasions. So much has happened to us through the four years of the programme's life, and a great deal of it has been mentioned during those midnight chats. It has been a rich and productive experience – one we would not have missed for the world.

Company's fourth birthday sees me at a turning point, a point where I haven't the foggiest idea what's going to happen next. I don't know where I'm going, or how I'm going to get there; I don't know what I'm going to do or how I'm going to do it; but I feel an odd mixture of uneasiness and anticipation.

When I told my eldest son, Matthew, that I was about to write the final chapter of this book, he paused for a moment in his activity of transferring great wodges of dried mud from the bottom of his football boots to the kitchen floor, and nodded with all the wisdom of the modern twelve-year-old.

'Oh yes,' he said, 'that's the bit where you have to say everything's all right now, and you and God get on very well and all that.' Matthew has read his share of Christian paperbacks!

He was right of course. Many, if not most, of the huge number of testimonial books that exist nowadays, end with a tidying-up chapter in which God, man and the universe are slotted firmly into their proper places, and the reader is invited to submit himself to a simple process that will ensure spiritual growth or transformation.

I would *love* to be able to write a chapter like that. If only it was possible to pass on the information that Jesus lives at Number Ten, Gorringe Road, Luton: ring three times and say that Adrian sent you. I know that many people would like it to be that easy, and I know that some folk think it is that easy. I even know a few people for whom it really does seem to have been that easy, but they are very few. Nothing in my recent experience has made me any happier with simplistic formulas for spiritual living than I have ever been, nor, I'm afraid, am I much more patient with those who peddle such recipes.

Not very long ago, for instance, a Company viewer stopped me in the street and asked me why 'that man in the wheelchair doesn't say the prayer of faith and get up on his feet'. I was almost dumbstruck. Philip Illot believes in, and has had experience of miraculous healing, but God is using his physical situation in a particular way, just as St Paul's physical suffering was clearly part of his ministry. I'm glad that Jesus didn't say the prayer of faith, and come down from the cross to live out his life quietly in some Jewish suburb. Neither Philip Illot, nor St Paul, nor Jesus, for that matter, actually wanted to suffer physically; only loonies want that; but more important to them was discovering what God wanted of them and obeying him despite the suffering that obedience would bring. I told Philip what this lady had said one day, and asked him what he thought about it. He answered without any hesitation.

'If you should happen to see that lady again, I'd like you to tell her, with my best wishes, that I say the "prayer of faith" every single day!'

Of course we should pray for healing, anoint with oil and lay hands on the sick, but they won't always get better. They *don't* always get better. Everyone knows that they don't always get better, and it requires a peculiar form of corporate dishonesty to claim that they do. God will do what he will do, and sometimes we can only live in the mystery of that fact, waiting for it all to make sense when the right time has come.

The disciples had this problem of course; wanting to develop systems and rules to make life safer and easier to handle. Every now and then they really thought they'd got Jesus pinned down.

'She could have sold the ointment and given the money to the poor!'

He was always going on about the poor. Surely they'd got it right this time. Sorry lads – wrong again!

'Shall we call down fire from heaven on this village, Lord?'

Jesus told them not to be silly.

'I shall never let you be killed, Lord!'

Peter really got an earful for that.

'Tell Mary to help me, master, she's no use to anyone sitting there!'

Poor, likeable old Martha was wrong as well.

God cannot be reduced to a set of simple propositions, however simple his dealings with any individual person might be. This was, in hindsight, a large part of my problem in the sixties. When the church tried to compete with other 'instant cures', or means of establishing identity, it was, and still is, offering a version of Christianity that is, in one sense, too simplistic, and in another sense too difficult. The hippie movement tried to say that love is free, that it can be given away with a flower. This was no more true than that Jesus saves without cost or complication. I don't mean that he doesn't want to – far from it! But an honest and genuinely open reading of the four books that record what Jesus said, shows me that there are two essential parts to the message he wanted to put over.

First, I read that God is passionately committed to a world that he is absolutely crazy about, and there is no doubt that he would go, and has already gone, to the most extraordinary lengths to open up the channels between him and us, channels which are *so* blocked nowadays that only a very few people are genuinely and specifically hearing God talking to them. A lot are pretending or imagining (I've done so often), but very few really hearing.

The other part of what Jesus says is about counting the cost, keeping one's hand to the plough, loving your enemy, using talents properly, and being able to lose or give away all that you value most, if that's what is required of you. In other words – turning your own world upside down! I believe that these things need to be preached as part of the Christian message, instead of being the small print that you notice with dismay after committing yourself to receiving the free gift. I can't believe that Jesus said them all for fun. He must have meant them.

The problem for me, and for many others, was how to reconcile these two areas in my life from day to day. I was glad that God loved me – although I, in company with countless other Christians, probably never quite believed that he did – but I was quite unable to comply with, or even comprehend, the awesome demands that were being made on me. This is made even more difficult by the way in which God is all too often presented in evangelical and charismatic circles. He tends to come over as either a sentimental softy with such a pathological need for human affection that, he doesn't really care what we get up to, or as a harsh, vindictive, austerely pure being, more concerned with narrow moral issues than people. I have seen so much fear and guilt transferred from speaker to listeners, disguised as 'conviction' and 'divine chastisement'. I recall one man who put an empty chair in the centre of the church, and invited us all to imagine that Jesus was sitting in it.

'Wouldn't you feel bad!' he said, 'wouldn't you want to hide your face and creep away, knowing the sin that's in you – the things that would make it impossible to meet his eyes!'

All I could think of as I stared at the empty chair, was how marvellous it would be to fling myself at him, like Peter dashing through the shallows to have an exciting breakfast with the risen Jesus. He didn't think of his own sin first, and remember, the denial business still hadn't been sorted out yet – he just wanted to get to Jesus because he loved him. Not want to see Jesus? I thought there must be something wrong with me!

I have begun to understand the way in which God is both loving and meticulously demanding by exploring an image used consistently by Jesus. He knew God as father. Now, as anyone who has read this book so far will know, that image presents problems for me, but there are good fathers around who I have been able to 'see in action', as it were, and I have been involved, directly or indirectly, with many children in care who needed to be fostered or adopted by families other than their own. Saint Paul says that Christians are the adopted children of God. God is their new father; so what does a really good father look like?

Well, first of all, joining a new family, adoption into a different kind of environment with different rules and different expectations, needs careful thought and preparation by all concerned. It isn't like joining a club; more a matter of deciding where to put down your deepest roots. The candidate for adoption will need to visit the home in which he has been offered a place so that he can see the head of the household in action, without the pressure of immediate decision or commitment. He will see this prospective father of his being very firm, punishing his children at times. He will see him being very loving and forgiving as well. He might well see him rolling on the floor with the kids, laughing and joking. He will see how he weeps when one of the family is hurt or lost, how everyone is encouraged to love and look after everyone else, and how all have direct access to their father, but show different degrees of trust and confidence depending on what kind of people they are and what their backgrounds have been. He will be intrigued by how different the children of the family are; some quietly, deeply affectionate, others loud and boisterous in the way they show love to their father, a few can manage only a small smile because they hurt too much to do anything else for a while. Some may just sit in the furthest corner of an empty room, paralysed with fear of rejection, but nursing the tiniest of tiny hopes that the smile they glimpsed on the face of the man in charge was meant for them as well as everyone else. They are all in the house. They all belong. The most fearful will be loved into happiness in the end.

If our candidate likes the place, and is happy to take the rough with the smooth, do what he's told when necessary, and accept his adoptive father's control and guidance as a sign of his care, then he'll probably move in. He doesn't have to be perfect, or even good, to qualify, and even after he's arrived, space will be allocated, allowances will be made, time will be spent and given. He'll be left in no doubt about what the house rules are, but everyone will be aware that it takes time to learn and adapt. Adopted children take ages to settle in sometimes. He'll be all right in the end. He might leave, but the offer of a home is forever;

he will always be able to come back if he wants to; his new father will never stop loving him, however annoying he may be. Eventually, the spirit of the place will get right inside him; he will mature and learn that he really is wanted. The rules will suddenly seem much easier to keep, in fact they won't seem like rules at all. He will probably be given one or two responsible tasks to perform on behalf of his father. In the end, he will be so well tuned in to his dad's voice, that a single word will bring him flying to his father's side, saying excitedly, 'Yes! What do you want me to do?'

The family image is reinforced for me by what I see in those who really have learned to trust the head of the family. They don't become narrower and more condemnatory, they become broader and more loving. They show little interest in gifts, but are profoundly fascinated by the giver. Their spirituality does not seem loony, it feels real; it fits, on some crucial but undefinable level, with everything else that is real. They may be travelling on the hard road that Jesus said was the only road for his followers, but something makes them smile even when their feet hurt. They have usually paid dearly for their joy, and the price seems to be, quite simply, everything. They are convinced that they are the worst of sinners, but equally convinced that they are the most forgiven of men. As far as they are able, they organise their priorities so that God is at the top of the list, knowing that an honest reading of the gospels makes it quite clear that all other things begin from that starting point. And yet, as I've said in connection with Peter Ball, the effect is not to make someone like me despair, and study my sins in a misery of self-loathing, but to feel that the source of all this love and warmth must be able to do something, even with me. I catch sight of God's optimism and feel cheered and encouraged. I remember visiting Peter once with my friend James, whose Christian life has followed an agonised path, not unlike my own. The three of us talked for an hour or so, then, as James and I drove away towards Hailsham, he said with a sort of wistful puzzlement, 'He knows a different God to the one I do. His God's nice!'

He didn't mean soft, he meant 'nice'. Warm and caring and consistent and reliable and firm and forgiving and competent – like a father. That same sense of rich, compassionate, intelligent care can be found in the works of Paul Tournier, a Christian writer who, again and again, has preserved my spiritual sanity. His book, *The Adventure of Living*, is an invigorating invitation to get off the Circle Line of religion, and explore the mystery of *really* living as a follower of Jesus in the *real* world. Because we do live in a huge and thrilling mystery. Whatever I may say here, the things that happen to me are not the things that will happen to the next man, and I have no right to try to crush him into the little box of my own experience. It is so easy to be wrong, so easy to decide that because God did 'X' on Tuesday, he will do 'X' on Wednesday; so easy to preach our own salvation as the way things should be, instead of acknowledging the excitingly complex and creative nature of God's dealings with men. I know a lot of Christians, they're all different – gloriously different. I used to think, for some strange reason, that our ultimate goal was to be exactly alike, but now I don't. I love the differences, and so, I believe, does God. Despite the fundamental similarities in faith, who could be more Paulish than St Paul, more Peterish than St Peter, more Jesus-like than Jesus? I don't want to be like anyone else, nor do I want to force anyone into being like me – God knows I don't want that! I want a hair-raising adventure of cosmic proportions with this God whose aim is to make me the best possible 'Adrian' that I could be. In the process I might even become a useful member of the family, and be able to lend a hand with the newcomers. I'd like that.

Meanwhile my own adventure doesn't look much like an adventure from the outside. Each day, after sharing the arduous task of producing three reasonably dressed and equipped children out of the morning chaos, I settle down to do three things.

First, I read a chapter of the New Testament. I read it in the Jerusalem Bible because I like the print and the headings and the lay-out. I have never read the Bible in a disciplined way before. When I have tried to do so, I've usually taken a couple of verses only, and squeezed them pessimistically in my mind, hoping to extract a drop or two of meaning or significance. Now, I read in order to grasp the broad intention of a chapter, happy to stop and consider a point if it catches my interest. I am reading the gospels at present because I am suddenly fascinated to know what Jesus really said. With my mind still cluttered with prejudices and preconceived notions, this isn't easy, but even I can see that the full gospel of Jesus Christ wouldn't go down too well in most churches that I know. I can also see, though, that he himself would bring healing and tenderness to individuals in those same churches who carry inside themselves a deep-rooted conviction that they are too bad or too insignificant to enter what Jesus calls the Kingdom of God.

Interestingly, as I discover a new freedom to be disciplined in Bible-reading, a close friend has discovered a different kind of liberty through his conscious and careful decision to postpone, for a few months only, the daily study of scripture that has been his habit for many years. I relish the contrast between the ways in which our individual needs are being fulfilled.

Secondly, I pray. At last I have found a way of prayer that is not excruciatingly boring or meaningless, or hopelessly fragmented. On the desk in front of me as I write, lies a pile of about thirty long brown envelopes. On the outside of each is written one or more names. Inside each sealed envelope is a written prayer for the people concerned. Each day I pick up each envelope, hold it up to God, and ask him to do whatever is needed for them. If I am in a grumpy, or sulky mood, I flick through them quite quickly, saying, 'Bless him, and him, and her, and them ...' If I am feeling more peaceful, I try to be creative in my prayers. I might, for instance, imagine Jesus administering communion to each person, and try to see what happens in the encounter. I might, on another occasion, hold the hands of each one in my mind, and say a prayer for both of us. Sometimes I picture Jesus standing by an open door, greeting people individually, and inviting them in. They all respond to him differently. Sometimes I see strange things occurring in these 'mind-pictures'. Whether they are purely imagination or something else, I have no idea. I begin to feel, nowadays, a real sense of responsibility towards this little group of people, and I enjoy meeting them and God every clay. I usually say a prayer of confession before doing anything else, and perhaps spend a few minutes after this trying to float in the warm sea of God's love for me. I try to do these things however I feel. In the old days I would have abandoned the attempt to make contact with God if I had been unpleasant since getting up, or if things seemed generally bleak, or if Bridget and I had gone through one of our monumental arguments over some trivial issue. I'm now much more aware of the difference between temperamental and spiritual failure, and far more conscious of the fact that God is as anxious – more anxious probably – to meet me when I've been a berk, as when I fancy I'm one of his little sunbeams!

Thirdly, I write – or try to. We have frequent visitors, and as others who work at home will know, this is a sweet-and-sour dish. I love seeing people – first, because I simply like people, and secondly, because they are a welcome addition to the long list of 'things that prevent you from getting started on filling up the horrific blank sheet of paper'. The list includes such essential activities as going to the lavatory, making coffee, answering the phone, scratching your ear, combing your hair, anything to avoid the moment when the pen first touches the paper.

As I've said, it doesn't look much of an adventure on the face of it, but I feel a growing excitement about the prospect of living in an upside-down world, presided over by a passionate, humorous God, who wants people to be as free and involved and creative and committed and tough as Jesus was. God forgive us for the way in which we have presented Jesus as a 'wet-willie' over the years; as an 'A-stream/doesn't play sports' type, who can't wait to leave this nasty world and get back to the sanitised environs of heaven. As I read the gospels now, I find a Jesus who was passionately involved, physically, mentally, and emotionally with people and with the natural world. Healing and helping and feeding and getting angry and weeping and eating and drinking and sweating and dying. His message to the world was uncompromising and impossibly demanding, but his way with hurt and sinful individuals was tailor-made and tender, unless the sin happened to be hypocrisy in church leaders, in which case he could be devastatingly angry. As far as I can tell, the invitation to continue his adventure and mission in this world is open to everybody, but it seems clear that nothing very startling happens in anybody's life until they start to do what Jesus laid down as a very clear condition of growth. Namely, to make the number one priority in your life, 'Seeking the Kingdom of God'. That's why I do what I do each day. I want to be in on the adventure. I don't want to huddle with other Christians twice a week for the rest of my life, indulging in religion as a hobby. I want God to take this grumpy, jealous, critical personality of mine, transfigure it somehow, and send me out to get my hands dirty in the real world, on his behalf. It's 'mission impossible' at the moment, but as Jesus himself said, 'What is impossible for men, is not impossible for God.'

My heart goes out to all those for whom 'being a Christian' has been like a marathon walk through ankle-deep mud. Some drop out, some keep going, all wonder what on earth it's all about. Why so many peaks and troughs? Why so little peace? Why do some Christians seem to have 'got it', whatever *it* is?

I've got no smart answers. I'm still trudging along myself most of the time, but I'm excited by three things. One is the person of Jesus, one is the fact that God likes me and wants me in his family, and the other is his assurance that nothing is wasted. To all my fellow-stragglers and Christian delinquents I say, with tears in my eyes as I write, God bless you in whatever way you need.

Be wary about those once-for-all solutions, but hang on – he'll rescue you.

> *That day – it is Yahweh who speaks – I will finally gather in the lame, and bring together those that have been led astray and those that have suffered at my hand. Out of the lame I will make a remnant, and out of the weary a mighty nation. Then will Yahweh reign over them on the mountains of Zion from now and for ever.*
>
> Micah 4:6 – 7

Book 2:

Why I Follow Jesus

My job involves meeting and listening to lots of people. Sometimes I feel overwhelmed by the sheer volume of folk who battle continually with deep hurts and chronic difficulties. When the dark cloud of pain seemed to be blocking out more light than ever, I wrote this poem. If it had come from another age and a different place and had been better written, I suppose it might have been called a psalm.

Winter waking, stretched across the moonstone sky,
Caring less than nothing for the destiny of man,
You see the crows, like ragged scraps of dustbin bag
Come floating down the wind to scavenge what they
*   can,*
And nothing need be spoken.
Deep in winter sleep is where you hear the saddest
*   cries,*
The wheeling dealing seagull souls,
Of men and women taught to stay a step ahead,
Who reached the edge,
But found that when they fell,
They had not learned to fly.
I tell you that it drives you wild,
It drives you out to march and march beside the heart-
*   less sea,*
To weep and rage and beg the only one who really
*   knows,*
To tell you, tell you, tell you, tell you why,
So many hearts are broken.

This book is dedicated to that special group of people so passionately loved by God the Father – the brokenhearted.

1
Why I Follow Jesus

Why do I follow Jesus?

It may be foolish to ask this question because, in these pages, I'm planning to answer it truthfully and, although the truth can certainly set us free, it can also cause an awful lot of trouble. Mind you, if I wanted I could avoid trouble by supplying an answer that would be entirely satisfactory to folk who prefer to cement over those cracks that create crazy-paving pathways through the lives of so many of us ordinary believers. Here it is: Christ died and rose again for us, and that act of redemption will save us from an eternity of separation from God, if we sincerely repent of our sins, become baptized and believe in him.

There we are. End of book. That is the technical truth of the gospel, a truth I accepted and responded to more than 30 years ago, and I believe it – most of the time. What better motivation is there? None, of course, and yet, that bald statement does not in itself embody the heart of my motivation for following Jesus.

You would think, wouldn't you, that after all these years I might have successfully identified the springs of my faith? It has been quite a long time, you know. I laboriously worked out on a calculator that I have probably attended something like 1,620 church services, plus an equal number of weekday meetings. This means that I have been exposed to the Bible, the gospel and fellow Christians on 3,250 separate occasions – at least! And that's not counting accidental ones on television. Frightening, isn't it? Surely

I must have sorted it all out by now? I'm afraid not. It takes so long to learn that you know nothing – or at best, very little.

Why do I continue to follow Jesus? I have burrowed down into the confusion of my feeling and thinking to produce quite a lot of answers for you, and the first one I'm going to mention is, for me anyway, one of the most important.

2

I Follow Jesus Because ...

I Want to Be with My Friends for Ever

Now, this is all very well, but it begs the obvious question, doesn't it? Who *are* my friends? Well, of course, when my thoughts turn in this direction I immediately include my wife, Bridget, and the family, and those close friends who love me and whom I love. Naturally I want to be with all those people who are so important in my life, but there's quite a lot of sorting out to be done in addition to that.

You can see how important this whole area is to Jesus when you read the later chapters in the Gospel of John. Jesus sounds rather like a mother trying to drum into her family that someone must take responsibility for feeding the canary while she's away, or it will die, because she's normally the only one who does it regularly and properly. Over and over and over again he implores the disciples to love one another. We are his friends if we obey his commands, and his command is that we love one another. And that love is to extend, he tells us, not just to those who are close to us and contained within our little corner of his kingdom, but to all Christians, everywhere.

His example is before us – Almighty God, who willingly sent Jesus to be the sorter-out of untied shoelaces. As it happens, Bridget and I know a bit about untied shoelaces. The church often reminds us of the country walks we used to do with children in care when we were residential social workers.

In the front during those memorable walks would be our colleague, Mike, an athlete with huge thighs, no imagination and proper walking equipment, accompanied by his terribly keen support group, all looking like an advert for healthy breakfast cereal.

Next, in the centre, would come me, supervising bright but troubled under-achievers wearing spectacles. We would be whimsically speculating on the poetic, philosophical and artistic significance of hiking.

At the back you would find Bridget, helping the fat ones and the slow ones and the ones whose shoes never stayed done up and the ones with bad feet who didn't believe they were ever going to make it, and the ones who only came because they wanted to get out of doing something else and wished now that they'd put up with whatever it was they'd wanted to avoid.

If you like, the triumphalists were at the front, the liberals in the middle and the servers at the back. I have to be honest and say that my vote goes to the servers every time. In fact, as you know, each group gets annoyed with each of the other groups at one time or another. The triumphalists at the front get annoyed with the group at the back for slowing them down when they want to move on at an even greater pace to even greater heights, and they get annoyed with the group in the middle because they're so unfocused, *abstract* and irrelevant. The servers at the back get annoyed with the triumphalists because they won't *wait*, and seem to want to be a little group all on their own, and they're annoyed with the group in the middle because they seem so *vague* and useless, and the group in the middle get annoyed with anything or anyone that threatens to move them to a position as vulgarly committed as the *front* or the *back*. If only we could swap around from time to time, we might discover some amazing things – not least that the final group will have achieved more than anyone else if they finish the journey, and that will indeed be a mighty triumph!

Just as those children used to squabble and fight, many of us Christians would have to admit, if we are honest, that our enemies are often drawn from among our friends, from the church itself. In certain parts of the world that I have visited, some religious groups are nearer to being enemies than friends. Where that is so, we would do well to remember that Jesus was just as insistent about loving our enemies as loving our friends.

I'm following Jesus because I want to be with my friends, and if I want to be with them in heaven, I've got to be with them now. I've got to own their sins and faults, because even if I don't like them they are friends of a friend, and that friend is Jesus, and he's the friend I most want to be with for ever. This church of ours is his body. Do I love it? How long will it take me finally to pick up my cross and take it to the place of death, to die to my rights and my resentments and my personal agendas, so that, if necessary, I can step out of the group that attracts me, or the mood that I'm in, or the character trait that tries to imprison me, and be what I need to be in the place where I'm most needed?

But it's not only a love for the body of Christ on earth that motivates me to follow. It's Jesus himself. By a miracle of kindness from God himself, I'm allowed to call him my friend. I really do want to be with him for ever.

3

I Follow Jesus Because ...

I Don't Know Where Else to Go And, in Any Case, I'd Find It Very Hard to Stop

Friends of mine who mistakenly fancy themselves as satirists enjoy offering their opinion that the main reasons for my continuing faith are practical and commercial. They suggest that, for someone who makes his living from writing and speaking about the Christian faith, it would be financial suicide publicly to announce my conversion to atheism or the worship of two-toed frogs. Warming to their theme, these alleged f.o.m. further suggest that any virtue I might display is based solely on the awareness that having an affair or committing some other major and visible sin would have a similarly disastrous effect on my career. (This latter theory is, of course, complete nonsense. We've all seen how it's done. Suppose you're a Christian writer who has an affair, for instance. Okay, all you have to do is repent after a decent pause and then write a whole succession of helpful and lucrative books entitled *Picking up the Pieces*, *New Buildings from Old Bricks*, and *God Will Forgive You*. A nice little earner, in fact.)

This is all utter rubbish, of course, although I do sometimes wonder if God, in his great wisdom and knowing me so well, has deliberately manoeuvred me into a position where several thousand people can keep an eye on what I'm up to. Who knows?

No, those silly negative reasons for staying with Jesus are as nothing compared with two quite different strands of motivation which, while still apparently negative in nature, are also highly significant.

The first is that I wouldn't know where else to go. Simon Peter, the fishy follower of Jesus, expressed it perfectly in the sixth chapter of John's Gospel. Everyone had been complaining about Jesus' extraordinary claim that he was bread come down from heaven, and that whoever fed on him would live for ever. As many of his disciples turned away and made it mutteringly, grumblingly clear that they no longer wanted to follow him, Jesus turned to his original 12 followers and said, rather plaintively I've always imagined, 'You don't want to leave too, do you?'

'Lord,' said old Simon Peter, 'to whom shall we go? You have the words of eternal life. We believe and know that you are the Holy One of God.'

And it's true, isn't it? We sense that Jesus holds the only available keys to real-life 'happy ever after'. We depend on him knowing the answers to those questions that loom like monsters from the darkness of our inner lives almost from the first moment we discover that death is inevitable. We feel in our bones that he alone can make sure that the narrative of life will have a beginning, a middle *and* a satisfactory end. He's the explanation and solution to the puzzle of why men and women, in their enjoyment and appreciation of theatre and fiction and story, experience a dimension of profound yearning for the clear and rational completeness that characterizes these ancient human pursuits. All of these truths, though dimly perceived much of the time perhaps, shine like beacons to the lost child inside us, making it very difficult, if not impossible, to do anything but hang around waiting to see where he will lead us next. Every road except his, however dangerously long, and however alluring, is a cul-de-sac.

The second negative reason for following Jesus is that I'm not at all sure I could stop if I wanted to. There are quite a few indications in the Bible (have a look at the beginning of the twelfth chapter of Romans) that faith is a gift placed into me, as it were, by God. It becomes a part of what I am, and is only very rarely visible as a discrete entity, rather as the end of my own nose is something I catch sight of only very occasionally. Certainly, the Bible says that some people will abandon their faith, but probably for the same reason that you would end up wanting to abandon your nose if you spent your entire life squinting at it instead of using it naturally and unconsciously in conjunction with the agents of your other senses.

Even on those occasions when I really think I'm seriously on the edge of unbelief or disillusionment, something happens to turn the whole thing upside down. Have you known those moments when, just as you're witnessing some unusually crass piece of behaviour on the part of what's called the Christian church, and you're about to turn away from the whole thing in disgust, you become aware that Jesus himself is watching the same thing over your shoulder and shaking his head as despairingly as you are? It's not easy to trudge dolefully away from an entire faith system when its founder trudges dolefully away beside you.

I heard somewhere of an occasion in one of the Second World War death camps when the suffering Jewish inmates put God on trial for failing them so badly. Eventually a verdict was about to be passed stating that he had not only failed, he did not exist at all. Proceedings had to be abruptly halted at this juncture, however, because it was time for synagogue. Making a decision to stop following Jesus is very much like that. I might decide that I do not possess nasal apparatus, but my decision will not affect the existence of my nose in the slightest.

Perhaps belief and unbelief are two sides of the same coin.

You can turn the coin over, but you can't make the side you're not looking at go away. There have been times in my life when I have been extremely grateful for that fact.

Where would I go? How would I stop? I have no answers to those questions.

I Follow Jesus Because ...

He's So Good at Judo

What?'
That was the initial reaction of a friend when I told him
the title of this section. 'I may not be the greatest Bible scholar in
the world,' he continued, in heavily ironic tones, 'but I feel fairly
confident in saying that there's no record in the Gospels of Jesus
heaving his enemies over his shoulder, even when the soldiers
came for him in the garden. Or have I crassly misinterpreted some
vital little passage involving an original Greek word that has a
very strong sense of kung fu?'

Well, of course that isn't what I mean. My dictionary tells me
that the literal translation of the Japanese word *jujitsu* is 'gentle
skill'. One aspect of that gentle skill is the way in which an oppo-
nent's weight, speed and aggression can actually be used against
him by an expert practitioner. And this is exactly what Jesus was
so good at. His gentle skill enabled him to use the weight of other
people's prejudices, or anger, or need, or attitudes, or desires, to
propel them, often to their surprise and bewilderment, into places
where he wanted them to be but they had never expected to find
themselves. Some obvious examples spring to mind.

Confronted with the woman taken in adultery, Jesus declined
to waste time arguing with the Pharisees and lawyers who had
tried to trap him with their question about the woman's punishment under the law. Indeed, his response when it did come was

more or less, 'Yes! Yes, of course she must be stoned, that's the law. Get on with it. Get on and stone her. One of you who's never sinned, step up now and throw the first stone.'

Over his shoulder, figuratively speaking, went the lot of 'em. Not a stone was thrown and the woman went away to sort her life out.

That story appears in the Gospel of John, but there are many other examples of divine *jujitsu* throughout all four of the Gospels. Read about Jesus' reply to the chief priests and elders when they questioned his authority in the twentieth chapter of Luke, and enjoy the way he dealt with a question about paying taxes to Caesar in the twenty-second chapter of Matthew. The same gentle skill was employed in many of his parables. The story of the Good Samaritan in the tenth chapter of Luke, for instance, made direct use of his audience's natural sympathies and sheer enjoyment of story to draw them into providing an answer to their own question, 'Who is my neighbour?' As we know, that answer was most certainly not the one they had anticipated.

Later in the New Testament, we find Paul the apostle taking a leaf out of his master's book. Quizzed about Christianity by curious Athenians in the seventeenth chapter of Acts, and faced with a pagan altar inscribed 'To an unknown god', he doesn't squeal, 'New age! New age!' as some of the modern brethren might. Instead he uses the words on that altar as a platform or starting point for his message about the one true God. Paul was quite good at judo as well.

It saddens me that, in this age, there remain so few practitioners of this art. It saddens me because people are so much more likely to return to God if they are allowed at least to *begin* the journey on a familiar road. Very few folk make a spiritually positive response simply to being told off, and yet, despite having the example of Jesus in front of us, that's what we very often do. There's a real fear in many Christians that creative interaction with non-Christians is a form of cheating. At best this can result in the sort of bloodless evangelism that won't attract and may well repel.

The other day, for example, an acquaintance named Robert rang to ask if I could offer him some advice. He had been asked to write six spiritually based pieces to be broadcast daily for a week from his local radio station. His producer's brief stated that these Thoughts for the Day should be short, bright and entertaining; they should make at least one good point as clearly as possible, and they should avoid the use of religious language that might be inaccessible to unchurched listeners.

'The thing is,' said Robert, 'I've written them, and I think they're more or less all right, but I wondered if I could drive over and read them to you and get your comments or criticisms. You've done a lot of these things, haven't you?'

I agreed to him coming, but not without trepidation. It was true that I had produced many similar pieces over the years, but I also had wide experience of people urging me to be absolutely frank about the things they had written, and then getting tight-lipped, tearful or just plain cross when I took them at their word.

'You are sure, aren't you,' I said, as I was about to put the phone down, 'that you want me to be perfectly honest?'

'Good heavens, yes!' laughed Robert, as though I was making some sort of silly joke. 'That's why I'm coming, for goodness' sake! What would be the point otherwise?'

As I finally put the phone down, I calmed my fears by reflecting on the fact that Robert was an intelligent, sensitive man who had known a lot of pain in his life. Surely his writing would reflect all those things?

As it turned out, some of them did, but there was one piece that seemed to me lacking in judo skills. 'Can we just look at that last one about the lottery?' I said.

'Right!' Robert nodded.

'Now, in your piece you say this is a very materialistic age, and that, instead of thinking about winning lots of money, people should be thinking about their spiritual lives and realizing how much Jesus has done for them. In fact, you're more or less telling them off for doing the lottery, aren't you?'

'Well, yes, I don't agree with it.'

'But don't you think there could be a more positive route to take than simply saying it's a bad thing – dismissing people's dreams so totally and unsympathetically?'

'Well …'

'Why do people play the lottery?'

'To get rich.'

'Well, that's one way of looking at it. The other way is to say that they yearn for something really wonderful to happen in their lives.'

'Yes, but money isn't – '

'Hold on, hold on! We haven't arrived there yet. They want something wonderful to happen in their lives, something that will change everything. Jesus coming into their lives might be something wonderful that would change everything, right?'

'Right, and that's why – '

'So they've got all the right appetites, but perhaps for the wrong things – do you agree?'

'Well, perhaps, but it's the desire for money that's wrong. I've got to say that.'

'Have you considered, Robert, the fact that, more than once, Jesus offered being rich as a reward for following him?'

Robert stirred uneasily in his chair and shook his head. 'No he didn't. He said it was pretty well impossible for a rich man to get into heaven.'

'What did he say we should store up in heaven?'

'Well – treasure, but he didn't mean money, he was talking about – '

'Hold on, hold on! We haven't got there yet. He was appealing to the part of humanity that wants to be rich, wasn't he? He tells us that it's fine to be rich as long as we've understood what the most important currency of all actually is. Right? And when we get to heaven and we're strolling through the divine shopping precincts, what will that currency be? What will be printed on the wad of heavenly banknotes that angelic bank clerks have issued to us from the account we've built up while we were on earth?'

'Love?'

'Exactly! The currency of heaven is love, and if Jesus comes into our lives we suddenly become heirs to a fortune, and we shall spend it in eternity, and that isn't just playing with words. Maybe we should be saying to the people who do the lottery, "This is great! You have all the right spiritual instincts. You want a real, significant change in your lives and you want to be rich. What you haven't understood is that you can have both those things without paying a pound, and at considerably more favourable odds." What do you think, Robert? Does that make sense as a way to approach that one?'

I looked at him hopefully. He looked back at me like a land-lubber cast adrift on a flimsy raft in a bad storm. 'Well – I, er, I think I'd rather leave it as it is, really.'

I was a bit thrown, but then that's judo for you, isn't it?

5

I Follow Jesus Because ...

He's Gentle with People Who Have Been Badly Hurt

Let me tell you now about one of the most important things that has ever happened to me. I hope it will mean something special to you, and that through it you might understand more about the compassionate heart of God and, much less importantly, a little more about me.

This experience happened in the early hours of the morning on British Airways flight BA 2028 as it droned through dark European skies from Baku, the capital of Azerbaijan, on its way to Gatwick Airport in England.

I was already feeling quite emotional. Baku was the place where my eldest son, Matthew, was teaching conversational English at a private language school. Sitting on the plane, I was remembering that incredible moment when, on seeing baby Matthew for the first time, I had whispered to myself that this might be the first toy I had ever been given that stood a real chance of not getting broken. Now, just as he was approaching his twenty-fourth birthday, I had spent a week visiting him and exploring a city of intriguing extremes.

Until recently a part of the Soviet Union, Azerbaijan is a Muslim country, shaped – very appropriately considering its geographical position to the east of Turkey – like an eagle flying from west to east. A great oil-producing nation at the turn of the century, it may become so again when the liquid gold begins to flow once more. In the meantime, the Soviets seem to have sucked the country dry and departed, leaving a people who have perhaps lost the will, the way and the means to achieve a reasonable standard of living. On every road and in every street I saw stalls selling either cheap plastic goods, spare parts for cars which suffer from the appallingly bad roads, or shoe-mending services, essential because of the equally uneven and unrepaired pavements. On several occasions I came across elderly folk sitting resignedly beside old, dusty domestic weighing machines, presumably hoping that odd passers-by might feel a sudden uncontrollable urge to pay for the privilege of knowing their weight. Some roadside stalls, often but by no means invariably presided over by children, were nothing more than cardboard boxes on which stood two or three bottles of fizzy orange drink of uncertain age. The streets were filled with taxis, mainly Russian-produced Ladas, in such profusion that it was difficult to see who the potential customers might be, other than fellow taxi-drivers whose vehicles had broken down. It had all been rather depressing.

On the other hand, some aspects of Azerbaijani culture were enviable. I came across small children walking home together in the dark with no apparent fear of attack, and all the women I spoke to had that same sense of being safe in most of the streets at any time of day or night. There is no unemployment benefit in Azerbaijan, and the old-age pension is only five pounds per month, but elderly people are not neglected, abandoned or benignly disposed of. They have a place in their families until death. I found the Azerbaijani people warmly hospitable and more than willing to share the little that they had.

Matthew's apartment, shared with two other teachers, was on the second floor of what must once have been a very palatial private residence. Baku was full of these reminders of a bygone age, splendidly ornate buldings that have been allowed to decay and crumble to the extent that the filthy stairwells and back yards resembled the set of *Oliver*, or those old photographs you sometimes see of poverty-stricken areas of Victorian London. I gathered that there was quite a problem with rats in Baku.

I stayed with Matthew for just under a week, greatly enjoying his company as always, and taking a particular pleasure in the experience of seeing him function so well in such a different context. Some aspects of my eldest son's childhood, especially the period when I was ill more than a decade ago, were far from easy for him, so it was good to see the present beginning to eclipse the past. It was hard to leave Matthew when my stay ended, but not at all hard to leave Baku Airport, which must be one of the most depressing places on earth, highly reminiscent as it was of a very low-budget set from the old television series *The Avengers*.

As I sat on the plane, bracing myself for a journey that would last for more than five hours, I thought about the people of Azerbaijan and about Matthew, about the rest of my family, with whom I would soon be reunited, and about the various challenges that awaited me at home. I found myself gradually slipping into an all too familiar mood of self-doubt and despair. There are times, and this point of transition was one of them, when faith and hope mean nothing, and all my reference points and benchmarks seem to become insubstantial and float away beyond my grasp. Some of you will know what I mean when I say that I almost shuddered with the complexity and puzzlement of simply being alive, and with a deep dread of something in the recesses of my mind that I could not (or would not) name for fear of acknowledging its existence.

Oddly enough, these alarming moments have quite often been the prelude to learning something important from God, perhaps because it's easier to fill an empty vessel than a full one – I don't really know. On this occasion, though, there was no immediate sign of such a lesson, because things started to look up.

It's amazing and faintly depressing, isn't it, to note how the arrival of a meal and a small bottle of wine can temporarily disperse such dark fancies and I was greatly pleased, in addition, to learn that the in-flight entertainment was to be *Good Will Hunting*, a film which had featured heavily in the Oscar award ceremony for that year. I had really wanted to see that film. Now I was going to. When the video began to play I clamped my headphones to my ears with both hands to cut out extraneous noise, and settled down to enjoy a solid hour or two of entertainment.

Good Will Hunting is about Will, a young man who, although gifted to the point of genius in the area of mathematics, is severely handicapped in his practical personal and social interactions because of traumatic experiences as a child. The first light of salvation comes through his encounter with an unconventional therapist, played by Robin Williams, who, after a series of sessions in which his patient becomes increasingly accessible, offers him a file containing details of his troubled past and says simply, 'It's not your fault.' The young man retreats, unable to handle such a proposition, but the therapist persists until, after the fourth or fifth repetition of this phrase, Will breaks down for the first time and weeps on his therapist's shoulder.

I wept as well. Buckets. Quite embarrassing really.

Who did I weep for?

Well, for a start I wept for the children in care I once worked with. I had been through the same process with many of them, saying as clearly as I could, 'Some things are undoubtedly your fault, and you must take responsibility for them, but these things, the things over which you had no control, the things which create a whirlwind of fear and anger and guilt in you whenever they rise to the surface of your mind – these are not your fault, and they never were. The time has come to accept that and move on.' Sometimes I had even gone through their files with them at bedtime, especially when they were just about to be fostered or adopted. It was a revelation to many of them. At such times I was privileged to witness a lot of bravery and tears.

I wept for Matthew, always deeply loved and cared for, but nevertheless with very real demons of his own to exorcise, demons whose presence is certainly not his fault, and I wished I could go back to help him do it, even though he appears to be managing very well on his own.

I wept a little for the people of Azerbaijan, seemingly always being used or abused by someone or other, and especially for the children, who are living through bewildering changes in the historical and political ethos of their country, reckoned to be the third most corrupt in the world. They have so little at the moment, and that lack, and the confusion many must feel, is not their fault.

I even wept a little for myself, and for the rest of my family when their lives are unfairly darkened by the indefinable shadow that has oppressed me since childhood.

Finally, and this is important to me because I believe God wants me to pass it on wherever I go, I wept for so many members of the Christian church who have been taught only about the anger and retribution and inflexibility of God. I wept for all the men, women and children who have never really understood that Jesus, the Lord of creation, who justly demands full repentance from all those who wish to come home to the Father, looks with deep compassion on those who struggle to live with wounds from long ago. Laying a hand gently on their shoulder, he says, 'I know what they did to you, I know how they hurt you and made you feel guilty and worthless. I know how, over and over again, the past rises in your throat to snatch away the very breath of life, and I also know that it's not your fault. Please hear me say those words to you once more – it's not your fault.'

6

I Follow Jesus Because ...

You're Allowed to Even If You're Useless with Practical Problems, General Technology, and Especially Computers

I have nothing but admiration and deep regard for those who are practically and technologically inclined. Good for them, I say. More power to their elbows or fingertips or whatever. It's just that the technological revolution seems to have passed me by, and I'm so glad prayer isn't conducted through the Internet. I have, it's true, just about mastered my computer enough to write on it (that's what I'm doing in a rather laboured fashion at this very moment), but it's so much cleverer than I am. Don't you just hate that message that appears on the screen after you've written something, saying, 'DO YOU REALLY WANT TO SAVE *THIS*?'

I'm similarly intimidated by the cashpoint machine next to one of the banks in our local town of Hailsham. After asking you to enter your personal identification number and the amount of money you want to draw out, the final question is, 'WITH OR WITHOUT ADVICE?' In this context, the word 'advice' presumably means 'information' or 'receipt', but I always opt for 'WITHOUT ADVICE', for fear that the machine might produce a slip of paper saying,

Doesn't it occur to you that you're going through your money at a rather alarming rate? You've asked for £50, but if I were you, I'd take £30. You know as well as I do that if you've got it in your pocket, you'll spend it, and you've got a lot of things coming up next month. Just for once, do think! Money doesn't grow on trees, you know ...

I really am defeated by most practical tasks (I've only just understood that WD40 is not a postcode), all machinery and every aspect of technology. A while ago, for instance, I purchased one of those items that purports to be a telephone, fax and answering machine all in one. My naive hope was that this incredible invention would make life much easier. After all, in theory it should have done, shouldn't it? I'm in need of all three of those functions on a regular basis. The blurb on the side of the box seemed to promise that my new toy would do just about everything except cook bacon and eggs for me before I started work in the morning. Encouragingly, it was accompanied by one of those user-friendly manuals that are supposed to allow the most thickheaded dumbo to programme his or her new purchase successfully for daily use.

Well, yes, but what the authors of this idiot-proof publication with the section headings in big black print and little cartoon figures pointing smilingly to things failed to realize is that I have taken ordinary, old-fashioned idiocy to new and giddy heights. Like the writers of just about every other easy-to-follow set of instructions that I've ever read, these well-meaning people had a tendency to make sudden, wild jumps between one stepping stone and an impossibly distant other, leaving me to flounder helplessly out of my depth in between.

One day I'm going to write a special instruction book for all the hollow-brains like me – if my computer is good enough to allow me to, that is. I can promise you that it won't just be user friendly, it will be user *intimate*. There will be chapters on such subjects as how to boil an egg, how to change a plug and how to put up a shelf that will actually hold things. These sets of instructions will take readers gently by their trembling, inexpert hands and lead them like little children into new worlds of confidence and achievement. The section about changing one of the wheels on your car, for instance, will begin in the following way:

1. Have a cup of tea (see Chapter One – 'Making Tea').
2. Read the paper.
3. Have another cup of tea.
4. Give up the idea of changing the wheel.
5. Decide you might as well do it in a minute, as you have nothing better to do.
6. Have another cup of tea.
7. Stroll outside and stand in front of your car (in the about-to-be-run-over-but-don't-care position). Behave in a casual fashion. If the car gets the slightest inkling that you're planning to do something to it, it will turn awkward and sulk.
8. Now, the first tricky bit. Do you see those four big round things, one at each corner of the car? Those are the wheels. One of them isn't working properly because the rubber thing called a tyre that runs round the outside hasn't got any air in it. We're going to take that whole wheel off and put a different one in its place. Do you believe in your heart that such a thing could be possible?
9. Go back in and have another cup of tea, revise what you've learned so far, then we'll go back outside and I'll explain how to work out which wheel is the one that needs to be replaced ...

Long before this point is reached in normal instruction manuals, technologically challenged folk like me will have been instructed to 'invert the lateral flange in relation to the inward angle of the outer rim', or some other such meaningless command. Ignorant of the nature or location of either flanges or outer rims, we will have given up and gone in to have a cup of tea and read the newspaper. I think my instruction book will sell like hot cakes, don't you? Come to think of it, I might include a chapter on making cakes. First, locate the kitchen ...

Anyway, the results of my attempt to get the phone/fax/ answering machine operating properly were disappointing to say the least. Friends who called for a little chat were instructed by a chillingly sepulchral voice to press something they hadn't got in order to initiate a procedure that they hadn't heard of; people who tried to fax documents were asked to leave messages after a 'long tone' which never actually materialized in any case; and those who attempted to leave messages found themselves verbally assaulted by a series of pre-recorded Dalek-like messages informing them, among other things, that they had performed an illegal action and were liable to prosecution. An expert, called by me from the public telephone box down the road, investigated the whole situation and detected a serious fault in my system almost immediately. Me. It was being operated by an idiot.

I've never got on with all these space-age watches either. Frustratedly trying to poke minuscule buttons in the right, impossibly complex permutation with a blunt pencil in poor light when you've mislaid your spectacles strikes me as an overrated pastime. I've tried and failed a number of times. If you were to sit in the confusion of my study for a while, you would hear abandoned digital watches intermittently peeping out obsolete or wrongly-adjusted reminders from hidden places, like little electronic frogs in a swamp of folders and box files and unanswered letters. I never see them, and I shall certainly never understand them, but I have to confess that I do take a quiet pleasure in their company, particularly in the morning. The dawn chorus of the lost digitals has become part of my life.

My daughter is quick with modern stuff, which is just as well, but one day, when she was about 10, she produced an ordinary cardboard box and asked if we could make a carriage for Honey, our foster-hamster. The gods of chaos relish my efforts with glue and scissors and cardboard. Katy and I share a staggering lack of talent in this area, but we love getting into a complete mess together as we feverishly try to *make* something. Isambard Kingdom Brunei may have been proud of his completed Clifton Suspension Bridge (go and see it if you're ever in that part of Bristol), but no more so than Katy and I were of our sticky, unstable, rickety collection of toilet-roll holders and bits of cereal packet. *We* had *made* it together. Honey managed to mime her intention of leaving home if we made her get in it, and I don't blame her, but it just about rolled along, and we thought it was wonderful.

So why did God not choose this age of superior technology for the visit of his son? Most people are not like me when it comes to these things. Surely, twentieth-century global communication systems would have been far more preferable than painstakingly passing on the message from person to person? Apparently not. But *why* not? Presumably because Christianity always was *about* person-to-person communication. It always was about individuals being special. More people come to the Christian faith through one-to-one contact than in any other way. It had to start like that. And, despite the worst efforts of some who call themselves Christians, Christianity survives. Unstable, rickety, homemade and in continual need of repair it may be, but it still rolls along – and, as the body of Jesus on earth, we have made it together.

I Follow Jesus Because ...

He's Interested in the Heart of Worship Rather Than the Form

I know as much about worship as the Pope knows about sharing toothpaste or hot-water bottles, but it has long been the case in Christian circles that specialized knowledge is regarded as a sort of public well. Anyone is entitled to go and draw a bucketful for distribution to others who aren't sure where the well is, or can't be bothered to go for themselves. That's why very married people are asked to do seminars on being single, and whimsical poets end up lecturing on practical Christianity. Do you think I'm joking? If only I was.

Having made this very defensive point, however, I must confess that I have both enjoyed and suffered an enormous amount of worship of many different kinds during my travels over the last few years. If you will allow me to cast a retrospective eye over some of these experiences, we may discover something about the way in which God regards these various expressions. (I only said 'may'.)

There are no fixed rules about the quality of worship, are there? Bad worship (like good worship) can be formal or informal, musical or unmusical, modern or traditional, long or short, prepared or impromptu. No doubt some or all of these are very important considerations, but they are not the criteria that, as far as I can see, bring joy or sorrow to the business of paying homage to God, which is what I understand worship to be. Let me tell you about two very negative experiences, and two very positive ones. (Forgive me – I'm hopelessly anecdotal.)

The first negative one occurred in a church in the north of England that, as a matter of interest (nothing to do with me, I hope) no longer exists. There were about 200 people present on this bright Sunday morning, and it must have been one of the best organized services I've ever attended. The notices were discreet, the prayers were beautifully worded and read by voices warm with sincerity, the Scripture readings were delivered with emphasis and feeling, and the music – oh, the music! You should have heard the music during the actual worship session. It rose and fell and ebbed and flowed and linked and joined and boomed and hushed like well-oiled, complex machinery, guided by a worship leader who conducted the congregation and, as far as one could tell, the members of the Trinity themselves, as though they were some great spiritual orchestra. At last, as we approached the time when I was due to speak, this same worship leader extended his hand dramatically towards me and, when the final chorus had sunk like a dying ballerina to its close, said in a voice that throbbed and resonated with feeling, 'Now, Adrian, will you come and speak to us?'

And I said, 'No.'

I wasn't just trying to muck up their wonderful event – I did get up and speak after that, of course – but the thing was that I'd hated that service. It felt terribly unreal and contrived, and I wanted to break the spell if it wasn't one cast by the Holy Spirit. Later, I learned that the church was suffering a great corporate hurt, and I realized that the 'perfect' service was nothing more than a huge piece of sticking plaster.

The second negative experience was almost an opposite to the one I've just told you about. In this case almost no preparations had been made for an event that had been in my diary for over a year. When I arrived there was much talk about 'letting the Holy Spirit take charge of events'. Well, all I can say is that if the Holy Spirit was in charge, he shouldn't have been because he didn't do a very good job. No one seemed to know quite what was supposed to happen next at any given point, and when the praise session arrived it threatened never to go away again. Those musicians and singers got completely carried away and gave us a real foretaste of eternity. An exaggeration, of course – it only lasted about three days.

Positive experiences? I suppose the one that stands out is an Easter Day service in Norwich Cathedral. The hymns were traditional, the spoken words were pure prayer-book, and the address was worthy without being inspired, but there are sometimes great benefits to be had from the democracy of a fixed liturgy. As the bright April sun streamed in through the windows that morning, my heart soared in worship. I wanted to fly up to the roof of that beautiful building and shout out my appreciation of the risen, living Jesus. It was wonderful.

Then there was that Pentecostal service in a kind of glorified shed in a depressed area of one of our large cities. The people gathered in this place were more like a bus queue than a congregation. I would guess that most of them were pretty hard up, and I'm quite sure that, in the view of many of my theologically expert brethren, some of them would be considered seriously 'off the ball', if you'll forgive the expression. But there was so much love there – such a sense of Jesus being present. And when the poorly played, cheap guitars and the squeaky violin got going, I found the tears coming to my eyes. We really worshipped.

What made these two services so much more relevant and meaningful to me than the two disasters I mentioned previously? Why did the worship touch my heart and spirit in such widely varying situations? I would suggest that the answer is something to do with reality, and something to do with what, for want of a better word, we might call 'heart'.

Reality demands that we allow for situations and people to be as they are when we come together to acknowledge God, recognizing and giving permission for pain and joy to rise with exactly equal validity to the heavenly throne when we give ourselves in worship. How many times have you heard worship leaders exhorting folk to leave their troubles aside for an hour and make a sacrifice of praise? That's not what it means, for goodness' sake! We don't leave our troubles aside. On the contrary, we collect up the baggage that's weighing us down so uncomfortably and carry it to God. That's the sacrifice – that we go anyway, and we say, 'Despite this weight, which I can't yet put down, despite this pain which fills me right now, I will worship you.' Check it out in the Psalms.

Heart is much more difficult to define, but wherever there is warmth, humour, goodwill, the glow of genuine kindness and a readiness in key people to abandon their personal agendas when necessary, worship will come alive, because Jesus inhabits all of those things, whether they occur in a cathedral or a shed. I wouldn't give you twopence for streamlined worship that has no heart.

Reality and heart – that's what I reckon. Within reasonable limits I would say that anything, anyone, anywhere, any music, any words can be relevant as long as those two little items are on the corporate agenda. Rather unsurprisingly, if you amalgamate ultimate reality with pure heart, you'll find Jesus, and if he's not there it's not worth bothering anyway.

In fact, of course, true worship is much broader than a few choruses, or an hour together on a Sunday. It's about giving all that we are and all that we do to God. The challenge is actually much greater than we think, but don't worry – as with everything else in the Christian life, Jesus has made it quite clear that failure is not only anticipated, but catered for as well.

I Follow Jesus Because ...

Now and Then I Get the Chance to Follow His Example and Stir People Up

The best two examples of this that I know, as far as my own work is concerned, are the following. The first, an imagined account of a meeting in my home, has previously only appeared on the Internet, where it attracted wide and wildly varying responses. I was glad, because that was exactly what it was supposed to do. What do you think?

Example 1

I'm taking advantage of a half-hour break to tell you about some of the people who are gathered in my sitting room at this very moment. Most of them represent oppressed Christian minorities, suffering brothers and sisters of yours and mine who have been dealt with very roughly by the wider church, and I just know that your hearts will go out to them in love and sympathy. I cannot be away for too lengthy a period, as some of these minority representatives are likely to exercise their proclivities rather indiscriminately on each other, if you see what I mean.

You don't see what I mean? Ah, well, let me explain.

Sitting side by side on the floor by the piano, for instance, are Phil and Bob, who run a helpline for those who see disembowelling as a natural and essential part of any intimate relationship. Some of us were in tears just now as we heard about the crass way in which these two fine young men were more or less rejected by their local church when they dared to suggest that the forcible removal of internal organs should become a regular feature of Sunday worship.

'The thing is,' said Bob, 'a lot of people have got a very blinkered and old-fashioned idea of what disembowelling is all about. We're not into rushing wildly around with knives from morning to night, are we, Phil?'

As we all laughed at this absurd caricature, Phil's good-natured face broke into an infectious grin. 'Good heavens, no,' he chuckled, 'we're not monsters, you know. We just think that if the need to 'disembowel and be disembowelled is part of the way we've been created, then there should be some recognition of that by the body of the church, and an opportunity on Sundays to express ourselves at least as openly as everyone else.'

At this point a member of the group rather insensitively put forward a suggestion that disembowelling was a grotesque and appalling practice that invariably resulted in a lengthy and agonizing death, and might therefore be outside the will of God. It was good to see how patiently Bob and Phil handled this, but the pain in their eyes told its own story of similar hurts in the past, and our hearts went out to them – metaphorically.

'Look,' said Bob, 'we're the same as everyone else, right? We go to work, go to the supermarket, watch television – all the things that ordinary people do. The only real difference is that in order for us to feel fulfilled on the deepest level we like to cut open abdominal cavities and drag out the contents. It really is as simple as that, and if anyone can find anywhere in the New Testament where Jesus in any way specifically condemns that kind of behaviour, well, I'd just like them to show me where it is.'

'And if *he* doesn't condemn it,' added Phil quietly, 'it's hard to see why anyone else should.'

Something in the calm dignity of these responses precluded further comment or criticism, and our attention turned to a reserved but pleasant-looking lady called June, who had been listening interestedly from a stool on the other side of the room.

'It's really encouraged me to hear what Phil and Bob are saying,' she began shyly, 'because I've been trying to introduce human sacrifice as a regular activity at church weekends, and so far I've met nothing but opposition from the leadership.'

'What exactly *is* their problem?' asked someone wonderingly.

June spread her arms wide and shook her head. 'That's exactly what I'd like to know!' she exclaimed. 'Apart from the personal outlet that it provides for me, I've tried to point out again and again what a good group activity it would be for people who don't always know each other very well.' June's eyes shone with the bright light of the enthusiast as she warmed to her subject. 'You break up into groups, you see, and each group has a different job. One lot gets sent off to collect dry paper and firewood, another sorts out a good strong stake and some rope and matches and that sort of thing, and the rest do sausages on sticks, and jugs of squash and sandwiches and whatnot, to have round the pyre when it really gets going.'

This happy picture of bright and busy mutual involvement was greeted by expressions of interest and nods of approval from most of us, but the same troubled person who had already carped at disembowelling seemed to feel it necessary to throw cold water over this idea as well.

'How do you choose which person is going to be sacrificed?'

This was met by little gasps and sighs of incredulity and a general shaking of heads from the rest of us, but we needn't have worried. June held her ground well.

'Nobody who doesn't actually want to be burnt alive should have any pressure put on them,' she declared firmly. 'That would be totally wrong, and, in my view, quite unnecessary. Church people do tend to be a little wary about trying out new things, as we all know, but I think once they'd understood what it was all about there'd be no lack of volunteers. I sometimes can't believe,' added June, her eyes suddenly filled with unshed tears, 'that people like Phil and Bob and me, whose only crime is to look for fulfilment through things like disembowelling and human sacrifice, are *so* marginalized by the church. Why are people so *frightened* by the needs of others?'

We all sat in silence for a moment, filled with unspoken sympathy as we pondered this seemingly unanswerable question. The silence was broken eventually by an elderly lady dressed in a rubber suit and carrying a spiked metal ball on the end of a chain.

'I suppose,' she said tentatively, 'that something like sado-masochism, which in itself is obviously morally neutral, tends to be given a bad name by a small number of irresponsible people who use it for their own selfish ends.' She sighed deeply, gazing into the distance as she went on. 'In the old days, you know, it was so different. We used to have our own rack at home when father was alive, and on special occasions we'd pull it out and put an aunt on it – it was usually an aunt, I seem to remember – and, you know, we'd all have a turn at the handle. It was *such* fun. A much greater sense of the extended family.' She giggled at her own little joke. 'Nowadays, if you bring, say, a thumbscrew into a prayer meeting everyone backs away and gets all sniffy. Church, generally, was so much better in the old days in every way. The traditional hymns were lovely, and we didn't get all muddled up, confusing what we believed with the way we lived.'

After that the floodgates were opened. A small, round, balding man who had said nothing until now, sliced the air with scything gestures as he described a lifetime of survival at church in the face of outright disapproval of his deeply felt decapitational needs. Asked if he had ever found a partner, the little man held his head in both hands and shook it miserably from side to side. Most congregations are a long way from regarding mutual decapitation beween consenting adults as an acceptable norm.

So much unhappiness! An athletic-looking young lady painted a vivid picture for us of what it meant to battle the widespread taboo against jumping out at people in dark, lonely places with a chainsaw, a middle-aged banker talked with pride of the stable, monogamous relationship that he has enjoyed for 20 years with a fellow arsonist, and we heard from a small group of professional men and women who are in the process of establishing an information and exchange service for those who describe their future lives as 'meaningless without access to napalm' – all folk whom the church has heartlessly rejected for the flimsiest of reasons.

I must go back to them now, but I do ask you to consider the fact that these poor folk are as much a part of the church as you and I. We've come such a long way in broadening our attitudes. Let's not stop now. Thank goodness we live in such increasingly enlightened times! Do you not agree that the spirit of tolerance abroad in the church at present indicates a strong chance that the so-called peculiarities of these persecuted ones will very soon become a normal part of everyday church life?

And isn't that what we all want?

Example 2

The second example appeared in a newspaper published in Holland, a country where the issues involved are particularly relevant ones, and it began with the following question.

Who is more dangerous to society, a murderer or a liberal professor of theology?

Forgive me for asking a question that is so easy to answer. It's just that I sometimes get confused about issues that other people seem to find very straightforward and simple to resolve. I suppose this particular question may have been complicated for me by the strange thing that happened as I was trying to work out our income tax on my computer the other day. What happened was this. Just as everything was beginning to make financial sense, the list of figures on my screen faded away, to be replaced by something that, at first, I took to be an extract from a film.

The scene before me was a superb baronial hall furnished and decorated in a style combining extravagance and good taste in such a startlingly attractive manner, that I felt a wild yearning to be able to leap through the screen of the monitor and enter that place myself. At both sides of a long, highly polished table running the length of the room, were seated cloaked figures who seemed somehow too serene and ethereally statuesque to be truly human. Sitting at the end of the table farthest from me sat a magnificent man with a huge beard and impossibly deep eyes. He was of the same type and quality as the others around the table, but more so, if you understand my meaning.

Happening to glance at the very top edge of my screen, I suddenly noticed that the legend {HEAVEN – FUTURE VISION. WPS} was visible in the place where the filename usually appears. So that was it! This was no film extract. For some reason I was in the privileged position of actually witnessing an event which was yet to happen in the heavenly realms, an event which must be linked to earthly matters, I surmised, since there is, of course, neither present, future nor past in heaven. And those creatures around the table – they must be angels! Yes, now that I studied them more closely I could clearly see the significantly large protrusions beneath their cloaks, just at the point where the shoulder blades would normally be located. As for the grand personage at the end of the table – well, who could he be but God himself?

And this gathering – was it possible that I could be witnessing a meeting of the committee for divine admissions?

Excited beyond words, I watched and listened as a bright-faced servant holding a large bunch of golden keys in one hand, a notebook in the other, and with a heavy book clenched under his arm, ran in through a door at the end of the hall without knocking and, standing at the head of the table, spoke with an intriguing blend of familiarity and respect to the creator of the universe.

'There's a man just turned up unexpectedly at the gate,' he said, 'who would like to come in. What shall I do?'

'Name?' enquired God interestedly.

The servant glanced at his pad.

'Er, Kuitert,' he replied, 'Harry Kuitert.'

God frowned and thought for a moment, then shook his head slowly from side to side.

'Never heard of him,' he said. He turned to the angel on his right. 'Mean anything to you, Gabriel?'

'Can't place him at all. What was the name again?'

'Harry Kuitert,' enunciated the servant slowly and clearly. 'Sounds vaguely Dutch to me.'

'Oh, dear!' muttered an angel near the bottom of the table.

'No,' pronounced Gabriel after staring into the distance for a moment, 'sorry, drawn a complete blank there.'

'What shall I tell him then?' enquired the servant.

'Well, tell him he doesn't exist,' said God. 'Tell him he only thinks he exists, but he's made a mistake. Easily done.'

The servant referred to his notebook again.

'He said some other things. Claims he was a professor of theology on earth, and – '

'Of course, that in itself doesn't necessarily rule him out of heaven,' interrupted God genially.

'And he says he wrote books questioning your omniscience and omnipotence.'

'Well, he's probably right,' chuckled God, 'because however hard I try I can't make myself remember anyone called Kuitert. That may be a source of satisfaction to him once he's got over the fact that he doesn't exist.'

'Well, he did give me this to show you as well,' said the servant, taking the heavy book from under his arm and placing it on the end of the table. 'He says he wrote it, and I've just had a quick read of it.' He thumbed his way through until he came to a specific page. 'There's a bit here about how Jesus' followers deliberately exaggerated his importance, and about how Jesus himself can't possibly have thought he was God.'

'Well, there you are, then,' said God, leaning back and smacking the table with an air of finality, 'he can't possibly exist. No one who's seriously interested in getting into heaven could possibly have taught dangerous rubbish like that. Why, that would be blasphemy! In any case, some old book doesn't prove a thing. This bloke's friends could have written it – made it all up. No, Harry Kuitert is a figment of his own imagination.'

'He did also say when he, er, thought he was alive,' persisted the servant deferentially, 'that he regretted robbing people of their trusted image of Jesus, someone they could speak to and trust and get close to and all that, but he had to do it to be honest to himself. Awfully strong on that, he was. Very clever man, he seems – I mean – he would seem, if he existed.'

'Oh, he seems clever, does he?'

The expression on God's face as he suddenly levered himself to his feet at this point was really quite frightening. He pointed towards the door and addressed the servant in ringing tones.

'You go and tell him that if one single person fails to come through that gate because Harry Kuitert was *clever* enough to know that they didn't need saving from an eternity of missing out on being here with us, he will spend the same amount of time wishing that we were right about him not existing. And for goodness' sake send in someone who really is clever enough to know me, a five-year-old would do, or one of my mentally handicapped friends.'

Just then the scene faded, and my tax calculations reappeared on the screen. That's what happened, and that's why, for a little while, I was confused about the answer to that question I asked earlier on. Silly, wasn't it?

Who is more dangerous to society, a murderer or a liberal professor of theology?

As if there was any doubt!

234

9

I Follow Jesus Because …

He's the Only One Who Knows the Path to Genuinely Solid Ground

You've heard of Tunbridge Wells, haven't you? It's famous as a symbol of conservatism, spelt with both a small and a large 'c', and is popularly supposed to be the home of a character who writes frequent, angry letters to *The Times* newspaper, signing them 'Disgusted of Tunbridge Wells'. Visually it's a rather beautiful place, with fine Georgian and Victorian buildings nestling in a valley at the foot of a magnificent piece of common land that's as relaxing to stroll in today as it must have been 200 years ago.

Now, before you begin to suspect that this section has been sponsored by the Tunbridge Wells Tourist Board, let me tell you something else about this charming collection of giant dolls' houses standing on the border between the counties of Kent and Sussex. I grew up there. This is not a fact that features heavily in the town's publicity material – in fact, it doesn't feature in it at all – but the 18 years I spent there were very significant ones for me. I roamed restlessly through the streets of Tunbridge Wells for hour after hour and day after day throughout the whole of my teenage period, searching for something or nothing or someone or no one. It was a depressing time, but it also had a sort of rotten richness, like leaf mould. I was quite relieved when I left. I had begun to think that this dismal decaying process was irreversible, and that I would never get away from the place or the negative image of myself that clung to it.

About 18 months ago I discovered in myself a need to be there again. Why? I was able to identify two reasons.

First, we were seriously on the verge of moving house. For 16 years we had lived in a three-storey Victorian house in East Sussex. We moved there when Matthew, our eldest child, was nine years old, and Joe, the next one down, was nearly four. It was the house in which our children grew up and it saw deep sorrows, great joys and an awful lot of ordinary day-to-day living. It was a house with many rooms, but not a great deal of space, except in the kitchen, which we knew we would miss very much, as my wife and I and most of our friends have been kitchen-dwellers all our lives. The house we were moving to was larger and closer to the countryside, and for those reasons we looked forward to the change. Bridget and I are fairly nomadic by inclination, and neither of us usually minds upheaval.

I found, though, that an unexpectedly dark place threatened to open up beneath me as a result of this plan for change in our lives. It was as though the ground was trembling very slightly under my feet, creating a quite irrational fear that some unidentifiable abyss was about to appear and swallow me. Every now and then, pictures of the streets I had known so very well in Tunbridge Wells flashed into my mind and I wanted to be there, unhappy, but in control.

The other identifiable reason for this desire to return seemed to be the fact of my mother's death in December the previous year. On a not very accessible level I felt my grown-up orphaning very deeply as the anniversary of her death drew closer, and the inner drive to be near to where she had been was strong.

Of course, I was wrapped round by the security blanket of my own immediate family, and that was why I knew I would not actually be endlessly roaming the streets of Tunbridge Wells for the next few months. But that tremor made me think.

What *was* my solid ground?

I wrote somewhere that the resurrection of Jesus redefined solid ground, and that once you have accepted that redefinition, there is a shakiness about any other support system than the one which upholds and protects the part of you that will one day live with him. I continue to believe that with all my heart, but I am aware that, every now and then, I still cling nervously to rocks that look solid, but are bound to sink into the sand when I put my full weight on them. Let us pray for ourselves and each other as we learn how to find our safety truly in Jesus.

Oh, and please don't be put off visiting Tunbridge Wells, by the way. It's a beautiful town.

I Follow Jesus Because ...

He Defends Us and Battles for Us, and Has Been through a Terrible Storm for Us

Do you like thunderstorms? I love them. The last major one in our part of the world was awesome and Armageddon-like, the mother and father of all thunderstorms. I had never heard such a volume of natural sound in my life before. It was as though some cosmic giant had tried to carry too many planets at once and ended up bouncing six or seven of them down the stairs of his giant mansion. The very air shook.

When such cataclysmic explosions vibrate the very foundations of the house in which we cower, and lightning splits the night sky into jagged fissures of blinding light, it really is very hard not to believe that God is trying to say something significant about someone or other. As I say, I love violent storms usually, but on this occasion, almost without thinking, I found myself reviewing the last week or two, just to check that I hadn't committed a sin worthy of such a dramatic response. Silly, isn't it, but there we are. I am silly sometimes.

The other thing that occurred to me was that when movie-makers like Steven Spielberg witness phenomena like this, they must itch to get their rich, ingenious fingers on the control buttons of such wildly spectacular effects. It's rather pleasant to know, isn't it, that all the wealth and persuasive power of Hollywood put together would never offer sufficient incentive to God to sell off his 'storm rights'.

The next day a friend called Helga rang to talk about two things. First of all she wanted to talk about the storm. Hadn't it been amazing? Yes, it had. Wasn't the thunder loud? Goodness, yes, louder than any thunder any of us had ever heard before! Wasn't it extraordinary how, every now and then, the lightning suddenly lit up every detail of the surrounding countryside in such a vivid way? It certainly was. A bit scary, eh? Well, yes, perhaps just a little ...

We enjoyed a good mutual chill and thrill about the storm, and then Helga started to talk about something that, at first, seemed quite unrelated to that subject.

'Did you know,' she asked, 'that I've got a young girl of about 18 or 19 living in the house next door to me?'

'Yes,' I replied, 'one of my sons knows her a bit. She's called Wendy, isn't she?'

'That's right,' said Helga, 'and she's a nice girl really, a bit all over the place, but then she's only young and she's living on her own. Anyway, this morning there was this bunch of neighbours discussing something very sort of intensely not far from my front door when I got back from shopping, and when they saw me they called me over. They were talking about Wendy – well, more moaning than talking really, and they seemed to be enjoying every minute of it. I asked what exactly she was supposed to have done, and everyone started rabbiting on all at once about the noise she makes when she gets in late at night. "But she's not always late," I said, "and anyway, she's only 18. We can't expect her to behave like a nun just because we all like going to bed at 10 o'clock in the evening, can we?"

'This didn't go down too well with the lynch mob, as you've

probably guessed, and there were more than a few glares in my direction, but they were obviously determined to get me on their side one way or the other, so then they produced their secret weapon. "Tell her," one of them commanded the person next to her, "what you saw during the storm last night." Well, then this sort of low hum of scandalized agreement rose from the rest of the bunch, and the commanded one gathered herself together all dramatically and spoke in low, carefully enunciated tones. "If you look out of my bedroom window you can see Wendy's back garden. And right at the height of the storm, when the thunder was crashing and the lightning was flashing, I happened to look out of my window, and there on her lawn I saw – well, I saw a young man doing somersaults on the grass in his underpants – in a thunderstorm, would you believe?"

'The lynch mob moved back half an inch at this so they could study my face for signs that this evidence of blatant evil had finally brought me round to their way of thinking. I looked at them for a moment, this little bunch of grim-lipped, respectable people, and I said, "Well, that seems quite a reasonable thing to do during a thunderstorm, if you ask me. Next time one happens I might go out and do the same thing. Although," I added to the lady who had told the story, "I don't suppose you'll be quite as keen to watch when it's me doing somersaults, will you?"

'I went through my front door leaving the lynch mob silent with their mouths hanging open, but I don't think they can have stayed quiet for long, do you? I'm afraid Wendy and I are both going to be in the firing line from now on.'

After my conversation with Helga had ended I sat by the telephone for some time, thinking about that young man rolling around on the grass in his underwear, celebrating his sheer excitement at witnessing the way in which the world performed its very own *son et lumière*. G. K. Chesterton, author of the Father Brown stories, and perhaps my favourite author of all time, would have so appreciated the fact that someone was doing something that felt entirely appropriate to those abnormal circumstances, even though that something seemed bizarre and excessive to others who dared not step beyond the bounds of what is expected.

I thought about Helga and felt glad that someone had been strong enough to resist joining in with the hymn of hate and disapproval that had obviously been getting nicely into tune when she first arrived on the scene.

And I thought about that little bunch of people who had discovered some unity in their common dislike for the way in which another person behaved. 'Ah,' they would want to say to me, 'but what about the underpants? What are the implications of the underpants? What do you have to say about that?' Well, I have nothing to say about that. It's none of my business. But whatever those sinister implications may be, they can't be much worse than ganging up on a young girl behind her back, when she probably needs real, warm, constructive support from her immediate community. Finally, I thought about God, and the way in which he must yearn for those of us who call ourselves Christians to be aware of the great storms of spiritual warfare that roll and crash around the unseen but crucial battlegrounds of creation. I thought about how much he would like to see us throwing off the stifling garments of meaningless religion so that we may vulnerably, wildly celebrate in the sight of others, the fact that however much thunder and lightning may be flung around the universe, the battle is won by the Lord, and has been ever since a young man called Jesus, dressed only in a loincloth, cried out in a loud voice, 'It is finished!'

11

I Follow Jesus Because ...

He Does Miracles

I'm enormously comforted by the resurrection. It is, of course, the greatest miracle of all as far as we humans are concerned, a shining and ever-present promise in the front or the middle or the back of our minds that, as Jesus himself told his disciples, God makes absolutely anything possible.

Crucially, the miracle of personal salvation is possible. We can, like the Prodigal Son, turn away from the wreckage of our Godless lives and warm the cockles of our heavenly Father's heart by starting the long or short walk towards home. So many people are homesick for a place they have never seen and find impossible to identify. Because of Jesus they can find that place and one day learn just how loved they are and were, right in the centre of their lostness.

Miracles of healing are possible. We get confused and puzzled and angry and passionate and dogmatic and despairing about this vexed issue, but the Bible tells us that Jesus responded with compassion to all who were in need. I think he still does. Having said that, I have no idea why only a small number of people are healed through prayer, while many, many more are not. And I absolutely refuse to concede that a sick person who feels a little bit better or a lot more cheerful has been miraculously healed. That isn't what happened when folk in need came to Jesus. He healed them.

I would *love* to see the healing hand of God on people's lives as it was seen by the crowds who flocked to hear Jesus, wouldn't you? I pray for that to happen and, in the meantime, I do my best to accept the mystery and to trust that God knows best.

Yes, anything is possible because of the resurrection, and that is very good news indeed for us human beings, lumbered as we are with options that, without the power of the Holy Spirit, are dismally finite. Thank God for the miracles that happen in our lives, the ones we know about and, rather importantly, the ones that we were never even aware of.

12

I Follow Jesus Because ...

He Doesn't Do Miracles

There must be people who are sick of reading about how I gave up smoking. (No, don't stop reading if you're a smoker – I'm talking about me, not getting at you.) But it is a very good example of what I'm trying to say in this section, so forgive me if I mention it briefly.

Sixteen years ago I was smoking 60 cigarettes a day. I knew I should stop, and I hoped that God would lift the problem painlessly out of my life. He'd done it for one or two others I knew. He didn't do it for me – thank God! When I was closest to giving in he almost certainly stepped in to top up my willpower just a tad, but that's all. Having to grit my teeth through nine months of absolute misery before the pressure eased was one of the most useful and constructive things that has ever happened to me. And, of course, God knew it would be. Like a parent allowing a child space in which to grow, our heavenly Father will sometimes stand back and let us amaze ourselves with our own baby-like achievements, simply because that character-building experience is very good for those of us who are programmed for failure. And when that's the divine intention, looking for short cuts is a waste of time.

Even as I write I'm reminded of something quite ridiculous that happened in our house the other day. How can I even begin to describe it to you? Well, I'll try. There's a game we have often played during long car journeys with bored children (and adults). This is what happens. One person describes a strange or bizarre scenario, and the others have to discover how the situation has come about. The guessers are only allowed to ask 'yes' or 'no' questions. Let me give you an example.

A man enters a saloon in the Wild West and walks up to the bar. A few seconds later the bartender suddenly whips a rifle out from under the counter and threatens the customer with it. There is a short silence, after which the customer expresses his sincere thanks for what the bartender has done. Why? What's going on?

The answer, if you can bear to hear it, is that the customer was suffering from a bad attack of hiccups. The bartender, knowing that a shock can often be an effective cure for this particular complaint, takes his rifle out and frightens the man into an instant cure. Silly, isn't it? But it does take people quite a long time to arrive at the truth when the only answers they're allowed are 'yes' or 'no', and those of us who have experienced the way in which cars can turn into red-hot ovens of discord and discontent will agree that even half an hour of harmony can be extremely welcome.

So, that's the game. You may have played it yourselves. You may be saying, 'Oh, yes, we've been using that boring old hiccup story for years.' Okay, well, now I'll present you with the challenge of this real-life situation that happened just a few days ago in my house. Here is the scenario.

Four people (I am one quarter of them) are roaming impatiently around the various rooms of the house, including the attached double garage. All of us are whistling the first line of the tune of 'Yankee Doodle Dandy', and all of us are becoming increasingly irritable. Every now and then one of us will stop and play the same note on the piano in the living room as the last person who passed through, before continuing on our whistling, irritable way. There you are. What was going on? See if you can work it out before reading the answer in the next paragraph.

Did you guess it? If your mind has turned to *keys* you're definitely on the right track. We were searching for the keys to our car, and if it hadn't been for the fact that we were already miserably late for the theatre I suppose it might have been hilariously funny.

My son's girlfriend, noting the sad and daily consistency with which we misplaced our keys, had very kindly bought us one of those key-ring attachments that are supposed to whistle back to *you* when you whistle to *them*. The theory is excellent, and there may well be versions of this appliance on the market that do faithfully perform exactly that function. Ours was not one of those. On the evening in question we were, unusually, all dressed and ready to go in good time to get to the theatre for the opening of the play. Our sole remaining task was to find the car keys. The general atmosphere as we searched was a pleasantly light and jovial one at first. This time it was going to be easy. After all, we only had to whistle a bit, the thing on the key-ring would chirp back at us, and that would be that.

Without experiencing it, you can have no conception of the speed with which you run out of the will and wetness essential for continuous whistling. Our confident, strident blasts quickly faded into thin, reedy piping sounds as we tried in vain to locate the missing keys. The original light and optimistic atmosphere turned into one of glum frustration, coupled with a growing sense that we were behaving like a bunch of demented loons.

This was nothing compared to what followed. Someone suggested we should dig out the packaging that our non-whistling thing had come in, and check we were doing it right. We found it – without whistling. The instructions, printed on shiny paper in a sub-Lilliputian font, were couched in that strange version of English that results from someone translating with a Chinese-English dictionary and no understanding of grammar. The most important piece of information, however, was quite clear. Unbelievably, the only way of getting the infernal thing to respond was to whistle the first line of 'Yankee Doodle Dandy'. After a moment of stunned silence three of us rushed off to whistle 'Yankee Doodle Dandy' all over the house, only to be arrested by a strangled cry from the person who had been reading the instructions on the packet and was busy deciphering the next bit.

'We have to whistle it in the key of C!' she screamed. 'It has to be in C!'

A stampede began in the direction of the piano, until we realised that only one of us actually needed to play the note. Thereafter, for 10 minutes or more, four relatively sane adults flew around the house whistling 'Yankee Doodle Dandy' in the key of C, fantasizing as they went about applying fiendish tortures to fleshy parts of the Chinaman who had devised the useless gadget that was still failing to respond to their wild but accurately pitched whistles.

The stupid thing never did whistle back at us, and we never did get to the theatre. We found the keys much later in a pile of gunge at the bottom of the kitchen waste bin where Bridget had accidentally dropped them earlier in the day. I washed them, and then whistled 'Yankee Doodle Dandy' in the key of C an inch away from the thing that was supposed to whistle back. It still didn't. I detached it from the keys, took it outside and smashed it with my heel. As I did so, it emitted one tiny and, to my mind, slightly sarcastic whistle.

Can you see now why this ludicrous little story reminded me irresistibly of those occasions, like my desire to give up smoking, when spiritual short cuts look more attractive than personal discipline. Take it from me, like the thing that was supposed to compensate for our lack of organization by whistling back, if God doesn't want it to happen that way, it won't work.

I Follow Jesus Because ...

I Want to Be More Like People I've Met Who Are Humble About Themselves, Make Others Feel So Much Better About *Themselves* and Are So Proud of Belonging to Him

Does your heart warm to humble people? Mine does. Are you humble yourself? I am, despite countless, obvious reasons to be otherwise. Does it not strike you as strange that one as gifted as I should have succeeded in achieving such a correspondingly high level of modesty?

Seriously, though, I'm sure you would agree that true humility is an exceptionally attractive virtue. I'm too fundamentally insecure ever to be one of the life-enhancing folk who possess this quality, but I have met a few during my life, and those encounters have always done me good.

During the course of our second trip to Australia, for instance, I met a man named Peter, who had spent the whole of his working life as a Methodist minister to various churches in different parts of the state of Queensland, and was now on the point of retiring at the age of 65. Peter was cleverer, more sensitive and demonstrably more experienced than I am ever likely to become, and yet he had that very rare and special gift of making the people with whom he came in contact feel far better about themselves than they usually did. As we drove along in his car towards the church where he had invited me to speak, I could feel my confidence opening and blossoming like a flower in the gentle rain of his affirmative manner.

'I cannot tell you,' he said, sounding like an excited small boy, 'how *thrilled* everyone is about you coming to talk to us tonight, and how grateful we are to God for enabling you and Bridget to travel right across the world to bring such a special ministry to us needy Aussies.'

It made me feel like crying. Not, I hasten to add, because I altogether accepted what he was saying, much as I lapped it up like a thirsty little doggy, but because the spirit of the man, inhabited for so many years by the Spirit of God, was so warm and loving and therefore empowering. Because, you see, he meant it! This warm stream of support and appreciation wasn't issuing from one of those irksome individuals who create opportunities for failure by randomly exercising what they call a 'ministry of encouragement' on all and sundry, but from someone whose heart had become, in the best sense, like that of a little child. I found myself actively looking forward to being able to see the smile on Peter's face as I spoke later that evening.

As it happens, my most vivid memory of Peter's inherent humility is connected with something quite practical. A little later during that same journey, the heat inside the car began to be almost unbearable. Summer in Queensland is a blazing affair in which the heat of the sun hits you like a hammer from dawn to dusk. The temperature inside Peter's car had risen to a level which I found very uncomfortable indeed. When I commented on it he must have seen how much I was suffering.

'Look, Adrian,' he said, as though I'd offered to do *him* a favour, 'I – er – I've got just a little bit of air-conditioning down here,' and, taking his left hand from the wheel, he pressed the square button on the dashboard marked A/C to bring what I always think of as a miracle of chilled air swirling through the inside of the vehicle within minutes.

The thing that moved me and made me chuckle inwardly to myself as we drove on was my companion's reluctance to claim an atom of kudos or credit, even for a thing as impersonal and practical as the air-conditioning system in his car. Peter did not have air-conditioning. Peter had 'just a *little bit* of air-conditioning'. I hope you can understand why the addition of those few words had such an effect on me.

Now, the interesting thing about humble Christians like Peter is that, while they may be very self-effacing and generous in giving ground to others, they are by no means pushovers in matters of fundamental standards of behaviour, nor do they compromise the faith that has been responsible for nurturing the fine qualities they possess. Peter was known in church circles as a man whose single-minded determination to follow Jesus, combined with sheer toughness of spirit, had enabled amazing things to happen in the congregations he had led over the years.

I used to find it very strange that Saint Paul appeared to be boasting openly in his letters to the young churches, But I have begun to realize that there is a proper pride that may and, indeed, *should* be felt by those who are as deeply subsumed into the will of Christ as my friend Peter, or the apostle Paul.

It's a justified and entirely legitimate pride in the God who loves them so much and has gone to such lengths to set them free. And we Christians do indeed have a reason to boast, not about ourselves, but about Jesus, who is our Saviour, our brother, our friend and our God. A great number of the Christians that I meet, and I have been one of them, don't walk with their heads held high, because they're so conscious of the extent to which they fall short of God's highest expectations. I can assure you that if the height at which I held *my* head depended on that comparison there would have to be a special ditch dug (like the ones they used to dig for tall female Hollywood stars who were playing opposite Alan Ladd) so that I could slither miserably along below ground level – or possibly I might have to learn to walk on my hands. Not one of us can walk tall on the basis of our own merits. We all fall dismally short of the glory of God.

But here is the important question. Will we be humble enough to be proud of the one who sets that uncompromising target? Will we lift our eyes and our chins as we march because we're filled with the warm, exciting, energizing knowledge that we belong to him and that he has rescued us from the Egypt of our old lives to be with him for ever, justified and protected, not by our own efforts, but by the blood of his son, Jesus? This is not hollow religious talk – it's the basis for everything that we do.

I meet so many Christians whose progress is paralysed by the low opinion they have of themselves. If you're one of those people, then here's a suggestion. Pack your low opinion at the bottom of a small rucksack (in case you need it later when real pride sets in), give yourself a little shake, stick your chin out and, like my friend Peter, walk humbly behind Jesus with your head held high.

14

I Follow Jesus Because …

He Knows That Evil Smells Often Have a Very Ordinary Origin

They say some stories are better left untold. The one I'm about to narrate is probably a good example of the genre. I was surprised when the person concerned gave me permission to tell it because, frankly, it doesn't show him in his best light. Indeed, immediately after the events I shall shortly describe, he begged me to tell no one what had happened. As well as being surprised I was pleased, because the story is a living example of how 'spiritual excess' can get us into trouble if we haven't checked our facts.

Here, then, is the true, cautionary tale of an evil smell.

One dark afternoon in winter the telephone rang. It was my friend Henry. Henry and I were both Christians, and had known each other for several years. Our close, almost brotherly relationship was punctuated by the occasional mild disagreement, but basically we were fond of each other. Henry's Christian walk was a tumultuous affair, swinging from wild, hectoring assurance to darkest despair and creeping doubt. Recently his state had been one of total assurance, a condition that was slightly wearying for his friends, but infinitely preferable to the mood of crumbling disillusionment that seemed to overwhelm him at other times. On the phone I detected an odd mixture of excitement and worry in his voice.

'Ah, Adrian, you're in. There's, er, a bit of a problem down here.'

'At your house, you mean?'

'Here, yes, that's right, and I'm not quite sure what to do.'

'Well, what's going on?'

'There's a smell in our house."

I was silent for a moment. I kncw nothing about plumbing and it was difficult to see how I could be more qualified than Henry himself to advise on any other kind of household odour.

'A smell?'

'Yes, a smell, but – not just any old smell.'

'Not just – '

'It's an *evil* smell, and I'm talking evil with a capital E.'

I was tempted to say something foolish, but a certain tension in my friend's manner made me check myself.

'Henry, where is this – this evil smell coming from?'

"That's what's so strange,' replied Henry, his voice trembling very slightly. 'When you go into one of the bedrooms it's there. Then, when you go into the bathroom it follows you. Then, if you go into the bedroom again, it follows you back!'

'Hmm, I see. Worrying. What have you done so far?'

'Well, I phoned Doris.'

Doris was an elderly Christian lady living nearby. She had a sizeable reputation for mystical insight and discernment, and had been contacted more than once by local people confronted with what appeared to be spiritual manifestations of the more *outré* type.

'What did she say?'

'She said she'd pray about it and ring back, and when she rang back she said she felt it was very serious and I ought to say the Lord's Prayer in every room of the house.'

'And – and you've done that, have you?'

'Yes, I've done that.'

'And the smell's still there?'

'Yes, it is. I wondered if I ought to get some of the elders round to pray and cast out – '

'Henry,' I interrupted, '*please* don't do anything else until I've been round. I'll be there in about five minutes. Don't ring *anyone* else until I get there.'

When I arrived at Henry's house a few minutes later he immediately showed me upstairs and into one of the children's bedrooms. Sure enough, after a few moments the air filled with a horrible smell that, though faintly familiar, I couldn't quite identify, nor track to a single source.

'Now,' said Henry excitedly, 'come into the bathroom.'

The same vile odour was undoubtedly present a few feet away in the bathroom, but much less strongly than in the bedroom.

'Now come back into the bedroom,' urged Henry, 'and you'll see what I mean.'

As we stepped across the landing and back into the bedroom I found that the smell had abated considerably. Within seconds, however, it had increased to exactly the same pungently unpleasant level as before. I peeled my jacket off and threw it out onto the landing.

'I'm going to take this place to pieces, Henry,' I said.

And I did. I pulled open every drawer and every cupboard, and emptied everything out of them. I shifted every piece of furniture that could be moved and one that theoretically couldn't. I didn't believe in the supposed supernatural origins of that infernal smell and I was determined to prove my instincts right.

After a quarter of an hour no dead rats or rotting pieces of meat had been unearthed, and the smell was worse than ever. It really did seem to be *everywhere* in the room. I sat back on my heels, mopped my brow, and gazed at the ceiling in puzzlement.

I think the truth must have dawned on Henry and I at almost exactly the same moment. He was standing in the centre of the room, immediately beneath the lightshade. I was staring in the same direction, still seeking inspiration. Suddenly everything clicked into place – the fact that it was one of those dark winter days, Henry's deep dislike for wasting money, the feeling that the smell was everywhere in the room at once, the particular fishiness of that loathsome odour – it all made sense!

'It's the light fitting,' said Henry.

And it was. A plastic fitting had somehow slipped down until it was in contact with the glass collar of the burning bulb. Henry's evil smell was the result.

'But why did it seem to follow me ...?'

Henry stopped speaking as he mentally answered his own question. On leaving the bedroom each time he had conscientiously switched the light off to save electricity, even when he was only crossing the landing to the bathroom. As a result the plastic stopped burning until the light was switched on once more, thus giving the impression, when he returned, that the smell arrived in the room at almost the same time as he did.

He looked at me, a hunted expression on his face. I knew what he was thinking. He was thinking about his call to Doris, her response, his saying of a prayer in each room of the house, his call to me and our lengthy and energetic search.

'Would you mind,' he said nervously, twisting his fingers together, 'not mentioning this to anyone?'

'No,' I said, with sinful reluctance, 'no, of course I wouldn't mind.'

Henry learned a lesson on that day, and so, I can assure you, did I.

15

I Follow Jesus Because ...

In His World, Love Comes First

We had just moved house, and for the first time since I began to be a professional writer I had a study, my very own little kingdom. It wasn't a large room; in fact it was quite small, with a little walk-in storage cupboard to one side, but, as I delighted in telling friends who dropped in to look around, it was *mine*. It belonged to me. It was a place dedicated to my use. It wasn't anyone else's. It didn't belong to another person. It was exclusively earmarked for the work that I did. It was *mine*. If I could have thought of another 35 ways of expressing that succulent fact, I would have used them to bore my friends to death at an even faster rate than usual. I was *so* happy to have my own space.

One of the first things I did on acquiring my citadel was to hunt through all our books (some were unpacked and on shelves, many were still in the cardboard boxes we used for the move) to find all the 'comfort books' that have meant so much to me throughout my life. These included children's books, particularly the 'Just William' series by Richmal Crompton, humorous works by giants of literary comedy like P. G. Wodehouse and Jerome K. Jerome, several C. S. Lewis favourites, and a whole other widely varying selection of writings that have enriched my life in one way or another. They're a shabby, overbrowsed bunch all-in-all, a few very unwisely read in the bath, but, for the first time, they were all standing richly together on rows of shelves beside the door, and just behind me as I sat at my desk. No longer would they have to be hunted down with the mounting fury and diminishing patience that has become my very own special trademark.

Because, you see, they were *mine*, and they were in *my* study.

I really enjoyed setting my desk up as well. On the left-hand corner at the back stood the white anglepoise lamp that I switch on every morning before starting work, however dark or light the morning might be – nowadays that small action seems to correspond with switching my brain on in some strange way. In the centre of my desk stood the computer, the one I mentioned earlier that's frequently rude to me, and on the right stood the printer. The printer is in league with the computer, but I have its measure now. Discipline is what works with a printer. Be firm. Simply refuse to accept any hint of failure to operate properly. My wife occasionally uses this machine, and regularly has trouble with it because she's too soft. On these occasions she calls me. The moment I appear the cowardly thing flings itself into frantic, chattering, panic-stricken action, hoping to win my approval and avoid a beating. Believe me, you've got to let a printer know who's boss.

At the front of my desk and to the left stood that combination telephone, fax and answering machine I told you about. I endure its leering presence only because I need it so much, but I'm only too aware that it secretly resents finding itself owned by a technological lame-brain like me. Some day the reckoning must come. I'm ready.

In one of the desk drawers beside my chair I squirrelled away a delicious collection of stationery articles which I planned to try very hard never to use. I have always been irresistibly drawn to stationery counters in newsagents' shops. I'm a loony about stationery. I love it all. I love the rubber bands and the sticky labels and the pencil sharpeners and the pencils and the Sellotape and the paperclips and the staple guns and the Blu-Tack and the drawing pins and the neat little packs of envelopes. I love their fiddly, twiddly, functional little beingness, and I love having them stowed away in *my* drawer. Yes, I do! In the other, lower drawer there were just under a million cheap biros. Resigned to the wretchedly shameful fact that every single member of my family is an incurable pen-thief, I asked only that *one* functional pen should be available when I needed it.

On the shelf to my right, a shelf miraculously fixed to the wall for me by a friend who has the Gift of Attachment, there were two things. The first was a little row of reference books. These were, in no particular order, the *Concise Oxford Dictionary*, *a Complete Concordance* of the New International Version of the Bible, H. L. Mencken's *Dictionary of Quotations* and a Chambers paperback *Thesaurus*. It's from these volumes that I frequently haul planks to facilitate crossing the yawning chasms of my thought and creativity. They stand beside me as I write today, sturdy forests of wisdom.

The second thing on the shelf was a pot containing three blooming hyacinth plants, bought for me by my wife. This was an act of profound generosity on her part, knowing as she does that buying a hyacinth for me is the equivalent of sending any other man off to Brighton for a weekend with Pamela Anderson. The way in which I wantonly soak in the scent of hyacinths is positively sinful. (I suppose that should be *negatively* sinful, shouldn't it?) I don't know why it is, but that particular heavenly aroma makes my eyes glaze over with pleasure. You can keep your hash and your Ecstasy – I shall stick to my hyacinths. I rather like the idea of clubs full of people with glazed eyes passing pots of hyacinths around.

Other features of my newly appointed little place of work included the chair I'm now sitting on – firm, yet sufficiently yielding in the seat to become formed by the force of gravity into my individual shape as the months went by, and another seat in the corner, not quite so comfortable, of course, for those who would be granted temporary residence in my kingdom from time to time. Add to all these things the walk-in cupboard where, for the first time in living memory, my files were stored in some kind of easily accessible manner, and you could hardly blame me if I began to feel that it would only really be necessary to leave this place in order to have the odd meal and to sleep.

Isn't it funny how God sends little things to teach you a lesson? I came into my study one morning soon after setting it all up, glanced pleasurably around for a moment or two, yet again relishing the fact that it was all *mine*, and sat down at my desk. I think I really had got a little bit carried away with the way in which the whole thing was so organized and self-contained and geared exclusively to what I wanted. Glancing down to my right, where a recently acquired memo board was leaning against the desk-leg waiting to be attached to the wall, I felt a sudden spasm of annoyance. The day before I had very carefully used my specially purchased, wet-wipe pen to make a list of the tasks that had to be performed on the following day. Some *evil* person had rubbed out my list and written something else instead. I was about to storm out and exact summary revenge on the only likely suspect, my 10-year-old daughter, when I happened to notice what had been written across the white surface of the board.

'IMPORTANT,' it said, in huge capital letters, and then there was a big arrow pointing to just four little words in the corner. So small were they that I had to get down on my hands and knees to see what they said.

'Remember to kiss Katy ...'

May God, in his mercy, grant me the humility and wisdom to remember, when I'm obsessed or caught up with my own possessions and concerns and accomplishments, that the demands of love and relationship will always be a first priority in the only kingdom that really matters.

Thank you, Jesus – and Katy.

16

I Follow Jesus Because ...

He's Less Narrow and Boring About Salvation Than an Awful Lot of His Followers

Who will be saved?

Let's have a little recap of what a question like this might mean before we try to answer it in any detail. Well – let's try, anyway.

Jesus made it clear that a disaster of cosmic proportions, one that our finite minds can only fleetingly grasp, is threatening each human being on this planet. His aim, directed by the profound love of God for mankind, was and is to save as many people as possible from what we rather shyly call 'hell'.

He explained that men and women can indeed be rescued by being figuratively or physically baptized in his name, by declaring their allegiance to him, by following him, by being obedient to him, by making him the first priority in their lives, and by assenting to the proposition that his death on the cross has been graciously regarded by God as a substitute for punishment that they should justly receive. God's act in bringing Jesus back to life after three days loosened the grip of death on humanity, thus defeating the devil, a fallen angel whose ongoing intention is to confuse and blind humanity to the truth, so that they cannot enter the heaven he has left and lost for ever. All of these things are, of course, no less true because we don't fully understand them.

The Spirit of God will live in us if we truly follow Jesus. As a result we will become committed to other people's physical and temporal needs, just as Jesus himself was. However, the major issue confronting us is not how we are to pay our rent, nor how we cope with illness, nor has it anything to do with whether we play the lottery or not, important though these things may seem to be or actually are. The major issue, the one we shall all have to face, preferably before death, is that, through Jesus, the love of God offers rich and eternal life with him as opposed to some unspeakably appalling alternative. Nothing is more important than that fact.

Jesus came to save sinners, and he wishes to continue through us, the body of Christ on earth. This, incidentally, is the ultimate reason for following Jesus.

Okay, that's the scenario, so back to the original question. Who will be saved?

A couple of years ago, soon after the death of Diana, Princess of Wales, some people took exception to a comment I made about the likelihood that she had met Jesus by then, and that the most important things in her life would have been resolved. Now, as then, I don't care to waste time defending that statement because, as it literally stands, I'm quite sure that it's absolutely true and thoroughly biblical, but I would like you to join me as I follow my nose in search of some kind of answer to my opening question. I'm very far from being systematic, as more discerning readers may already have noticed, but I feel sure, we shall arrive *somewhere*.

Who will be saved?

As we have already mentioned Diana, let us begin with Mother Teresa, who died at almost exactly the same time. Don't you think it was wonderful, first of all, that God managed to slip her out of the back door and home, at the only point in modern history when the ending of her life would be eclipsed by the death of somebody else? The meaning of the parable of her life was confirmed by the manner of her passing. She was not important, but Jesus is.

Now, still hanging on to our initial question, I have just stated that God has taken this remarkable woman home to be with him in heaven.

But has he?

I have recorded elsewhere my meetings with people who countered my enthusiasm about Mother Teresa with the dark words, 'Ah, yes, but is she saved?' What they were really asking, of course, was whether she had gone through the established set of procedures that evangelical Christians have decided is the only respectable path to salvation. Was she aware of the four spiritual laws, and did she proceed accordingly? Did she repent of her sins, asking Jesus into her life to be her Lord and Saviour, and did she confess him before God and men? I haven't the faintest idea whether or not Mother Teresa selected a conversion package that would satisfy the sterner brethren, but I do know some things.

I know that she saw Jesus in the eyes and faces of starving, filthy beggars, and that she cleaned and fed and comforted them because she was doing it for him.

I know that Jesus pointed out in the twenty-fifth chapter of the Gospel of Matthew that it's those who feed him, and quench his thirst, and clothe him, and ask him in when he's a stranger, and look after him when he's sick, and visit him in prison, who will receive the inheritance – the kingdom prepared for them since the creation of the world. And I know, because he said so, that many of those will not even realize that they did it for him. Woe betide us if we arrive at the gates of heaven with a 'perfect' conversion and no loving works.

I know that if I were to arrive at those same gates and find myself behind Mother Teresa in the queue, I would hide behind her skirts and, when some eagle-eyed angel spotted me, tell God she was a friend of mine in the hope that such a claim might influence him.

I know that if Jesus was in hospital he would rather be visited by someone with warmth, humour, kindness, a box of chocolates and a shaky understanding of the things of God, than some miserable character with a perfect theology who was only there out of duty. I recall with blushing horror a much earlier period of my life when, as predatory members of our college Christian Union, we lured members of obscure sects to speak to us under the pretext of wanting to learn about their beliefs, then hacked savagely and triumphantly at them with specially sharpened shards of Scripture when they admitted that they had never invited Jesus into their lives. We showed them a thing or two about the love of God, I can tell you. If you have not love ...

Who will be saved?

'Of course,' someone cries, 'those involved in great ministries, those who have healed and cast out devils in the name of Jesus, surely they *must be* saved.' Well, I expect many of them will be, but Jesus makes it quite clear that some so-called followers who present themselves to him with what appear to be perfect credentials on paper will be greeted with those dreadful words, 'I never knew you.'

'Ah, but you don't quite understand,' they'll say, 'we really did do marvellous things in your name. We were leading lights in our church movement. We were – look, we were important!'

'Yes, you were,' Jesus will quietly reply, 'you were very, *very* important, and I never knew you.'

'But we prayed – we prayed! We prayed a lot – loudly. We called on your name every Sunday.'

'You did,' Jesus will say, 'but not all who cry, "Lord, Lord!" will enter the kingdom of heaven, only those who are obedient. I never knew you.'

Who will be saved?

You are dying to say to me that I surely must agree with the proposition that Jesus is the one way to the Father. *Surely* I must agree with that. Yes, I do. Jesus himself said it. Therefore it's certainly true. But Jesus also said that those who give as little as a cup of water to his servants for his sake will receive a reward. What will that reward be? Will it be a weekly day-pass to heaven from hell? Will it be a special concession of air-conditioning in whatever variety of accommodation they occupy in the infernal regions? Or will they be saved? You tell me, because I really don't know.

What will happen to the men who nailed Jesus to the cross? Jesus prayed that his Father would forgive them for what they were doing to him. What is the implication of this prayer for those men? At the tomb of Lazarus Jesus thanked his Father for always hearing and answering his prayers. If the prayer for those who hammered the nails in has been answered, those men are now in heaven. Do you believe that? They weren't even evangelicals, let alone born-again believers. They killed the Son of God. Could it be that Jesus is allowed to be The Way for absolutely anyone he chooses? No, surely not ...

Who will be saved?

What about nasty, horrible people who happened to say some sort of prayer of commitment one day, but have slid disastrously away from the path of rectitude and religion ever since? What about them? Are they saved because they said the right words and meant them for three and a half minutes? Or not? What about babies and small children? What about people whose brains don't work properly? What about dogs and cats? What about fleas?

Enough of this nonsense. I have no idea who will be saved and who will not, because it's none of my business. God will save whom he will save. I know the basic spiritual mechanics of salvation just as well as anyone else, but I also know that salvation isn't actually a mechanical process. It's about following and loving Jesus, and if there are any non-Christians reading this, I'd like to point you to that part of the Bible (the twenty-first chapter of the Gospel of John) where Peter suddenly recognizes Jesus on the bank of the Sea of Tiberias, and is so excited that he leaps into the water and splashes his way to the shore to be with him.

Why did Peter rush so precipitately to be with his master when, only a short time before, he had denied him? Why wasn't he too embarrassed to go near him? Was it because he was worried that he might have lost his eternal life and was anxious to get it sorted out? Was it because he was hoping to be given clarification on one or two matters of doctrine about which he felt a little unsure? Was it because he had just formulated a new statement of faith for potential believers and was keen to get it ratified? Was it because he wanted to impart a vision he had just had of the distant future, featuring groups of Christians who were as richly relaxed and kind and caring as their master?

No, it was none of these things. I'll tell you what it was. Peter wanted to be with Jesus because he loved him *so* much, and nothing else in the universe mattered.

But here is a paradox. The more uncertain I become about who is saved and who is not, the more certain I become that I must preach Jesus as the only way. Strange that, isn't it?

Never mind who is saved, unless God has specifically made it our business. Let us fall in love with Jesus and, when the time is right, tell people about him.

17

I Follow Jesus Because ...

He Encourages Me to Live 'Now'

One of our longest-running television programmes is the show called *This Is Your Life*. I don't know exactly when it began, but it must have been shortly after I was born because I can't recall a time when it didn't exist. Most people must surely have seen the programme at least once, but in case you haven't, I'll explain how it works so that you know what I'm talking about.

The general idea of *This Is Your Life* is that some unsuspecting famous or worthy person is ambushed by the presenter of the programme (Eamonn Andrews in the early days – remember him? – or Michael Aspel nowadays) bearing a large red book with the victim's name on it, and hauled off to a studio theatre to have the story of his or her life told in front of a live audience and, of course, vast numbers of television viewers as well. In the following 30 minutes a variety of surprise guests, who may be friends, family or admirers of the subject, make dramatic appearances through the curtains at the back of the stage to share personal anecdotes and memories. The climax of the proceedings tends to be the entrance of some especially significant individual separated by many years or thousands of miles from the star of the show. A tearful reunion followed by swelling music and embraces all round is the final course on the menu of this carefully planned feast of emotion.

In all the years that *This Is Your Life* has been running, I think only a couple of people (the footballer Danny Blanchflower was one) have ever actually refused to be dragged off to have their lives publicly reviewed, but that was two too many embarrassments for the television company concerned, who, after the second such negative encounter, decided that from then on the show would be recorded to avoid the risk of having to fill an empty half hour.

The vast majority of the victims have always seemed more or less to enjoy the experience, and as a child I found it very difficult to understand how they could possibly react in any other way. Just imagine, I thought, having all the people you've ever known turning up one by one to kiss you or shake your hand and tell the whole world how wonderful you are. What more could you possibly ask for? As a rather complex and troubled child, I found the programme becoming, almost unconsciously, a symbol to me of an inner yearning that, one day, everything in my life would sort itself out and I would arrive at some kind of glorious, *This Is Your Life*-like climactic moment in which, with tears of joy, I would discover that all my hurts were healed, all loose ends tied up and all my chronic problems solved.

The absurdity of such a specific notion caused it to fade as the years passed, of course, but for the first 40 years of my life I did remain trapped in the grim prison of believing that true happiness could only lie in the future, and that the things I was doing and experiencing *now* were of such little value that they were hardly worth regarding. What a recipe for the wasting of days!

As I approached my fortieth birthday, I wrote a song for a revue which included the following verse:

And good old Eamonn Andrews
Would come smiling round the corner
With a big red book and people
Who would say, 'We always loved you!'
And you'd wonder why on earth

They never told you when you needed
All the love that they could offer
What a shame
But as he moved towards you
You would know it doesn't matter
As it's just another way
To lose the game that you are playing
For in letters that are golden
On the big red book he'd show you
There is someone else's name
And the dream of being special floats away
And the whole sad world looks so grey.

General pessimism about potential prospects, of which this verse is an obvious symptom, was a bleak but very necessary part of my transition from being someone who relied on phantoms of the future to being someone who is able truly to enjoy the things that are happening to me and around me *today*. The process is by no means completed, but it's well under way.

C. S. Lewis said that, if the world were to become perfect, God would look down and see a man reading a book in a garden. I needed to understand that so-called prosaic or trivial activities happening right now are actually at the heart of real peace and contentment. This awareness might take us a long way towards understanding what Jesus was talking about when he spoke of the kingdom of God actually being among us, and it may also be the key to a special kind of joy that's much deeper and more spiritually nourishing than mere happiness. I suspect that Jesus looked fondly around at the faces of his disciples as they all ate meals together and knew with a sweet mixture of joy and pain that this was as good as it was likely to get on this side of heaven.

These thoughts arose in me on the day following my return from a summer holiday I once spent in France with the other five members of my family. It was a good and enjoyable experience to be away together, despite the occasional (and in our case seemingly inevitable) arguments and tensions, but two things particularly spring to mind in connection with the things that I have just been saying.

The first was a couple of hours spent in the beautiful forest on the hills overlooking a little cottage in Normandy where we stay quite often. We took bicycles with us on the back of the car to ride along the tree-lined tracks, a rug to sit on, a ball to throw, a bottle of orange squash to drink, a big bag of crisps to eat and a book to read. As we sat in the dappled coolness of the cathedral-like forest, throwing our ball to each other and listening as Katy (aged 11 at the time) read to us, I very nearly managed to allow *now* to be eternal.

The other occasion was earlier in the holiday, when we were staying at a place much further south, quite near to the wonderful city of Chartres. Four of us hired putters and golf balls so that we could play on one of the Crazy Golf courses that the French seem so keen on. We were the only people there because a light rain was falling, and it turned out to be one of those God-given times when the silliest things seem screamingly funny and you don't care whether you win or lose and the weather can do what it likes. We were people who loved each other, being happy for an hour. For me, at least, nothing else mattered. When we returned to the place where we were staying, I wrote the first poem I had written for quite a long time:

> *There is not much more*
> *Need not be more*
> *Than playing Crazy Golf in France*
> *Laughing in the summer rain.*

Sufficient unto the day is the evil thereof – the good as well, one suspects. Thank God for the *now*.

18

I Follow Jesus Because ...

He's More Interested in What Happens behind the Scenes Than in My Public Posing

I travel frequently to Europe – sorry, I mean to other parts of our great brotherhood of nations. A small but important lesson made one journey particularly memorable.

This trip was already different from others I had done in one significant way. A Christian television company, based in the United Kingdom and calling itself Christian Television Associates, had decided that they would like to make what is sometimes called a 'fly-on-the-wall' documentary programme about the wide variety of work and leisure activity that fills up a year of my life. As you know, the 'fly-on-the-wall' aspect simply means that the television cameras record what happens both formally and informally, as opposed to concentrating only on specially prepared and presented set pieces. By the time I had experienced the continual presence of a TV camera probing every intimate corner of my existence for only a month or so, I frequently found myself wanting to roll up one of the heavier quality newspapers in order to swat this 'fly', and I think I would have done exactly that on the trip I want to tell you about if the CTA camera operator who accompanied me hadn't been as likeable as he was infuriating.

Crawford Telfor is a Glaswegian distinguished by his small stature, extraordinarily bad jokes and incredibly thick skin, who once worked for the BBC but is now a director of Christian Television Associates. He was waiting for me as I walked up to the Lufthansa check-in desk at Gatwick Airport, armed and ready to poke his lens into every crack and cranny of my bleary-eyed progress towards the plane that was scheduled to take both of us to Stuttgart in an hour's time.

The girl on the check-in desk was amused but faintly nervous to find that her security-related questions were being recorded for posterity, but many of the other passengers in the terminal were completely gobsmacked as I approached them pushing a luggage trolley containing not cases and bags, but Crawford, lying on his back with his feet in the air, filming upwards in order to get an interestingly angled view of my face as I approached the departure gates. Don't ask me why I let him do that. I just don't know.

On the plane itself things got worse. Crawford was determined to film me actually arriving at my seat and depositing my hand luggage in the overhead locker. This he proceeded to do, much to the annoyance of a fellow passenger, who strongly resented access to her own seat being used as a vantage point for my little one-man camera team, who, for all she knew, was simply co-operating in the production of a ludicrously egocentric amateur holiday video.

'Is this really essential?' she enquired in acid tones.

I wanted to die. Crawford calmly filmed me wanting to die, and continued filming from his seat by the window as I ate my airline snack, read my airline magazine and dozed my airline doze. Finally, I cracked. I couldn't stand it any more. Turning to face the camera lens, I spoke in low, ominous tones.

'If you don't take that camera out of my face,' I threatened,

271

'I shall insert it so far into you that you'll require microsurgery to remove it.'

He lowered his camera for an instant. 'I didn't quite get the beginning of that,' he said. 'Would you mind just repeating it ...?'

Over the next 24 hours it didn't get much better, but the next day I got my own back a little when we ate lunch in a Japanese restaurant with Christian Rendell, a splendid fellow who translates my books and interprets for me when I speak in Germany. This was one of those Japanese restaurants where the centre of the table at which you sit to eat is also the metal hotplate on which the meal is cooked. Having ordered our dishes from a waitress, we sat and waited for the chef to complete his work for diners on a table at the other end of the restaurant before coming to ours.

Needless to say, Crawford had already checked with the manageress of the establishment that filming was allowed, but for some reason this information had failed to filter through to the chef. When he did finally arrive, Crawford happened to have put his camera down and was sitting quietly, looking strangely naked but reasonably normal for once. Our cook was a very impressive figure, far from tall, but intensely serious in manner, dressed in pristinely white garments and surmounted by an unusually tall chefs hat, which lent immense dignity to his slight figure. At his waist hung a leather belt, cunningly designed to accommodate a range of lethal-looking metal cooking implements of varying length and design.

With nimble-fingered skill and a hiss of frying ingredients, this master of the oriental arts began to slice, turn, mix and flavour the combination of rice, chicken and prawns that would shortly become our lunch. Christian and I were concentrating hungrily on the culinary process, but out of the corner of my eye I did notice that, predictably, Crawford's hand was stealing down towards the camera that lay on the floor beside him. Seconds later he was on his feet, eye firmly against the viewfinder, circling and advancing on the chef from behind, so that, eventually, the long lens was actually pointing down over the little man's shoulder and beside his face towards the food that he was preparing.

I cannot tell what the chef thought this thing was that had suddenly appeared over his right shoulder, but I shall never forget his reaction to the sight. In the best Samurai tradition he sprang back into a defensive posture, a loud, guttural cry of shock and aggression issuing from his throat. He lifted the implement that happened to be in his hand at the time as though seriously intending to impale Crawford on the end of it.

You have to give it to my small Scottish friend (and someone nearly did on this occasion) – his ubiquitous camera-work may have been intensely irritating, but he is courageous to the point of near death. Not only did he continue filming, but I could have sworn that he moved a little closer, presumably hoping to get a really good close-up of the murderous expression on his assailant's face as the blow landed.

All of us, including Crawford, survived this experience, although the chef took a little while to calm down, and Christian, who regards Japanese restaurants as sacred temples of Epicurean delight, was deeply embarrassed.

Over the next three days Crawford continued to be a constant presence. We got used to him and his camera in the same way that you get used to a small wound that refuses to heal properly. He filmed Christian driving, me sleeping in the back of the car, both of us eating, several members of the public minding their own business, and a bit of countryside. When we crossed the border into Holland he filmed my translator's wife offering her opinion that the nicest part of England was Scotland, he filmed me getting annoyed with my Dutch publisher because the cartoon on the cover of my latest book made me look like an alcoholic barrage balloon, and finally he asked if he could do some recording in the hotel room where I stayed on the night before flying back to England the next morning.

By then I felt genuinely exhausted, and when Crawford

pointed his camera at me as I lay flopped on the bed and asked me why I do what I do when it gets so tiring, I found it very difficult to produce a coherent answer.

It was when I was waiting to go to sleep a little later that the significance of Crawford's eternal 'thereness' really struck me. I pay general lip service to the idea that the eyes of God are always on me, but the fact of that camera pointing relentlessly at me when I wasn't in the public view as well as when I was standing and bleating behind a microphone was leading me to wonder just how much of a reality the presence of God was for me. After all, I reflected, when the time comes to face my maker, and he announces that we're to watch a heavenly video rerun of my life, he's likely to fast-forward the public performances and concentrate on the fly-on-the-wall stuff.

'So what it amounts to,' I muttered to God just before I fell asleep, 'is that if I want to follow you there's no such thing as being "off duty". That's hard, God, that's very hard, but I do see your point.'

As I drifted into unconsciousness, I could have sworn that I heard the voice of a small Scottish angel saying, 'Would you mind thinking that thought just one more time ...?'

19

I Follow Jesus Because ...

He Helped Me to Write Him Back into My Life

Every now and then, after a talk, or in the course of a workshop, someone will ask me if any of the things that I write have been directly inspired by God. My answer never varies very much. I don't believe that the things I produce are any more or less directly inspired than, let's say, a specific leg of lamb selected by a Christian butcher to buy and chop up and sell to his customers. Please don't misunderstand me. I certainly hope that God approves of my stuff. I continually ask him to make sure that I avoid the temptation to get too carried away on unproductive or harmful flights of fancy. I pray for those who read the platoons of sentences that come marching out of my mind, that they may feel just a little warmer towards Jesus as a result of what meets their eyes. I do all these things, but were you to ask if the Holy Spirit sits on a stool next to me, dictating every word of the text, I should have to reply firmly in the negative, cosy though such an arrangement might appear. I'm glad really. I think I might get rather bored with the post of God's full-time stenographer.

If, on the other hand, you were to ask if God uses my material – well, there we're definitely talking about something else.

God, as you know, is a great opportunist. He happily seems to use any old rubbish when nothing else is available. And you can't predict the post by looking at the postman, so – yes, the Holy Spirit does sometimes speak to people through my words. Thank God he does. What a privilege that is.

Now, having said all this, I want to tell you about an occasion when the content of my writing was so infused by the spiritual battle raging for my soul, that I might have been excused for beginning to wonder if the divine hand was placed upon my own as it moved across the page. And the extraordinary thing about it is that this was one of the very first things I wrote. It's called *The Visit*.

The Visit is a story in six short parts, and it concerns the unexpected return to a very ordinary High Street church of the 'Founder', a figure who is clearly meant to be Jesus, though he's never actually named during the story. The first part of the story was written in the early 1980s, at a time when, although neither my wife nor I were aware of it, I was heading for a stress-related illness that was to change the course of my life. One evening Bridget and I were sitting in front of the television after the children had gone to bed, when, quite abruptly, I had an idea for a story. It was an idea that filled me up with itself. It choked me. It took my breath away. As it developed in my mind I began to feel an absurd concern that if I moved my body too abruptly the whole thing would somehow be spilled and lost. Finally, I switched off the television and asked Bridget to find writing paper and a pen so that I could dictate something to her. Taking a pad of lined paper to the dining table at the other end of the room, she sat down and looked expectantly in my direction.

The next 30 minutes or so turned out to be one of the strangest, most intense half hours of my life. Fuelled, as I perceive in retrospect, by a desperate desire to establish the reality of Jesus at a time when that reality seemed to be drifting away, the story poured out in a stream that remained unabated until the last word was safely down on the page. Both of us were in tears throughout the process. At the end we were emotionally exhausted and rather puzzled by the experience, but we did sense that something important had happened. Unlike almost everything else I have written since, I hardly altered a comma or restructured a sentence in subsequent drafts, and I wouldn't think of doing so now. The style has a freshness and immediacy that's very hard to recapture in these days when my writing has become a source of income, and my style suffers as much as it benefits from professional objectivity.

The rest of *The Visit* was written a year or two later, as I was beginning to emerge from the aforementioned illness. Indeed, those who knew me well at that time might easily trace the path of my spiritual and emotional fragmentation as it winds through the landscape of those additional five sections. The writing of this extra material wasn't accompanied by the same intensity as the first part, but there were some memorably odd moments. The fifth story, for instance, concerns a crucial choice needing to be made by the man who, throughout *The Visit*, is narrating his experiences with the Founder. Basically, his choice is between good and evil – between physically following Jesus or being drawn away by a strange, shadowy figure approximating, I suppose, to the devil. I wrote the first half of the story, the part leading up to the point where this choice had to be made, during the morning and then left it, intending to continue on the following day. However, our house seemed to be filled with darkness and oppression that afternoon and evening, and Bridget, who had read my output for the day, suggested that until I had finished the story in a satisfactory way, there would be no peace for us. I did finish it, and she was right. I don't attempt to explain that sequence of events. I simply record it as further evidence that there was something oddly significant about this particular piece of work.

Eventually *The Visit* was published in Britain as part of a book called *The Final Boundary*, a collection of short stories that appeared immediately in the wake of *The Sacred Diary of Adrian Plass*. I was very proud of *The Final Boundary*, but quite a lot of potential readers were thrown by its appearance immediately after such an apparently very different book. Why wasn't I producing another three dozen volumes in the *Sacred Diary* mould? After all, that was what usually happened when a book was successful. Perhaps because of this reaction, *The Visit* was somewhat lost over the following years in this country, although it has always had a real popularity with those who happened to discover it. For years, Bridget had been urging me to find a way to make these stories available to more people in an accessible and attractive form, and in 1999, to our great excitement, that's exactly what happened.

As we approached the millennium, *The Visit*, a book about Jesus returning to his own, was published by HarperCollins as a large-format book with superb illustrations by Ben Ecclestone, also my collaborator on such projects as *Learning to Fly* and *Words from the Cross*. Words cannot describe the pleasure with which I saw these plans come to fruition. *The Visit* is a crucial part of my personal history, an important hinge on which my life turned. God didn't write it, but, in some indefinable way, he certainly seemed to stand over me to make sure I got it right, and in the writing of those words, I remembered who I had met and why I had become a Christian all those years ago.

And the central message of the book? Well, it concerns the forthcoming and decidedly nonfictional return of Jesus, and was the same when this century began as when the story was written in the 1980s: Would you be ready?

20

I Follow Jesus Because ...

He Forgives Me for Sins I'm Not Even Aware Of, for Being Extremely Silly, and for Sometimes Being Very Annoying to Other People

It's funny, isn't it, how we Christians talk mainly about the more cataclysmic sins, when the faults that actually beset us most are either ones we're not even aware of, or else are scratchy little offences that seem hardly dignified enough to talk about or confess. Let me give you an example of each.

Example 1

First of all, there are the sins or failings that we don't notice in ourselves. Take self-delusion, for instance.

Have you ever found yourself engaged in conversation with someone who suddenly says something that completely robs you of the power of speech? There was a time when this happened to me twice over a period of a few weeks, and on both occasions for more or less the same reason.

The first was in the course of a celebratory meal of some kind, when I was sitting next to a man whom I shall call Ronald. Ronald is famous – well, infamous, really – in our immediate circle for his tendency to say hurtful and insensitive things to friends and acquaintances. Inwardly blessing my hostess for deliberately placing me beside such a delightful dinner companion, I was doing my very best to make pleasant conversation when Ronald adroitly turned the subject to a mutual friend called Jill, who happened to be sitting further down the table.

'I'm very fond of Jill, of course,' said Ronald, leaning towards my ear and lowering his voice so that nobody else could hear, 'but don't you get a bit annoyed by the way she talks to people sometimes? I know I do.'

Conscious that my mouth had started to open and close like a goldfish out of water, I tried to say something, but the words wouldn't come.

'The thing is,' continued Ronald, warming to his theme, 'I've always thought that an important part of being a Christian is making sure that you don't hurt other people by the things you say. I'm *very* careful myself.'

My mouth no longer opened and closed – it just hung open. I stared blankly at Ronald as he developed his argument.

'I never say anything that's likely to upset the person I'm speaking to,' he explained. 'That's how I manage to maintain such good relationships with everybody I know.'

Just for a moment I wondered if he might be making a joke at his own expense. Could it really be possible that this was the same Ronald who had once said to me, 'My poems are about things that appear trivial to everybody else,' and had then, without drawing a breath, announced that he had written a poem about *me*? Was he seriously claiming to be scrupulously aware of the way in which his words might affect others? I peered hopefully into his eyes, hoping to detect the merest sparkle of self-mockery somewhere in their depths. Not a flicker could I see.

'B-but ...' I began, then gave up, aware that this was probably not an ideal situation in which to revolutionize Ronald's view of himself as the most tactful person in the universe. In any case, I don't think he would have believed me. Was Ronald going mad? No, but he was seriously self-deluded.

The same sort of thing happened no more than a fortnight later. A very close friend called Julia came for coffee and, in the course of our chat, informed Bridget and me that she disapproved strongly of those parents who make a regular habit of complaining to the local school about the way in which their children are treated. This time we *both* sat there with our mouths hanging open. Bridget recovered first.

'But, Julia,' she said gently, 'you've been up to the school to complain ever so many times since your two started going, haven't you?'

A look of mystification and slight annoyance appeared on Julia's face. 'No I haven't,' she replied. 'I've hardly ever been up there – once or twice, perhaps, but certainly no more than that.' She shook her head in puzzlement. 'I really don't know what you mean.'

Bridget and I exchanged glances. How many times over the last few years, we silently asked each other, have we sat in this very room listening to Julia's latest account of how she 'went up that school' and gave them a piece of her mind that they wouldn't forget in a hurry? Many times, we silently answered each other – too many times to count. Were we going mad? Was Julia going mad? No, but she was terribly self-deluded.

I mention these two incidents because they set up a small but persistently worrying question in the back of my mind. It was very easy for me to conclude that Ronald and Julia were deluded about those aspects of their behaviour that I have mentioned, but what about me? Do I sometimes confidently assert that I *never* do this and *always* do that, while others listen with incredulous, dumb disbelief?

Having considered this question carefully, I'm absolutely sure that, in fact, I *never* do such a thing – but, on the other hand, it's just possible that I'm chronically self-deluded. How about you?

Example 2

Secondly, there are the petty, silly little, things that can cause real annoyance to other people. I feel myself blushing as I enter the confessional.

It was late December, and Christmas fever was upon us all once more. The change of atmosphere in the streets and shops was as pronounced and difficult to define as ever. People went about their business with just a little more briskness than usual, and there was a heightened sense of excitement as life flowed, like water in an emptying bath, towards the plughole of that single, confusedly significant day.

In case any of you think that the image I have just employed is wholly inappropriate to the blessed season of Advent, all I can say is that it was absolutely in line with the way I was feeling at that particular time. The preceding 12 months had been one of the busiest years I had known for a long time, and I was running out of steam. I thanked God for the work, but I couldn't wait for the new year to come, because, in 1998, I was planning to take a whole year off from all public speaking and performance. This was happening for a number of reasons, not least among which was the fact that I was simply sick of the sound of my own voice. I intended to spend a year writing more material and actually *living* life, rather than seeing it as a series of repeatable anecdotes.

Another part of my motivation was connected with an observation that Christian initiatives and ministries never actually seemed to end. Have you noticed that? They either dribble away into nothingness, or they're enshrined inflexibly and eternally in a form that's quite often a travesty of the original. Or sometimes those involved continue to go miserably through the motions, assuming that lack of finance, support or any visible success is some test of faithfulness imposed upon them by the Lord. I intended to use my free year to check that God really did want me to continue with the things I had been doing, in the way that I had been doing them. I hoped that those who had been displeased by my writings would pray with particular faithfulness that the Holy Spirit would make it clear to me that they were right. And, of course, I had absolutely no objection to those who liked what I wrote throwing up the occasional prayer as well. Just in case I was right, you understand ...

Yes, I was certainly looking forward to it. It should be good. For a whole year I would be a 'local person', a regular attender at my own church, a person who made family plans for the weekend. I would still be writing, but that was more like a 'proper job' anyway. I was really relishing the prospect.

In the meantime, however, as I said just now, I was running out of 'oomph', and getting mean and petty and irritable as a result.

One day I had to walk into town to post a parcel and some letters. Quite apart from my general feelings of tiredness and harassment, I had been obliged to wrap a parcel before coming out, an activity which has always reduced me to teeth-clenching, quivering fury within minutes of starting. Why *can't* I do it? Why *can* others do it? Why do rolls of Sellotape, pairs of scissors and sheets of brown paper start distorting themselves and sticking to the wrong things and leaping about and misbehaving like delinquents in a bottom-set maths class as soon as I come anywhere near them? It's not fair. I come away from wrapping parcels like a seven-stone weakling who's just done 12 rounds with Lennox Lewis. I arrived at the Post Office clutching a few letters and the strangely shaped, sticky, sulking mass that was my barely vanquished parcel, needing to buy stamps and hoping the queue would be short or nonexistent. It wasn't. It was long. I breathed heavily through my nose and joined the end of the line.

Seconds later, two women attached themselves to the queue

behind me and began to talk in loud voices about someone at the place where they worked who had earned their disapproval in some way. With considerable relish they swapped anecdotes about how they had *really shown* this unfortunate offender what they thought of her. I listened without appearing to listen, my already dark mood deepening as I listened to such a hymn of unpleasantness. It was then that I gave in to the temptation to play my dreaded 'Post Office Queue Game' for the first time in many years.

When the people in front of me in the queue moved forward a yard or so, I pretended not to notice because I was so absorbed by a notice on the wall. There was a lull in the dialogue behind me. I sensed the minor frustration of these two ladies as they willed me to move into the space that had been created, thus allowing them to move forward as well. I waited until the queue in front of me had progressed yet another pace before appearing to notice for the first time that a gap had opened up. Then I moved on at last – but only about 12 inches. At this, billowing waves of annoyance began to wash over me from behind. Why hadn't I moved right up behind the people in front of me, leaving room for the rest of the queue to do the same? I sensed that a major component of this frustration was the awareness that no logical complaint was justified because we would all be served at exactly the same time, regardless of gaps in the queue.

'But,' they must have been seething and burning to point out to me, 'you *feel* as if you're getting somewhere when you move forward, so why don't you blinking well *move*!'

The discussion about the enemy at work continued, albeit rather disjointedly, but there was no doubt about who had become *numero uno* villain as far as the immediate environment was concerned. I continued to not fill the available gaps in the queue all the way up to the point where it was my turn to be served, preserving throughout an air of innocently detached absent-mindedness which, from time to time, I have found highly successful in deterring open criticism. The two ladies, who happened to end up in the serving position just beside mine, darted little malevolent glances at me as I had my sticky bundle weighed and bought stamps. I smiled at them in an innocently mild, friendly sort of way, and set off home.

It was only as I opened my front gate a few minutes later that I was suddenly filled with shame over my silly game in the Post Office. What right had I to judge the way in which those two people were talking about their workmate? Hadn't I done the same in the past? How could I possibly justify the fact that I had deliberately created anger and frustration in them, just because I was fed up with my messy parcel and my wearying year? I asked Jesus to give me a gift of awareness concerning the things I do to others, things that are so lost in the ordinariness of life that I hardly recognize them as sins, and I asked him to forgive me for being so childish and silly and annoying in the Post Office – and for enjoying it so much.

21

I Follow Jesus Because ...

He Sometimes Lets Me Visit Him in Prison

The year of abstinence from public speaking that I mentioned in the last section was a strangely heavy time. Not once did I miss the business of going off to speak to groups of people, much as I enjoy that when I do it, so there was no sense of loss in that area. I suppose it's just that when you stop doing what you do, you tend to discover what you are, and that can be alarming. We very easily talk about the idea that we Christians are nothing and that God is the one who does the business, but it seems to take a lifetime for that piece of knowledge to make the journey from head to heart.

Because of all this, I had rather hoped that my initial re-entry into the world of religious bleating would happen in an environment offering minimum challenge and maximum benefits, but in the event, thank God, I only scored one out of two. Let me explain.

Ever since moving to the town near the south coast where we now live, we have been friendly with a local family made up of two boys, three girls and their mother, June. June is a splendid lady who battled to bring her children up on her own since her husband left in the early years of their marriage. Despite her best efforts, one of the boys, Daniel, got into trouble with the law on many occasions as he was growing up, and as an adult has spent two or three periods in prison, usually for drug-related offences of theft and violence. Despite the fact that Daniel has done some very unpleasant things over the last few years, Bridget and I have always maintained our friendship with him and continued to hope and believe that a change would come about in his life one day.

Just before Christmas on my year off, I was contacted by a man who runs a special project at a prison down in the south-west of England. He explained that he was responsible for a wing that is staffed by Christians and run according to a model that originated in a Brazilian prison where the inmates volunteered to organize themselves because of staff shortages. The unexpected result of this was wide-scale revival in the prison.

Each prisoner who successfully applies to come onto the wing, my caller went on to explain, has to attend a weekend of intensive instruction and discussion on the subject of the Christian faith and its relevance to him as an individual. The weekend then ends with a service involving all those who have attended, as well as people from outside the prison who provide regular visiting support. This meeting, or 'Closing' as it's known, is normally an occasion of much emotion and shedding of tears, as men face the darkness within them and the light that beckons. Their stay on the wing continues with considerable Christian input from staff and outsiders, together with involvement in a system that is self-regulating and therefore quite demanding on men who are used to surviving in the normal prison ethos.

'Daniel Scott's down here at the moment,' said my caller, having explained all this, 'and he said you'd come down and speak at one of our Monday evening meetings if I asked you.'

And that was why I found myself, one January morning, sitting on a train bound for the West Country, wondering how it was all going to go, and feeling deeply intrigued about Daniel's involvement.

After my five-hour train journey the prison itself turned out to be as depressing as all prisons inevitably are, a grey hulk of a building lowering grimly from the top of a hill across the bay below, but the aggressively dull environment was more than compensated for by the warmth of Daniel's greeting just inside the door of the wing where I was about to speak. To my surprise, there was another old friend of mine with him, a man called Jack whom I had known when, as a boy, he had been admitted into the secure unit where I worked. It was *so good* to be greeted with such enthusiasm.

A little later, though, as I watched 60 – 70 men troop into the meeting room, my confidence dipped a little. I knew, because I had been told, that not all these men were Christians, and I sensed from the general atmosphere that an easy ride for outside speakers was by no means guaranteed. I felt quite nervous as I began to speak, but after a few minutes I was overwhelmed by the realization that God wanted to reach out to these people, and I began to relax as I talked simply about the love of God, the heavy demands he makes on our lives and the excitement of wondering exactly how he will use us. Afterwards, I chatted with several of the men, including Daniel and Jack. The change in Daniel was a fascinating one. He seemed almost puzzled by the shift of perspective that he was experiencing.

'The thing is, Adrian,' he said, 'in the past I was so angry, and I tried to solve everything by lashing out, but now – I dunno – there's these new ways of doing things. I really want my life to be different.'

The impression I got from Daniel and other inmates I talked to, as well as from the man who ran the project, was that change in individuals almost invariably begins with encountering the possibility of unconditional love, a love that demands much but will never let go. Nothing has changed much in 2,000 years.

Later, as I was being driven down to the little guesthouse where I was to stay that night, I really thanked God for the privilege of being allowed to be part of what was going on in the prison for just one short evening, and to meet Jesus in the hearts of those men who so wanted their lives to be different. My first engagement of that year had been in the dullest environment you could imagine, with a smaller audience than I was likely to encounter for the whole of the rest of the year, and for the least financial return possible. And yet, I couldn't conceive of a better way for a Christian to begin a busy 12 months of travelling and speaking.

If you have a moment, please say a prayer for Daniel and Jack, and all the others in that wing who are daring to believe that change is possible.

22

I Follow Jesus Because ...

Among the Good Things He Offers Us Is the Gift of Speaking in Tongues

Recent involvement in a debate concerning the gift of 'speaking in tongues' triggered memories of when I first encountered this interesting phenomenon for myself. As a teenager of 16 or 17 in the mid-1960s, I travelled to the town of Sevenoaks every Thursday evening to help at a church-organized event called 'The Cavern' (nothing to do with The Beatles, I'm afraid). Here, a mixture of Christian and non-Christian young people met in a converted cellar under the parish church to drink very weak coffee and listen to very loud music. I had been recently converted, and was determined to pluck as many lost souls from the fires of hell as possible. On reflection, I suspect that I might have repelled many more than I attracted with my hectoring approach to evangelism, but I meant well – I think ...

A Christian girl called Marian also came along to The Cavern fairly regularly, and it was from her that I first heard about 'tongues', this strange gift, mentioned in the New Testament in some detail, which apparently enabled those who had received it to speak in languages they had never learned. With the crassness of youth, I asked Marian if she would give some of us a demonstration of her gift and, with great courage, because she was actually a very shy girl, she did. A little circle of us, Christians and non-Christians (the latter even more bewildered than I was, of course), sat in a back room and waited expectantly for the 'magic' to begin. Marian asked the Holy Spirit to help her, and then started to speak softly in something that certainly sounded to my ears like a completely different language.

I don't know how anyone else reacted to what they heard on that winter evening in Sevenoaks, but I was fascinated and deeply excited. It was my first real intimation that God could be present in the lives of his followers in a much more immediate way than I had ever imagined. On investigating (that means I read about it) the scriptural basis for such things, I was even more enthralled to discover that 'tongues' appeared to be the *least* of the gifts, and that we were exhorted by Paul to ask even more earnestly for the gift of prophecy, which would be vitally useful to the whole body of the church. I started to visit a local Pentecostal church in the mornings, as well as continuing to attend Evensong at my usual Anglican church, so that I could see gifts being used in the services.

In the course of the next year I started to speak in tongues myself, although, try as I might, I cannot recall a specific moment when this began. I found and still find this gift richly valuable in my private prayer, as it seems to excavate love and longing from the depths of my psyche, but – let me be absolutely honest with you – for a long time I felt a tinge of doubt about the whole business. Was my tongue really a tongue, or was I kidding myself? Was it just a meaningless babble that made me feel a bit better?

Then, one Tuesday evening, four or five years ago, something happened. The Bible study group which Bridget and I were leading at the time had been listening to a visiting speaker who had come with his wife. After the talk, which was excellent, a member of the group asked about the gift of tongues, and was prayed for by our visitor with no immediately apparent result.

I was feeling very uneasy. I had almost never spoken in tongues in front of anyone before and, unlike my old friend Marian, I didn't have the courage to volunteer a demonstration now, good idea though it might well have been. As soon as I could decently do it, I began one of those comfortable mopping-up prayers that always precede the coffee and biscuits. Imagine my horror when the prayer that I had begun in English moved seamlessly into being the most fluent tongue that I had ever heard coming out of my own mouth. When I finished, our visiting speaker's wife interpreted the message (interpretation being another distinct gift, of course), although I registered nothing of what she said, and I had to sit down as I was feeling rather shaky. You just can't trust God at all, can you?

I greatly value these experiences, but I would like to be absolutely clear about where I stand on this matter. Many, if not most, followers of Jesus have never spoken and will never speak in tongues. The Bible teaches that this, the least of the gifts, is not in any sense an essential part of Christian experience, whatever some misguided teachers might suggest.

Having said that, why shouldn't we ask Jesus to give us as many gifts as will be useful to us and to the churches where we worship? Whether it's tongues or teaching, hospitality or healing, each one is valuable, and God is a generous giver to those who are ready to gratefully receive.

23

I Follow Jesus Because ...

He Truly Understands What Being Part of a Human Family Means

There was one week last year when two apparently uncon-
nected but significant events occurred. The first was the
birth of Thomas Patrick McCusker, and the second was the
departure of the priest in charge of our church.

A few years ago I collaborated on a book with Paul McCusker,
an experienced American writer who has been extremely successful in the United States in the field of radio drama. Our jointly
written book, *You Say Tomato*, is a collection of fictional letters
exchanged by George, an Englishman, and Brad, an American.
We wrote the book in three weeks, sitting at our individual word
processors in a rented cottage near Hailsham, finding the process stressful, combative and fascinating. The result, published
in 1995, was greeted in America and England with resounding
puzzlement, positive appreciation and silence. Paul can't have
found this unusual experience too negative, because later he and
his wife Elizabeth moved to England, where they now live in the
same town as us.

Thomas Patrick, their first-born, arrived at half past eight one
Friday evening, and we first saw him on the following day.

There is, of course, an important ritual to be observed with new babies. First, you ask about the birth weight. If it was more than eight pounds you utter a gasp of approval. If the little scrap was at the lower end of the scale you sigh fondly. Thomas Patrick emerged weighing six pounds six ounces, a weight which leaves one rather dumb. Bridget and I still felt vaguely obligated to respond rapturously, but it would have sounded odd to say with enormous enthusiasm, 'Gosh! Six pounds six ounces! That's – that's really, amazingly average, isn't it? Wow!'

Fortunately, Tommy himself was enough to produce genuine rapture. We're suckers for babies, and this one, besides being nothing more than an alimentary canal in a bag, like all babies, was beautiful. The sight of him triggered part two of the ritual. Which parent did he most resemble, and which features provided the clues? No room for debate there. If a fierce, head-shrinking South American tribe had blow-piped Paul in the Amazon forest one day, removed his head, taken it back to camp and reduced it to a third of its original size, the face on it would have been exactly the same as Tommy's. That baby was the image of his father. You could see it in the eyes, the mouth, and – to be noted with gentle sadness – the ears.

What has this to do with our minister moving on?

At a party held for the aforesaid minister and his family a couple of days later, we discussed which of Jeremy's many qualities as a priest had been most appreciated. The one that sprang to my mind was his habit of producing little nuggets of original thought in sermons, nuggets that I always tucked away at the back of my mind for possible use in my writing. Often these little gems were throw-away comments, things that we shameless, vulture-like scribblers leap upon and consume with hasty relish.

On this farewell evening, probably because of Tommy, I remembered Jeremy saying that, as well as having the spiritual characteristics of his heavenly Father, Jesus must also have inherited physical features from Mary, his mother. This self-evident fact had never occurred to me and after rolling it around my mind I stored it away, filed in my imagination, as it were, under 'Nose'.

Thinking about Tommy and Mary and Jesus provoked one of those chewy questions that are exciting because they force me into producing an answer, or at least a guess, in the form of poetry, story or drama.

When Mary first saw the resurrected Jesus, did she consciously or unconsciously check that the little parts of him inherited from her were still intact? We shall never know on this side of the grave, of course. One day we can ask Mary herself, but, in the meantime, isn't it interesting to conjecture?

Those real-life, legendary, famous men
Who ate the Sabbath corn with him a thousand puzzled
    memories ago
Are far more confident today
They play their humble trumpets in the market place
Clarion the truth
How Jesus was and is the image of his Father
Full of love and grace and truth
And yes, of course – of course he was and is his Father's
    son
The Holy One, the Saviour
Yes, of course
And yet, you know, that baby, once so closely mine
That baby who became a boy, a man, and much, much
    more
Inherited from me the things my mother's heart loved
    best
His nose
His ears
That way he had of lifting up his chin when the road
    was getting rough
Such special joy to see those sweet, sweet things all risen
    with the rest
Not much perhaps, but privately, for me – enough.

I wonder what Jesus and his mum talk about nowadays.

24

I Follow Jesus Because ...

He's Kinder and More Merciful Than Those Who Have Done Dreadful Things in His Name during the Last 2,000 Years

I started to cry as I watched the television one night. This sudden descent into tears was not because the quality of the programme that happened to be on at the time was so poor, but rather because the events depicted in this particular episode of *Cadfael* made me remember, with a sudden overwhelming rush of feeling, how deeply attracted I am by the mercy and kindness of God.

Cadfael, a fictional but beautifully drawn character created by the writer Ellis Peters, is a highly intelligent, sensitive monk who specializes in solving mediaeval murder mysteries. As you probably know, the *Cadfael* books are immensely popular, as is the television series of the same name starring Derek Jacobi, for my money one of the finest stage and screen actors of his generation.

In the episode that affected me so much, Cadfael was

investigating two deaths, one that of a rather satisfyingly growly and unpleasant monk who had recently arrived to take up the position of Prior at the monastery in which the story was set, and the other a single girl who had become pregnant by an unknown man. This young girl had approached the new Prior seeking confession and absolution for her sin, but had been cruelly repulsed and branded an evil woman. All the evidence available to Cadfael suggested that, in response to this rejection, she had committed lonely suicide by casting herself into a millstream that ran behind the Priory.

At the point of history in which *Cadfael* is set, suicide was regarded by the church as a mortal sin. Those who successfully sought such a cataclysmic escape from their problems were invariably buried in unconsecrated ground and reckoned to have certainly forfeited their salvation. Cadfael's hope was that by discovering she had in fact been murdered, he might ensure that her body would receive Christian burial.

Now, I'm afraid that's about as much of the storyline as I can share with you, not because I'm worried about spoiling it for you if you see it one day, but simply because I have never in my life understood more than about a tenth of what's going on in *any* whodunit that I have ever read or watched. I enjoy them, you understand, but my brain is simply not up to following the twists and turns of the plot. Even when I watch *Columbo*, perhaps my favourite detective series of all, where in every single episode you *know* who did it from the very start, I'm in a complete fog from beginning to end.

From out of the fog on this *Cadfael* occasion came two things that made me tearful.

The first was a moment when another monk from the monastery declared loudly that the pregnant girl had been nothing but a useless whore, and Cadfael said with a mixture of quiet indignation and sorrow, almost to himself, 'She wasn't a whore, she was a child.'

The second was an incident at the very end of the episode, after it had been clearly proved that the young expectant mother had indeed taken her own life, as had originally been assumed. Going out secretly to the place where her body lay in unconsecrated ground, Cadfael buried a little crucifix on a chain in the freshly turned earth of her grave.

Tears filled my eyes. Perhaps you will think me foolish, but I don't really care. Those two moments reminded me with an extraordinary power and abruptness that the God whom we try to serve is far more compassionate than most of his followers, let alone his opponents. We all fall woefully short of the ideal, and we thank God for Jesus who forgives sin and binds up the brokenhearted and understands and allows us to begin again.

In a very different work, *Three Men in a Boat*, written around the turn of the century, Jerome K. Jerome describes how he and his friends discover a young woman's corpse in the river, and learn later that, having given birth out of wedlock, she became so oppressed by poverty and loneliness that she ended her own life.

'She had sinned,' says Jerome. 'Some of us do that now and then, you know ...'

Well, yes, we jolly well do, and most of us know well enough what we've done without having our noses rubbed in it by the sort of tight-lipped harbingers of doom who have hurt so many Christians who were already hurting more than they could imagine. Thank God Jesus is in charge.

As I watched *Cadfael* I found myself thanking God that all through history there have been people who, often against the spirit of the age or the spiritual fashion, really are inhabited by the sweet Spirit of Jesus, that Spirit who never compromises, but is always ready to forgive and embrace those who have been cast out by men but are still able to turn to him. Thank God for those people who keep alive the essential truth that God is wise and warm and sane and adult and understanding and forgiving and

298

full of divine common sense, because they are the people who show the Saviour to the world.

Don't laugh. I know it was only a fictional programme, but God created television as well as everything else, and on that particular evening, he used it.

25

I Follow Jesus Because ...

He Values Everyone Equally and Is Teaching Me to Do the Same

This is the story of how a journey into the past affected the present.

My father-in-law, who has lived in Norwich since before Bridget was born, celebrated his ninetieth birthday by spending a week in the beautiful county of Lancashire where he was born and raised in the early part of this century. My wife's brother and sister-in-law and their two children joined the whole of our family for this significant event, the mark of a long life which, in its own way, is a powerful advertisement for moderation.

Bridget's father, George Ormerod, who was employed as a clerk in one of our major High Street banks for the whole of his working life, has been quite immoderately committed to moderation for the whole of his 90 years, and therefore leads a more exciting life than anybody else I know. This is bound to be so when *everything* unexpected is an adventure. On those rare occasions, for instance, when an unscheduled visitor knocks on the door of the Ormerod home in Norwich, life moves swiftly into *Raiders of the Lost Ark* mode as George half-rises worriedly from the chair in which he always sits, nervously conjecturing about who could possibly be disturbing the pattern of his normal life in such a dramatic fashion.

He has eaten exactly the same healthy combination of things at breakfast-time for as long as anyone who knows him can remember, chewing each mouthful of food the same number of times, exactly as he was instructed to do as a boy, and he never eats between meals, except at Christmas, when a discreet sweet and a very small glass from the bottle of liqueur that has already lasted for three years are entirely permissible, because they are tiny but unvarying details in the overall moderate pattern.

Over the years George has enjoyed visits from his son and daughter and their families, although the healthily anarchic tendencies of our respective children have disturbed and confused him from time to time. One of the most fascinating aspects of George's fanatical drive to avoid excess has been his quite amazing ability simply to avoid seeing those things that blatantly deny his perception of his own attitudes and habits. Sometimes, for example, the children will turn the television on in Nanna and Grandpa's house and a situation comedy will be announced.

'Oh,' says Grandpa uneasily, as the opening music is heard and the titles appear, 'we never watch this. We don't find it funny.'

Throughout the programme (which Nanna insists on allowing because the children enjoy it), George guffaws and chortles with laughter at the jokes, clearly enjoying every minute. As the credits come up at the end, however, he shakes his head and announces once again to the world at large, without any trace of self-consciousness, 'We never watch that programme, you know. We don't find it funny.'

One of the major benefits of this very regular way of life, apart from the constant excitement, of course, is that George is extremely fit for a man of his age. A little more wheezy than in the past, perhaps, but still able to enjoy not only regular swimming sessions at a local pool, but also those evenly paced walks that have been a favourite habit since he first met his wife on a walking holiday in the Lake District before the war. For nine decades, George has been going 'steadily on', as he puts it, and, at the time of writing, there's no visible reason why he shouldn't go 'steadily on' for another 10 years and reach the century that, as an ex-cricketer, would greatly appeal to him.

Relations between my father-in-law and I were, you won't be surprised to hear, more than a little strained when we first met. I was about as far from being moderate as it's possible to be. Poor George must have felt that his only daughter was being swept up into some kind of emotional and social 'twister' that would inevitably leave her damaged and disappointed. It took many years for him to understand and accept that Bridget has a tendency towards doing a spot of twisting of her own, and that we have always hung onto each other in the centre of the storm.

I have had to do some understanding and accepting as well. As a child of the '60s, I wore contempt for what I thought of as the stuffy old previous generation like a cheap badge. I was unthinkingly intolerant and scornful of those who appeared reluctant to explore extremities of experience in the way that 'free spirits' like me were prepared to do. What did a career matter? What did money matter? What did the future matter? Why should we be concerned about such trivial issues? Those were the sorts of intelligent thing that I was saying. George must have been utterly bewildered by me and my unexpected intrusion into his family. As far as my future father-in-law was concerned, an alien had landed and communication was a problem, to say the least. Now, I can understand why it was so difficult for him, and trips like the one we made to Clitheroe, his home town, have deepened that understanding.

The part of northern England where George grew up was cotton country, a region where hundreds of mills turned out cotton for markets all over the world. In those days it would have been reckoned more or less inevitable that George should go into that same trade, just as many members of his family had done before him. Instead, young George Ormerod, a mild, undemonstrative lad with a rather attractive blue-eyed smile, brought up in a house where the atmosphere was permanently hushed because of his mother's chronic illness, and with a record of considerable academic ability at school, managed to secure a job at the bank in Blackburn at the age of 15. At that time, and in that part of the world, this was a considerable achievement. It was a breaking away from what was expected, an opportunity to move upwards and onwards, a chance for George to really build a future for himself. Nowadays, it doesn't seem like much, but then, in the early 1920s, it was quite something. George was a child of the '20s.

While we were in Clitheroe on this occasion we drove past the small, stone-built house where George was brought up, and parked beside the cricket pitch on the other side of the road, where, in the recently modernized pavilion, we found an old black-and-white photograph of the Clitheroe cricket team of 74 years ago. The picture showed not only the 11 members of the team, but also the scorer, G. T. Ormerod, 15 years old, smiling nervously but proudly at the camera from his humble position behind the heroes of the side.

George went on to play for and captain one of the Clitheroe teams, and he also became superintendent of the children's Sunday School at his church, a massive responsibility in those days, when large numbers of children attended every week. All in all he was an involved and integrated member of his community, a person who did things and went to things and belonged.

I don't suppose George and I would ever have been soulmates exactly, but my early negative feelings have given way to a realisation that his humanity is, in the context of his own growing-up and development, as rich with the stuff of life as anyone else's, including mine. I trust that he has adjusted his view of me as well.

May Jesus help us all to avoid falling into the trap of believing that any other person is automatically worth less than us because the way they are, or the way they have lived, is beyond our understanding and experience. We shall all be making the same journey home in the end, so we might as well start learning to understand and appreciate each other now.

26

I Follow Jesus Because ...

He's Not Meteorologically Selective

Do you have faith in the weather forecast? Agnostic? Nonbeliever? Recent convert? Follower of the great prophet Fish?

Believe it or not, but I have detected a most interesting link between the way in which television weather forecasts are delivered in this country and the problems that many Christians have with understanding the place of suffering in their lives. Now, don't flick on to the next section. I know it's an unlikely connection, but read on.

First, let's just reflect on how this sort of programme has altered over the last few years. There was a time when weather forecasts had a narrowly defined function – namely, to forecast the weather. Crudely simple, eh? A smartly respectable, inexpensively suited gentleman with a vaguely scientific air would apologetically suggest the kind of weather we might possibly experience during the next 24 hours. Having delivered his faltering prediction, this prophetic rabbit would dive back into the meteorological burrow from which he had emerged, and not reappear until another forecast was due. He was never right, of course, but that in itself was most helpful when planning activities. If the expert proclaimed that the weekend was going to be cold and wet, we dug out the suntan oil and headed for the beach. If he said it was going to be warm and sunny, we ordered in an extra load of coal and got angry because someone had pinched the dice from the Monopoly set.

Nowadays, weather forecasts bristle with high-tech gadgets and snappy little cartoon-like symbols, and are almost always delivered by young, beautiful people who wouldn't know a warm front from a deep depression, but see pop-meteorology as a handy backdoor entrance to fame and fortune. Indeed, one or two of these incredibly white-toothed, professionally engaging men and women have actually gone on to minor stardom in isobar-free areas of entertainment.

One consequence of this changed style has been a tendency on the part of the forecasters to inject personal bias into what they say. Thus we have acquired a whole new set of values for each type of weather, largely based on the way in which Bright Young Things tend to see the world.

Rain, for instance, is always bad, despite the fact that, for excellent and obvious reasons, it's actually very good. 'Bad news, I'm afraid. We're in for a few showers,' says a Bright Young Thing sadly, dismissing our forthcoming copious supplies of a substance that some people value beyond gold. Bright Young Things have no use for rain. Call me weird, but I'm so glad that we get lots of rain, and I *love* walking in it.

Sunshine is always, always good. 'I'm pleased to say that I can promise you some sunshine!' trills the B.Y.T. chirpily. I agree that sunshine is very often good, but an unrelieved diet of sunny days would bore me stiff. Like Chesterton, I can enjoy all weather except what the English call a 'Glorious Day'.

Snow is always bad if it stops you getting to the wine bar from the studio, but it's allowed to be good if it falls in places where the Bright Young Things are hoping to ski at the weekend.

And so on, and so on. Day by day, bit by bit, a whole generation of telly-watching kids has been taught to celebrate the sun and rage against the rain.

Now, leaving aside your growing and ludicrous conviction that I'm actually talking about my own resentment at being dull and middle-aged instead of bright and young, there's a parallel here with the kind of teaching on suffering that the church has mistakenly offered over the last 20 years. Perhaps because we Western Christians are always trying – albeit unconsciously – to justify the luxury of our lifestyle, there has been a tendency to teach that the rain of suffering is a sign of spiritual weakness or inadequacy, whereas the sunshine of health and prosperity is an indication that God is smiling on us.

I regard this as dangerous nonsense.

A cursory reading of the Gospels makes it plain that this isn't the case at all. Jesus clearly warned his disciples to expect some very tough times indeed. 'If you think I've had it difficult, wait until you see what happens to you,' might be a rough but fairly accurate paraphrase of his words to that little band of followers, who really hadn't the faintest idea what he was talking about at the time. Later, they knew.

I don't mean that we have to like bad things happening to us. Jesus wasn't a loony and he doesn't expect us to be either, but our very right to go home to God was bought with the most significant act of suffering in the history of our planet. I don't think we should despise our suffering. I think we should offer our pain to God and tell him to do what he likes with it. We may be amazed.

Having said all that, what really happens when the crunch comes and we're right in the middle of genuine agony? The book of James instructs us to regard all trials and difficulties as pure joy. Help! What sense does that make in the real world?

This stark question takes me back to a time when I had cracked or broken one of my ribs. Stepping into the shower one day, I slipped on the bottom of the bath and fell backwards, hitting the right side of my upper back on the rim of the bath

307

with a sickening crunch. Those who have seen me in the flesh (evil word!) will know just what a crunch that must have been. Remembering that injunction from jolly old James, I obediently sang a bright little chorus of appreciation as I was in the act of falling, and celebrated the impact itself with a loud 'whoop!' of pure joy.

The whole of the previous sentence is, I humbly confess, totally and outrageously untrue – but isn't it interesting how many things do go through one's mind during that short, dramatic, involuntary journey from the vertical to the horizontal? In an oddly dispassionate, detached sort of way, I recall finding myself thinking about the implications of the fall – mine I mean, not the one that has slightly more profound theological implications – even as I descended. Would I be injured so badly, I wondered, that Bridget would have to get help to remove my naked body from the bathroom? Please, God, let it *not* be so. Would it be necessary to go down to the accident and emergency department of our local hospital? If so, would they admit me for a night or more, and how many of my engagements would be affected as a consequence? Might I be so seriously hurt that my general mobility would be reduced for the rest of my life? Had I damaged the bath? By the time I actually hit the side of the bath I seemed to have thought the whole thing through quite thoroughly. It hardly seemed worth the bother of actually landing.

As it happened, I was immobilized to the extent that I had to cancel a whole month of speaking appointments, and, as day after day of stillness passed, I developed a deep sympathy for those whose pain is chronic and incurable. Inevitably I was also drawn once more into this consideration of the meaning and significance of suffering in the lives of Christians, not least because I had a very particular and accessible case to study – my own. I had always adhered to the view that suffering is by no means an exclusively negative experience for those who wish to follow Jesus. To what extent was that really true in my own immediate circumstances? Did the 'pure joy' principle mean anything at all? I examined the evidence.

First of all, there was the fact that, to all intents and purposes, I was anchored to one end of the sofa that stood against the wall in our sitting room. One corner of this specific piece of furniture was, for reasons that I didn't quite understand, the only place in the house where I was able to experience reasonable comfort for the first week or two of my injury. Since I was unable to lie down at all, that same corner was also the place where I slept at night in a sitting position, but only for smallish chunks of time. Occasionally, when I was awake, I used my remote control device to surf through the endless Sky channels on television, seeking company from flickering screen images through the long watches of the night. In the early hours of the morning I was sometimes confronted by wild-eyed, ranting evangelists. I owe a great debt to these men. The therapy they offered was immensely effective. Emotions of anger reminded me that I was still alive and reacting to things, a very good thing for one who is obliged to remain virtually motionless.

Was this enforced anchorage a negative aspect of what happened to me? Well, yes, but not as far as my 10-year-old daughter was concerned. Katy just *loved* having her daddy pinned down to one near-permanent spot. She knew exactly where I was at any given point during the night or day. When she went to bed, there I was on the end of the sofa. When she got up and came down in the morning, there I was on the end of the sofa. She set off for school leaving me on the sofa; she returned to find me in exactly the same place. I became a sort of 'pet daddy', a large, uncaged hamster, always available to cuddle, or talk to, or ask for money. She really enjoyed it and so, I must admit, did I. Perhaps I should have realized long before then how positively my children would benefit from seeing me sit still for a while.

Then there was the fact that I was unable to do any work that involved travelling. At first that certainly seemed a 100 per cent, definite, cast-iron, indisputable negative, but after a couple of weeks I wasn't so sure. In the fortnight following my last meeting before getting crocked I received so many visitors who really only needed the ear of someone who had enough time on his hands to hear them out. These people most decidedly did not come because they knew I was stranded at home for a while. Rather, it was as if some kind of vacuum had been created by my inactivity, allowing those with troubled hearts to flow in and fill the space. Most importantly, perhaps, very close friends who lived nearby and had hit a very rough patch in their lives at this particular time desperately needed help and support in carrying their burdens. I thank God that, inadequate as I was, I was able to be there for them. Positive wins again.

What about sheer physical discomfort? Am I about to claim that excruciating pain proved, against all reasonable expectations, to be really rather jolly? No, I make no such claim, for the simple reason that it wasn't the case. The pain was awful, and would have been worse if it hadn't been for the use of powerful painkillers prescribed by my doctor. (You may be interested to learn, by the way, that the label on the bottle containing these tablets conveyed a stern warning that drowsiness might occur, and that it would therefore be unwise for me to operate agricultural machinery. Can you begin to picture the inner battles I fought and won to resist my natural inclination to operate agricultural machinery at every opportunity?) No, the pain was horrible, but, as I have already mentioned, my sympathy for folk who are never likely to see an end to their suffering deepened with every day that brought me nearer to relief and healing. I thank God for that as well.

Speaking of God – did he do it? Did God, out of the goodness of his heart, hide in the bathroom and pop out to give me a little shove as I was about to step into the shower, knowing that all the aforementioned subtle benefits would accrue to me if I broke a rib? Or might it conceivably have been the devil who did the shoving, hoping to drive me into a position where, just as he had vainly hoped with Job, I would wail and complain about the unfair way in which my creator had used me? Or could it possibly be that the absence of an anti-slip mat on the bottom of the bath, an omission I should have rectified ages ago, was the main reason for my accident? I don't pretend to know the final answers to such questions, but I must confess that the last one, deeply mystical as it is, seems the most likely to me.

Whatever the truth may be, I'm sure of one thing – and herein lies the 'pure joy' that really might underlie and contain all misfortunes – I'm sure that God is in charge and that he loves us. Whether he causes situations of this kind, or whether he simply uses them, we can be certain that, in the most important sense, we're perfectly safe.

Just occasionally, you know, even as I sat nursing my injury, the knowledge of his caring parenthood made me want to laugh out loud. I didn't give in to the temptation because it would have made my ribs hurt.

27

I Follow Jesus Because ...

He Brings Something Good out of the Most (Apparently) Awful Events

Early one morning that phone of mine rang. I have very mixed feelings about the sound of a ringing telephone, don't you? When I'm expecting good news it's a sweet, hopeful sound, whereas, when it rings in the middle of the night, when no one should be calling anyone else, my heart sinks in anticipation of some terrible information flying into my life like a missile to destroy sleep and peace. Or it might be an Australian. The rest of the time – well, I suppose that shrill call to communication is a neutral sound, until you pick up the receiver, that is.

The ring I'm talking about was from a man calling to say that a friend of ours had died in the early hours of the morning after a fall in her house the day before. My wife and I knew that Shelagh had been injured, but, as far as we were aware, she had simply banged her head after tripping on the stairs, and we assumed that she would recover after appropriate treatment. After all, we had seen her only a few days ago, and she was as right as rain. I now learned that this fall down the stairs had caused internal bleeding, which, despite an emergency operation, ultimately proved to be fatal.

How silly and trivial the causes of death appear sometimes. Somebody knocks on your front door, you hurry to the stairs to go down and let them in, your foot slips on the carpet, you fall awkwardly and suddenly the whole thing is over. No more questions, no more conversations, no more prayer, no more sips of wine, no more love or anger or tiredness or elation – not in this world, at any rate. How was it possible for someone who had been so whole and complex and human to be gone so completely? There are no degrees of death, are there? You can't be fairly dead, or very dead indeed, or less dead in comparison with someone else. You're just dead, and there's an end of it.

Shelagh, a single lady, was a Christian, a firm believer in the living Jesus – he who just that morning had received her with great joy even as we were releasing her from the landscape of our minds with such sorrow. She was a priest in the Anglican church, a writer of some accomplishment, and the editor of *New Daylight*, a booklet of daily Bible notes published by the Bible Reading Fellowship, which appears at four-monthly intervals and is read all over the world. Each edition features contributions from several writers, of whom I'm privileged to be one.

Some editors of Bible note collections are almost destructively censorious towards the work of their contributors. One well-known writer who's involved with a different publisher told my wife the other day that she had to search carefully through the printed sections that bore her name to find some trace of the pieces that she had originally written. This wasn't Shelagh's style at all. She was insistent that the very varied personalities of her team members should be allowed to give flavour and interest to the notes they wrote, so that, like the prophets of the Old Testament (I should be so lucky!), each one might emphasize a different facet or attribute of the nature of God. Shelagh's view appeared to be, 'If God isn't ashamed to be closely associated with Adrian Plass, then neither am I.'

It will take me a long time to get used to the fact that Shelagh is no longer with us, and a lot of people will miss her very much.

So, what is it possible for the Holy Spirit to teach us from what many regarded as the untimely death of this individual Christian person? Well, let me begin by saying that I meet quite a lot of vicars and church leaders who have lost heart or become worried because congregations are not as co-operative as they were, because there seems far too much work to do for one man or woman, and because the changing, evolving world threatens to overtake and engulf their role in society. I think the problem is a universal one, but let's not lose heart.

Here are some things that, through the death of Shelagh, have been brought into my mind.

First, the human being to whom she owes the greatest debt of all is that person who led her to a belief in Jesus many years ago. When the chips are down (an old theological expression), all that matters is the future of our eternal souls. We don't want to die the second death, as it's called in the book of Revelation, and it's because of vicars and church leaders all over the world that people like Shelagh walk straight into the arms of Jesus when their mortal bodies cease to function. They will live for ever because they belong to him. Church leaders shouldn't despise or lose sight of their high calling as harvesters for the Lord. The world is never going to evolve into a place where eternal life is no longer an issue. They are the guardians of this knowledge. They should be proud in the best sense, and pray for chances to lead others to the one who feels such compassion for those who live in ignorance.

Secondly, I think of Shelagh's passion for the personality of God to be expressed in different ways through the variety of people who wrote for *New Daylight*. God isn't calling leaders to produce a group of people who are all exactly the same. They're agents of divine freedom, that freedom which allows followers of Jesus to be extravagantly authentic versions of themselves. God isn't interested in religious conformity, or safe and stolid Christianity. He wants followers who will dive into the deep water of faith like babies who have never had drowning explained to them. There's nothing wrong with allowing folk to thrash about and make mistakes as they learn to swim. Rather, we should celebrate the profound truth expressed in the thirty-second verse of the eighth chapter of the Gospel of John and pass it on with joy to our congregations, praying that they will be submissive to Christ only.

Thirdly, I think of Shelagh's openness to advice and guidance from others. Is it possible, dear one-man-band ministers, for you to become just a little more vulnerable to those whom you serve? When I first began to speak to groups of Christians, I assumed it was essential for me to keep my problems entirely to myself, so that God would be given a 'good reference' whenever I spoke about him. Then, one day, when I was supposed to be delivering a talk on parenting, I confessed that I had been shouting at my children for 24 hours and that my wife and I were not speaking because of an argument on the way to the conference. I thought the audience would walk out in disgust, but the opposite happened. They were released to talk about their own family problems, which was, of course, the reason they had come to the seminar in the first place. There's something very intimidating about being addressed by perfect beings. If you're weary and failing because you feel unsupported, try telling people. It may be embarrassing, but it may also change your ministry.

Finally, my dear fellow lovers of Jesus who aren't ministers, can we try to be gentle with those who carry the burden of being signposts to heaven for us? There are no sinless human beings remaining since Jesus returned to his Father, and church leaders have no special dispensation in this area. In fact, the Bible tells us that they are to be judged more strictly than others because theirs is such a great responsibility. If somebody in our church offers us a criticism of the minister, how about resolving to answer it with a positive comment? We certainly won't be thanked for ruining the 'gossip game', but we will at least have supported the person who, contrary to what many worshippers think, is often the most easily hurt member of the congregation.

My friend has gone to be with Jesus, but we must continue with the work that we're doing here. May the inspiration of those who have, like Shelagh, done their best and departed to Paradise sustain and strengthen us in our resolve to seek the kingdom of God above all things, both for ourselves and for others.

28

I Follow Jesus Because ...

I Don't Want to Get Stuck or Left behind in Someone Else's Camp

Do you belong to a Christian camp? Keep that question in the back of your mind while I ask you another. What do you like doing best?

One of my favourite activities in all the world is to be with other Christians (preferably ones who are unlikely to start spraying condemnation or ministry around too freely), just nattering and gossiping about God. The wonderful thing about such encounters, whether they happen in a church or a pub or a car or a walk in the country or around a kitchen table, is that they become a kind of prayer in themselves. It's strange and significant, isn't it, that some of the most profoundly spiritual moments of our lives tend to be dismissed as merely secular events. It has taken me most of my 51 years on earth to understand that God finds arthritically religious activities as abominable as I do – almost certainly more so.

I remember, for instance, an evening when three of us met at a friend's house to eat a supper of bread and cheese and wine, and to engage in exactly the kind of nattering and gossiping that I have already mentioned. These two friends of mine are elders in a lively church in the local seaside town of Eastbourne, one that my family and I don't attend. We know each other very well, though, having met socially on as regular a basis as possible for the last 11 or 12 years. In the course of those many meetings we must have discussed everything under the sun, including just about every aspect of the faith we share. Nevertheless, because of the way the Holy Spirit is, and because of the way good friends are, there's always something new to talk about, especially when there are no silly restrictions on subject matter, and no negative kneejerk reactions to unpalatable truths.

The occasion in question was a little different. All three of us had been nursing a growing feeling that we would like our meetings to have a slightly more specifically religious seal set upon them, but none of us quite knew how this should be done. James, who was our host on this occasion, suggested that we should hold a little private Communion at the beginning or end of each meeting, and at first this seemed a very good idea. A few minutes of structure and formality would just about fit the bill, we reckoned, lending, as such an arrangement surely must, a reassuringly spiritual authenticity to our gatherings.

I can't tell you how glad I was that we abandoned this idea in the end. Almost simultaneously the three of us realized that our motivation for seeking ceremony and form was based much more on fear and the need for a feeling of worldly security than on any spiritual instinct. The desire and drive within human beings to make camp, to build a home, to establish a base, is so strong that it can easily be mistaken for Christian common sense, and end up ruining a God-given situation in which we have found ourselves riskily, excitingly, disturbingly, usefully free. The itch that James and Ben and I had actually been attempting to scratch was a vague feeling that, if we weren't some kind of recognizable *churchy thing*, we didn't really exist in the eyes of God.

I would hate you to misunderstand me. I love the Communion service. It's part of my joy and my duty and my life. Similarly, I love the church in Hailsham of which I'm a member. I want and need to belong to it. A church doesn't have to be a camp. But if, at some point in the future, those activities and that community were to stop being a caravan and become a settlement, I might have to move on, because I want to follow Jesus, and I feel a new gratitude that God has given me my two friends to accompany me on these very special occasions as I trudge along behind him.

This issue was highlighted for me a few days later when I met a man (let's call him Derek) who for some years had been an important figure in one of the largest and best known church communities in Great Britain. He described to me his feelings when, after being one of the founder members of the church and serving as an elder during the crucial years of its development, he found himself 'sidelined' for reasons that were as flimsy as they were cruel.

'To be honest, Adrian,' he said, 'I feel as if I've been dumped outside the camp, and that's a very lonely place to be.'

'There is no camp, Derek,' I said, 'and if there is, I offer you my congratulations on getting out of it. Jesus still walks the road ahead of us, just as he led his disciples 2,000 years ago, and we're still called to trudge along behind him, talking nonsense and doing what we're told, just as they did. If some people want to stop following him and make a nice tidy camp by the road-side – well, that's their business. We must walk on, because we never were supposed to have anywhere to lay our heads, and we won't have, not this side of heaven. I understand how hurt you feel, but I reckon you're in the right place.'

After that, I'm glad to say, there seemed to be a new spring in Derek's spiritual step.

As for James and Ben and me, well, we have agreed that our meetings will now begin with a prayer in which we offer *every-thing* that's said and done and eaten and drunk and thought to God. Apart from that, though, nothing will alter our regular trudge unless the suggestion for change comes from the Holy Spirit. Our most fervent prayer as the years go by is that our feet will hold out, our ears will stay tuned, and we will continue excitedly to follow the truth.

29

I Follow Jesus Because...

He Doesn't Ask Me to Adapt as Much as Saint John of the Cross Would Have Had to If He'd Been Booked to Address the West Fittlewick Over-Sixties Interdenominational Ladies' Afternoon Club at Three O'clock on a Wet Thursday Afternoon in November

Would it surprise you to learn that, every now and then, I complain about certain aspects of my life? No, I didn't think it would. I've been much too honest in this book. I sense that the stage of being seen as endearingly vulnerable has passed. You just expect the worst now, don't you? Oh well, never mind.

Yes, sometimes I do complain, and recently my complaints have been about the extraordinary degree of on-the-spot adaptation required for various speaking engagements. When I'm not feeling tired or sad, I actively enjoy the process of selecting the next piece of material even as I'm in the middle of delivering the present one, but it can be very hard going at other times.

In this connection I do have to confess that at first a little resentment crept in when I thought about spiritual communicators of the past. How would they have coped? Take Saint John of the Cross, for instance. A great thinker, writer and man of God, naturally, but if he had ever made the foolish mistake of getting himself booked to address the West Fittlewick Over-Sixties Interdenominational Ladies' Afternoon Club at three o'clock on a wet Thursday afternoon in November, might he not have given up mysticism altogether and run away to join the circus? I think he would, don't you?

I mean, just allow your imagination to picture the scene for a moment. A grave, bearded figure, dressed in the monk-like costume of his own era, gets off the bus just outside West Fittlewick village hall and arrives 15 minutes early, as arranged, to be greeted at the door by Mrs Stamford-Jones, the club president. Ushering him through the porch and into the body of the hall, she whispers with chatty confidentiality in his left ear.

'Word to the wise, Saint John – may I call you Saint John, or do you prefer Mr Cross? – some of our more elderly ladies will more than likely drop off after about 10 minutes, or start needing the – you know – the facilities, so if you could speak up nice and loud and cheerful and keep it to no more than about 15 minutes, that would be lovely. And then we all have tea. To be quite honest,' she giggles a little, 'our ladies really look forward to that more than anything. And we've allocated a nice piece of cake for you, so don't worry.'

Several minutes after this inspirational first encounter, it's time for the public introduction. Mrs Stamford-Jones rises to her feet and clears her throat. Saint John of the Cross, strangely unreassured by the fact that a nice piece of cake has been allocated to him, shifts wretchedly and uneasily on an orange plastic chair, his thoughts already straying to the attractive prospect of high-trapeze work or lion-taming.

'Right, ladies, let's make a start, shall we? *Nice* to see so many of you here today – nearly 20 at a quick count – and we do hope those of you who've come for the first time will have a really lovely afternoon and want to come again. Now – last month Mr Simmonds came with his projector to give us slides of West Fittlewick As It Was, and as usual a wonderful time was had by all, as I'm sure we'd all agree, wouldn't we?' Invitational pause. Murmurs and clucks of agreement from the ladies. 'Now, this month we are extremely fortunate to have secured Saint John of the Cross as our speaker for the afternoon, and he has offered to address us on the subject of – ' a glance at her notes, made several weeks ago whilst conversing with the speaker by telephone, ' – on the subject of the Dark Side of the Knoll. Over to you, Saint John.'

She sits amid a patter of applause.

Saint John of the Cross, looking and sounding faintly irritable, half stands, pushes the hair back from his forehead, and addresses the club president *sotto voce*.

'Er, excuse me, sorry, actually it's not the Dark Side of the Knoll. That sounds like the back of some gloomy little hill. It's actually the Dark Night of the Soul.'

Mrs Stamford-Jones, unperturbed and still smiling proprietorially, rises to her feet once more.

'Sorry, everybody, silly me. Right! Saint John of the Cross speaking on the Dark Side of the Soul.'

'No – no, it's not. It's not the Dark *Side* of the Soul, it's the Dark Side of – wait a minute, I can't remember what it is myself now – oh, yes, that's it, it's the Dark Night of the Soul. The Dark Night of the Soul. Right?'

Mrs Stamford-Jones' smile remains intact, if a trifle rigid. Although getting on in years now, she's a retired infant teacher who has dealt with any number of awkward children just like Saint John of the Cross in her classes over the years. She intones with patient precision. 'Saint John of the Cross, speaking on the Dark Night of the Soul.'

Saint John of the Cross opens his mouth to speak.

'Is there slides?' The dispassionate query arises from somewhere in the audience.

'No!' Saint John of the Cross is very close to losing it in a big way. 'No, there is – I mean there *are* no slides. I do not *do* slides! I'm a contemplative and mystic who has been divinely vouchsafed insight into an extremely complex and profound phase in the spiritual development of the Christian soul, and I do not – repeat *not* do slides!'

After a short, shocked pause the dispassionate voice is heard again.

'Ooh – cross by name, cross by nature! It's like that Julian man from East Anglia who turned out to be a woman and come to speak to us last year. Got ratty when I said what she was on about boiled down to all's well that ends well. Not sure I want to do this Dark Noel thing if you end up like this bloke.'

Saint John of the Cross, who now sees his future as one of those clowns with the huge check trousers, big red noses and enormous boots, finds his voice rising to an undignified, hysterical squawk. 'Look, it's not something you *do* like going up the gym! I can't possibly talk about it in 15 minutes. It's a very serious and meaningful state of being, and it involves – oh, what's the use? I'm giving it up anyway. Anyone know where the nearest circus is …?'

No, on reflection, I'm more than content to do the little bit of adapting that I have to. And I do rather like cake.

30

I Follow Jesus Because ...

He's a Stickler
for Accuracy and Truth

One of the most sublime experiences of my whole life was
hearing my wife ask an elderly French farmer whether it
might be possible at some time in the future for her to rent a small
strip of his bedroom. She went on to point out with great earnestness that such an arrangement would cause little inconvenience
because she would ensure that a small but attractive fence was
erected between her section and his. The old Frenchman frowned
and scratched his head in bewilderment at this bizarre proposal,
lacking, as he did, the essential extra item of information that
Bridget, whose French is usually very good (and much better than
mine) had got mixed up between the French words for 'field'
and 'bedroom'. Truth overcoming gallantry compels me to report
that the look of relief on the face of the elderly Frenchman as he
realized that a mistake had been made illuminated his granular
features like the sun coming up over the French Alps.

It's so easy to make mistakes. Here's another example.

Our last minister was about to move on to take up a different
post. An interesting slip of the tongue occurred as he was celebrating his final Holy Communion at the church where Bridget
and I worship. It was rather an emotional occasion, of course, and
I know from personal experience that when an excess of feeling

creeps into any formal proceedings, it's possible to tie oneself in verbal knots with even the most familiar words and phrases. I don't know if I was the only one who noticed this particular example of the genre, but it was, in any case, one of those times when mistakes really don't matter too much.

It happened when the priest was well into that marvellous piece of biblical prose which begins with the words: 'Who in the same night that he was betrayed ...'

The bit about the bread went fine, but after that our beloved leader's concentration must have dipped, because he very seriously intoned the following: 'In the same way, after supper he took the cup and gave you thanks; he broke it and gave it to them, saying, 'Drink this, all of you; this is my blood of the new covenant ...'

All the regulars would have known perfectly well what he meant to say, of course, but any nonreligious stranger who had chanced to wander in might have been just a little puzzled, to say the least. I found myself reflecting on how lucky we are that Jesus himself managed to be word perfect when it came to these crucial, one-off occasions. The parables would have been told over and over again, so there was little chance of later writers going too far wrong with them, but it wasn't as if they had a Penultimate Supper before the Last one, a sort of dress rehearsal for the real thing. It had to be right first time. Just consider, for one moment, the consequences if Jesus had made the same mistake as our minister.

Every Sunday, in churches all over the world, church leaders of every denominational shade and variety would have found themselves breaking little pieces from a chalice cunningly fashioned out of thin biscuit (or chocolate, perhaps?), dropping them into liquid of some sort, then offering them reverently to members of the congregation, so that they could be drunk in their dissolved state as the Scriptures so mysteriously commanded. There might even have developed a schism between those of the chocolate persuasion and those of the biscuit brotherhood, who were unwilling to expose their members to temptation in such a way.

Irreverent fantasy pictures Jesus paying a surprise visit to one of these churches and scratching his head in bewilderment like that old French farmer on witnessing such strange behaviour.

'Excuse me,' he would tentatively enquire, 'I, er, I was just wondering why you use those – those chocolate cups at Communion.'

'Ah,' would come the confident reply, 'because they dissolve better, of course.'

'They dissolve better?'

'Yes, you know you said we should break the cup and drink it – well, this is the easiest way of doing it.'

'I said what? Oh, dear! I'm most awfully sorry. I meant *take* the cup. And you've been ... oh, you haven't, have you? For 2,000 years?'

Son of God collapses in fits of helpless laughter.

A ridiculous scenario? Well, perhaps, but a little thought suggests that we would be very fortunate indeed if the Lord were to react with laughter to all our mistaken habits and practices. The fact is that we in the church have had the greatest difficulty in preserving essential truths that he made perfectly clear and expressed with complete accuracy, so it really is just as well that he wasn't guilty of any verbal errors.

'What?' he might say, as he surveys the church worldwide. 'I distinctly remember making it perfectly clear that you were to love one another. Why have you started a new religion under my name that doesn't just allow but encourages bitter division and unloving conflict? *Why* have you done that? Why?'

'What on earth are these?' he might further ask, as he encounters a succession of dumbly unwelcoming church buildings catering for the sterile religious habits of a few. 'I thought I called you to be fishers of men, not respectable, inward-looking, ignorers of the real world. I told you about the harvest. I was *passion-ate* about the harvest. Why aren't you out in the fields? People are dying out there! And another thing. Tell me why there are still Pharisees and hypocrites in the church that bears my name, people who continue to put impossible burdens on the shoulders of the men and women I died for, my brothers and sisters who should be free and rejoicing instead of shackled and guilty. Tell me why you put up with them. Tell me now!'

Never mind chocolate chalices and slips of the tongue. The truth is hard enough to handle, but that's what he wants and that's what he's determined to have. I'm glad.

31

I Follow Jesus Because ...

He Doesn't Insist That We Must All Have Scottish Accents

One summer morning I was awakened in the early hours by what sounded to my sleep-befuddled brain like a Presbyterian prayer meeting happening in the field behind our house. Getting up quietly so as not to wake Bridget, who deserves her sleep and is in any case a somewhat exclusive Anglican, I peered through the window, half expecting to see a posse of sombre-faced elders petitioning the Lord on the other side of our garden fence. As my eyes grew accustomed to the faint light shed by a handful of stars, it dawned on me that either a number of these pillars of the church community were down on all fours tearing grass up with their teeth like a herd of mad Nebuchadnezzars, or my slumber had actually been disturbed by the flock of sheep that appears in the meadow adjacent to our house at the beginning of each summer.

Lingering by the window, I marvelled at the extraordinarily human sound made by these gentle creatures and the variety of expression possible within the limitations of a simple bleat. Given these two observations, you may ask how I could have believed that a Presbyterian prayer meeting was in progress. Well, it may have been the fact, newly registered at this deeply contemplative moment, that all sheep bleat with a Scottish accent. Now, you may laugh, but consider – isn't it true that every single sheep you have ever heard giving voice, whether in Holland, Israel, New Zealand or Guatemala, has done so with a distinctly Caledonian inflection? I'm right, aren't I?

Jesus likened his followers to sheep for excellent reasons, but might there have been moments during the last 2,000 years when he wished he had chosen a different simile? You can watch the Scottish sheep behind our house cramming themselves into ridiculously inappropriate situations, simply because it feels safer to do what everyone else is doing. This aspect of sheepish behaviour is surely *not* one we're supposed to emulate, yet we do it continually, particularly when it comes to different 'waves' within the church.

A while ago, for instance, I visited a church in the north. Soon after I had taken my seat the woman beside me doubled up, expelling a loud grunt of pain, as though someone had punched her hard in the solar plexus. Deeply alarmed, I asked if she wanted me to get help, but she just smiled beatifically and said, 'Don't worry, love, it's just the Holy Spirit.'

'Just the – oh, I see ...'

I didn't see. I was bewildered by my neighbour's explanation of her violent convulsion. I was doubly bewildered when the minister climbed onto the platform at the front and exhibited the same symptoms – only more so. His delivery was so heavily punctuated by 'holy grunts' and clutchings of the stomach that he reminded me of one of those characters being attacked by nobody in films about the Invisible Man. By the end the whole affair was beginning to sound like 30 or 40 heavyweight boxing matches all going on simultaneously. This, apparently, was the way the Holy Spirit had chosen to manifest himself in this particular church. Who was I to argue? People were absolutely sincere about these manifestations. All I can say is that, looking back, I seem to recall a subtle but unmistakably Scottish flavour in those violent utterances.

Passing swiftly over the list of other phenomena spreading like bizarre rashes through our churches in recent years – such things as barking, mooing, laughing, falling over and roaring – we come to the business of dental fillings that miraculously turn to gold.

Our friend was so convinced by a visiting speaker that the fillings of all those present had turned to gold, that she publicly testified to the miracle having happened in her own mouth. Later, after asking a very good friend to inspect her fillings closely, she returned to the church, apologized for getting carried away, and withdrew her testimony.

Set against this is the fact that we once met an evangelist from South America who appeared to have genuinely experienced this strange work of God at a time when it really mattered to him as an individual.

And this must be the important point. God will do *anything* that's truly necessary for any one of his followers at the particular time when that person needs it. Problems arise when the special experience of person A is slavishly copied or imitated by the entire alphabet of other persons in the church because they're frightened of being left out or left behind. How much of what God offers me do I miss because I conform and imitate without really thinking?

Let us love the flock and enjoy being part of it, because that's certainly what Jesus wanted, but let us also be glad that God is, was, and ever will be creatively ingenious in his dealings with individual men and women. I find that very exciting. Do you find that exciting? Are you going to follow me slavishly in finding that exciting?

And all God's people said, 'B-a-a-a-a-a-h!'

32

I Follow Jesus Because ...

He Takes Responsibility for Problems I Haven't Got a Hope of Solving on My Own

We have more and more palatial shopping precincts in this country, but still no sign of a Wisdom shop. I wish there was somewhere where you could buy wisdom. There are times when I feel sadly lacking in that commodity. The Bible says God will give us wisdom if we need it, and I do believe that, but some situations are so taxing that we can easily lose awareness of the Holy Spirit touching what we do and say.

Here's just one example.

One day I was at my desk, busily writing Bible notes, when – yes, you guessed it – the jolly old phone rang. Now, before I tell you about the phone call, I should explain that these Bible notes related to the first book of Corinthians, chapters four to eight, in which Paul has much to say to the unholy church at Corinth about sin, sex, immorality, divorce, getting married, not getting married, and all that sort of thing. My mind was awash with thoughts and feelings about the conflict between carnality and holiness, and Paul's way of dealing with it in this particular case. It was as I completed note number nine out of fourteen that the phone did its invariable thing.

My caller was a friend (I shall call him George) who for some years has been the highly regarded leader of a large English-speaking church in one of the smaller European countries. I have known George and his wife Martine for many years and, as well as having great respect for their joint ministry, I'm very fond of them both. George sounded very subdued.

'I'm calling to tell you,' he said, 'that I've resigned from my church, and that Martine and I and the children have moved to a different city.'

I groaned inwardly on hearing these words. What disaster could have overtaken my friends?

George cleared his throat uneasily before continuing to speak.

'You see, Adrian, I've been secretly having an affair with someone in the church for over a year now, and the other day it all came out in the open. As a result we've moved right away, and I've been lucky enough to find temporary employment, but at the moment I just can't decide what to do. Poor Martine spends most of the time swinging from sobbing grief to wild anger, and I – well, I feel terribly guilty, but all I want is to be with this woman who's made me feel alive for the first time in years.' He paused for a moment. 'I really do need to come and speak with you, if it's possible.'

'Well, of course,' I responded, trying not to allow the shock I was feeling to sound too much in my voice. The marriage of George and Martine had seemed one of the few still points in a tumultuously turning world. 'Of course you must come if it would help.'

'I'm so glad you said that,' he replied, clearing his throat nervously again, 'because I'm already here.'

'You're already – '

'Just down the road in a phone box. I got the early ferry. I hope you don't mind.'

I told him to come on up to the house, and put the phone down in a state of considerable shock. This minister of the gospel, my friend George, had committed adultery, yearned to continue committing adultery, and would be with me in minutes to talk about it. There, on the desk in front of me, lay the notes I had been making, and the Bible I had been using, still open at the book of Corinthians. I stared at them. George's situation was not theoretical, it was real, and he would be here at any moment. What would I say to him when he arrived? Where did my duty lie? What would Jesus have said? What did he want *me* to say?

I found myself mentally rehearsing different ways of responding to George when he arrived. The voice of my early evangelical upbringing suggested the following: 'You know perfectly well, George, that adultery is against the will of God. The clear path of obedience that lies before you now is one of complete repentance and a new commitment to Martine and the divinely approved marriage that your sinful indulgence has threatened.'

Paul would approve of me saying something along those lines, surely, and there could be no divine comeback later, as far as I was concerned. It was the truth, after all, wasn't it? Was it? I shook my head and sighed. No, it was only a form of truth, truth without a heart, without compassion or understanding. Who was I to tell someone else what they ought to think or do?

Maybe I ought just to create space for George to make his own decisions. Something of this sort: 'George, you have to follow your own heart. The most important thing is to be true to yourself, as the Bible says – no, as you were, it was Shakespeare who said that, wasn't it? Still, same sort of thing – just know what it is you really want, and go for it with all your heart until you've got it. Be the authentic you, whatever anyone else says.'

Paul certainly wouldn't approve of that, I thought, and, to be honest, neither would I, really. I didn't want George to go off with this woman and leave Martine and the children behind. I wanted him to be strong and obedient and to discover that, if he was, God would support him. I wanted – well, mainly I wanted to avoid saying or not saying the very thing that might mess up God's best plan for solving the problem.

I said a prayer: 'Lord, I feel useless and troubled as my friend gets nearer and nearer to my front door. At the moment, I really don't know what to say to him, but there are some things that I do know. I know that Jesus always dealt with people according to their individual circumstances, and that he reacted in ways that were quite surprising and unexpected as far as onlookers were concerned. I know that Jesus only did what he saw the Father doing, rather than using fixed rules or methods. I know that he could be very tender with repentant sinners and very tough with people whose hearts were hardened, and, perhaps most importantly, he could always tell the difference. And I know that you love George and Martine and want the very best for them. Please give me as much of the mind of Christ as I'm capable of making space for, so that I open my mouth and shut it again at the right times. Amen.'

The actual substance of my subsequent conversation with George isn't terribly relevant. I still felt inadequate and lacking in wisdom as we spoke, but I also felt that I had truly released responsibility for my friends to the only one capable of making a real difference. That seemed important to me.

Do say a prayer for all those couples who are facing similar problems.

33

I Follow Jesus Because ...

He Offers Hope
for the Future

Just before the millennium someone invited me to address a meeting on the subject of 'Hope for the Future'. The organizers suggested that I might like to talk about how the Christian faith enables me to look with hope and serenity to the future, as far as my children and grandchildren are concerned. As I said in my response to their invitation, there are problems with this proposition as it stands.

First, there are major difficulties with the whole idea of Christians being filled with hope and serenity. Contrary to what some shiny-eyed enthusiasts might claim, the Holy Spirit doesn't issue regulation hope-and-serenity kits to all new believers when they turn up at the divine quartermaster's store. Living out the Christian life – actually following Jesus – can be a tough and perilous business, and it certainly offers no earthly guarantees. In the course of his work for God, the apostle Paul experienced many harsh discomforts, including hunger, beatings, shipwreck, imprisonment *and* despair. As far as we can tell, he was more than happy to endure all those things as long as Christ was being preached. Read his letters and his speeches in Acts, and you will see that he was full of hope in the power of the resurrection to save men and women for an eternity with Jesus, and serenely confident that the Holy Spirit would lead him along the right paths to make that possible, but in terms of comfort and physical safety – well, anything could happen.

I certainly don't have Paul's faith and perseverance, but I do think that his priorities were absolutely right, and that's why I look to the future for my children and grandchildren with a mixture of hope and fear. I want them to love Jesus as Paul did, and therefore have the same priorities as him, but I have to confess that my heart almost fails me when I think of the hardship that such a commitment might involve for them. I ask God to give them wisdom, strength, and a love for him so great that it overcomes all obstacles. You see, as I said right at the beginning of this book, I want to be with them in heaven, just as, for instance, I look forward to one day being reunited with my own mother, whom I mentioned earlier. She's the second thing I would like to talk about, because it was her death in particular that enabled me to focus on the priority of eternity in a new and spiritually energizing way.

My mother died towards the end of 1996, and my wife and I found it very hard to come to terms with our loss. To be honest, we didn't want to come to terms with it too quickly. Bridget regarded her mother-in-law as her best friend and so, in many ways, did I. These things always need to take the proper amount of time. But it was so *sad* that we could no longer jump in the car and drive up from Hailsham to Tunbridge Wells to spend a morning or an afternoon with my generous, stubborn, accepting mother. Every now and then I momentarily forgot that she was no longer there, and the words, 'Let's pop up and see Mum,' were on the tip of my tongue. Then I would remember, and the sadness would flood in again. Bridget experienced exactly the same thing. There really is no easy way around grief. You just have to go straight through the middle of it and, for a time at least, accept pain as a constant companion.

One of the saddest things about the death of a close family

member is the business of going through their possessions, sorting things into different piles and categories to be thrown away, or sold, or taken home, or given to friends of the person who has died. It felt like a sort of sacrilege to be taking the furniture of Mum's life apart in that way, especially when it came to the things that would be valueless to anyone else but meant a great deal to her. One of the most poignant examples of this was a brochure brought back from a voyage on the *Queen Elizabeth II*. All her life Mum had dreamed of taking a cruise on the famous passenger ship, and finally she had managed to afford a very short trip from the French coast back to England. That glossy brochure was the symbol of a dream fulfilled, and Bridget was about to drop it into one of the black rubbish bags when she stopped and said, with a little catch in her voice, 'I can't throw this away. I know it's silly, but it meant so much to Mum.' We took it home and put it in the cupboard in our bedroom. Mum would laugh at such sentimentalism, that's for sure.

It was strange to see the house eventually completely clear of any trace of the person who had lived there. The accumulated possessions of more than 70 years had been bagged, bought, bequeathed or binned within the space of about three days. All that was left was a shell, as empty of the person who had once inhabited it as the body that I had sat next to for a few minutes after my mother finally gave up the battle for life on earth and went to meet her God.

The sadness involved in disposing of her possessions and the grief over her death would rage with wild meaninglessness if I didn't have the confidence that she has gone to be with Jesus, and that we shall see her again.

> *But for you who revere my name, the sun of righteousness will rise with healing in its wings. And you will go out and leap like calves released from the stall.*
>
> Malachi 4:2 NIV

This Old Testament verse provides us with a graphic picture of the experience my mother will have had immediately after her death. We may be sad, but I can assure you that she is not. After spending four tedious, frustrating years in a wheelchair, don't you think that being able to leap like a calf released from its stall must be a heavenly pleasure? If you have ever seen calves when they're first released after being confined, you will know that they bounce more or less vertically into the air. They go boing! boing! around their pasture as though they're on springs instead of legs. Healed in the sunshine and leaping for joy. I wish Mum was here, but I'm glad she's there.

There are countless numbers of people all over the world who have never heard of Jesus, let alone learned to revere him as this passage teaches us we must. My mother didn't leave much behind, but her faith, the most valuable asset in her possession, went with her. My prayer and hope is that my children and their children will be part of God's work in bringing those people to the same faith, because nothing is more important. I honestly don't feel very serene about it, but my hope is in Jesus, and if we follow him he will not fail us or them.

34

I Follow Jesus ...

For Reasons That Are Almost Impossible to Explain

I had to add this last little section because it may be more important than any of the others, and yet I hardly know how to write it. I must, though.

You see, it all falls apart sometimes. The whole thing just crumbles and turns to dust. I don't mind admitting it any more, because I know now that I can only be the me that God has called, just as you can only be you. Sometimes a sad darkness comes and for a little while I can't see my faith in front of my face. When I'm rescued from that darkness, it's not by glib statements, nor by the light of technical theology, but by the living memory of those rare, wonderful, insubstantial, essential, fleeting moments when, in a world where faith and doubt are equally irrelevant, I have simply known that he's there, that he loves me, and that there are important things to be done.

After all, what is Christianity but God driving a jalopy to work with a smile on his face?

Thank you for reading this book.

Silver Birches

A Novel

Adrian Plass, Internationally Bestselling Author

When David Herrick receives an invitation to a reunion from a long-forgotten acquaintance, his first reaction is to refuse. He isn't feeling very sociable since his wife, Jessica, died six months ago.

But the invitation comes from Angela, one of his wife's oldest friends – and mysteriously, she has something for him from his beloved Jessica. Reluctant but curious, he visits Headly Manor.

When the friends gather, they no longer resemble the fresh-faced group of twenty years ago. One has been deserted by her husband, another has lost his faith, and another is filled with anger and bitterness. As they have less than forty-eight hours with each other, they decide to be vulnerable and bear their souls.

This poignant and moving story blends Adrian Plass's rich style of writing with his knack for addressing the deep issues we all face, such as faith, grief, love … and fear.

Softcover: 978-0-310-29203-6

Pick up a copy at your favorite bookstore or online!

The Sacred Diary of Adrian Plass, Aged 37¾

Adrian Plass

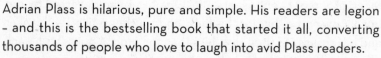

Saturday, December 14th

Feel led to keep a diary. A sort of spiritual log for the benefit of others in the future. Each new divine insight and experience will shine like a beacon in the darkness!

Can't think of anything to put in today.

Still, tomorrow's Sunday. Must be something on a Sunday, surely?

———

Adrian Plass is hilarious, pure and simple. His readers are legion – and this is the bestselling book that started it all, converting thousands of people who love to laugh into avid Plass readers.

The Sacred Diary of Adrian Plass, Aged 37¾, is merriment and facetiousness at its best – a journal of the wacky Christian life of Plass's fictional alter ego, who chronicles in his 'sacred' diary the daily goings-on in the lives of ordinary-but-somewhat-eccentric people he knows and meets. Reading it will doeth good like a medicine!

Softcover: 978-0-310-26912-0

Pick up a copy at your favorite bookstore or online!

The Sacred Diary of Adrian Plass, Christian, Aged 45¾

Adrian Plass

Adrian Plass lovers got their initial baptism of laughter through his bestseller *The Sacred Diary of Adrian Plass, Aged 37¾*. The author's account of 'serious spiritual experiences' naturally made him in demand as a public speaker – so of course another diary was inevitable.

The Sacred Diary of Adrian Plass, Christian Speaker, Aged 45 ¾ continues the misadventures of Adrian's fictional alter ego. As Plass gathers regularly with his support group, we meet old friends, including his longsuffering wife, Anne; son, Gerald, now grown but no less irrepressible; loony and lovable Leonard Thynn; Edwin, the wise church elder; and Richard and Doreen Cook, who are just as religious as ever. We also meet some new characters, such as Stephanie Widgeon, who only seems to have one thing to say, ever … and who knows, we might even find out why Leonard Thynn borrowed Adrian's cat all those years ago.

And finally – what is a banner ripping seminar?

Softcover: 978-0-310-26913-7

Pick up a copy at your favorite bookstore or online!

Share Your Thoughts

With the Author: Your comments will be forwarded to the author when you send them to *zauthor@zondervan.com*.

With Zondervan: Submit your review of this book by writing to *zreview@zondervan.com*.

Free Online Resources at
www.zondervan.com

Zondervan AuthorTracker: Be notified whenever your favourite authors publish new books, go on tour, or post an update about what's happening in their lives at www.zondervan.com/authortracker.

Daily Bible Verses and Devotions: Enrich your life with daily Bible verses or devotions that help you start every morning focused on God. Visit www.zondervan.com/newsletters.

Free Email Publications: Sign up for newsletters on Christian living, academic resources, church ministry, fiction, children's resources, and more. Visit www.zondervan.com/newsletters.

Zondervan Bible Search: Find and compare Bible passages in a variety of translations at www.zondervanbiblesearch.com.

Other Benefits: Register yourself to receive online benefits like coupons and special offers, or to participate in research.

ZONDERVAN®

ZONDERVAN.com/
AUTHORTRACKER
follow your favorite authors